ROMANIAN

FOLK ALMANAC

Compiled by Ion Ghinoiu

Foreword by
Katherine Dimancescu

Translated by Doina Carlsson
from the
"COMOARA SATELOR:
Calendar Popular"

NOTE:

The cover displays various expressive folk motifs evident in peasant architecture, folk costumes, carved wooden staffs or masks.

The design of the cover and contents of this book are by Dan Dimancescu, author of "ROMANIA REDUX: A View from Harvard" published in 2004 by BTF, Cambridge, Massachusetts.

Type faces used in this book include Bradley Hand for titles, Garamond for main text and for illustration titles and footnotes.

The translation from Romanian into English is by Doina Carlsson from the original text: *"COMOARA SATELOR: Calendar Popular"* published by the Editura Academiei Romane, Bucharest, Romania, 2005.

Cover and page design by Kogainon Films (Boston).

ROMANIAN
FOLK ALMANAC

First Print Edition

All Rights Reserved
Published by BTF Press
For Details Email: tsgdd@aol.com
Concord, Massachusetts
Copyright © Ion Ghinoiu

ISBN13: 978-0-9758915-3-7

TABLE OF CONTENTS

MAP of ROMANIA	p 4
FOREWORD	p 5
INTRODUCTION	p 7
January	p 13
February	p 44
March	p 71
April	p 97
May	p 126
June	p 158
July	p 185
August	p 212
September	p 239
October	p 265
November	p 290
December	p 311
BIBLIOGRAPHY	p 336

MAP OF ROMANIA

Profesor Ion Ghinoiu

He is presently the Scientific Secretary of the „Constantin Brăiloiu" Institute of Ethnography and Folklore (Bucharest) and has been at the Institute since 1967. He is also Associate Professor since 1991 at the University of Bucharest where he lectures in Ethnography-Folklore in the department of Sociology and Social Assistance. His Ph.D. was awarded in Geography at the University of Bucharest in 1978. His main fields of interest are customs and feasts, mythology, the ethnology of habitation, ethnographical cartography, and the taxonomy of popular culture. He is widely published in these fields including one hundred scientific studies, nume3tous boos, and lead editor of the monumental *Ethnographic Atlas of Romania* (5 volumes).

FOREWORD

"Apa trece, pietrele raman." [Water flows, boulders remain.]
Old Romanian Saying

The *Romanian Folk Almanac* is a unique contribution to our understanding of world culture. What makes this work so vital is a new respect for what is often generalized as 'peasant culture.'

Seen in this light are two profound legacies. One is a visceral and instinctive respect for nature or what in today's language we might call 'environmental harmony.' A second legacy is an evolved moral code born out of millennia of adaptations to natural cycles of birth, life and death. These codes are a foundation to modern-day conduct embodied in religious practices, spiritual beliefs, and civil behavior. Wherever one looks, one knows that the tales and belief embodied in folk wisdom are at the very roots of European civilization. They give us a direct link to the "Old Ways." It was from Nature's Laws that the first cultivators instinctively created an "Almanac of Traditional Knowledge" to guide them in the annual ritual of their day-to-day of lives. This was founded on a balance between man and animal and plants. Fundamental to it was the ritualized cycle of birth-life-death and rebirth of all nature's creatures.

How fortunate we are that these founding stories are still ours to discover. They have been passed from generation to generation because they connect us with our "mother earth", the most basic of teachers. To overlook this folklore that comes alive in Professor Ghinoiu's *Romanian Folk Almanac* is to loose a vocabulary that links us to our earliest beginnings as civilized people. Sadly, just as many ancient languages vanish and varied animal and plants go extinct, so is our awareness of the diversity and inner quality of our cultural roots.

Romania, as I have discovered, never lost its connection with nature and especially to its forests, its "forest woman spirits," to its wolf, bear and other inhabitants that populate the pantheon governing early animistic beliefs. Villagers, past and present-still, remain faithful to such symbols knowing that "She" protects and preserves the fertility and creation of all those who inhabit this cosmic space. The magic of life generated by these great forests resonates in the passages shared with us in the

"Folk Almanac." As we read them, they become instantly recognizable, and fascinating, as an unending umbilical cord stretching back into Neolithic or even Paleolithic times.

Those origins come alive with vivid clarity as documented and described by Professor Ion Ghinoiu. Millennia of evolved folk traditions, many of which remain actively practiced in Romania, are explained in an engaging 'Almanac' format. His work, confined to Romanian folklore, complements in scope that of Joseph Campbell in its breadth, insight, and perhaps most importantly in the universality and contemporary relevance of these legacies. It builds, too, on the enormous body of knowledge cumulated by Marija Gimbutas on ancient 'goddess cultures' of the lower Danube River basin. And, so too, on the pioneering ethnographic work in Romania by Dimitri Gusti in the 1930s, and ethno-musicologist Constantin Brailoiu as well as pioneering photographic recording styles by the likes of J. Berman.

Through them we better understand how ideas, beliefs, and practices came to be in our own contemporary lives. Sadly, these legacies are fast vanishing under pressure from the ubiquity of 'industrial' and 'postindustrial' social behavior. These forces of change are so pervasive as to have almost erased modern man's understanding of basic earthly rhythms as ritualized in the daily life of peasant communities.

The *Folk Almanac* may well be the record of an epoch tens of millennia long in which nature forced its will upon man. The transition, irreversible in its scope but uncertain in its ultimate outcome, brings us into the fast-forward industrial era only centuries in duration in which man has come to impose his will upon nature.

Katherine Dimancescu, *Concord, Massachusetts (USA)*

INTRODUCTION

s recently as the beginning of the 20th century - and indeed in some cases into present times - many Romanians used a different but unofficial calendar of annual events. Transmitted from generation to generation over the ages, I have termed it the *Folk Almanac*. It predates, the *Church-based Calendar* that attributes days of the year to the Holy Trinity (Father, Son and Holy Spirit), to the Holy Virgin, to Saint John the Baptist and to thousands of canonized people ranked hierarchically. And so, too, does it predate what we might now call the *Civil Calendar*, which is simply a table of workdays and holidays divided into months and weeks.

Only recently did I confront the challenge of making this more opaque work more accessible not just to the specialist but as importantly to the layman. In this way the *Folk Almanac* might better introduce the reader to some of the fruits of my life-long research on Romanian traditions. To do this I have linked specific folk events, beliefs, and artifacts to specific days and months of the year. Hence the 'almanac' title. Days with no associated folk holidays are used to describe traditional celebrations of the birth, marriage and death as experienced in the family life-cycle, popular sciences such ethno-botany, medicine, and astronomy, or social history. In this manner, the person interested in folk culture, psychology and philosophy can more easily discover a wide selection of folk holidays and customs observed during extensive field research or recorded in archives and libraries.

In the *Folk Almanac* human activities categorize themselves according to seasonal rhythms, to lunar months, to days and to parts of the day. The yearly almanac identifies the most suitable times for planting and sowing, for forming and dispersing flocks of sheep, for wooing and getting engaged, for spiritual rituals.

The unique and ancient characteristic of the year and its subdivisions - seasons, months, weeks and days - is embedded in their mythical personifications. These subdivisions are born, live, get old and die and then are reborn to start the cycle all over again. The most important *spiritual figures* of the almanac are *old*-aged ones, Father Christmas at winter solstice and Mother Dochia (Mother Carey) at the vernal equinox.

On January First, the New Year is born. As the months go by, it matures and into a young man, then from adulthood into an old age and then death, only to be born again on New Year's night of the following year. The mythical characters populating the *Folk Almanac* are metamorphoses of the year, some of them younger, others older, according to how long after the New Year comes their celebration day. Thus, *Sanvasai*, celebrated on the first day of the year is a young man, sitting on a barrel, who loves women and enjoys parties; *Dragobete* (February 24) is the God of Love in the Carpathian Mountain lands; *Sangeorzul* (April 23rd) is a young warrior, riding a horse; *Santilie* (July 20) and *Samedru* (October 26) are adult figures, followed by the generation of old age saints: *Father Andrei* (November 30), *Father Nicolae* (December 6), *Father Christmas* (December 25) who mark the coming death of the year in almanac time.

The female mythical representations, related to Dochia, the Neolithic Mother Goddess who dies and is reborn on vernal equinox, are arranged similarly to those of the Indo-European Father God, Christmas, and his annual metamorphosis. They, too, age as the year goes by. Beginning with Dochia's Day, March 9, the vernal equinox of the old almanac, the female representations of the *Folk Almanac* are grouped into three generations: *Maiden Goddesses,* (Floriile, Sanzienele, Dragaicele, Lazaritele, Ielele), *Mother Goddesses,* (the Virgin Mary, the Holy Virgin, the Woods Mother, the Caloian's Mother and other mothers) and *the Old Goddesses* (Saint Friday, Saint Varvara, Dochia).

The *Folk Almanac* preserves traditions that determine the New Year from traditions established by the ancestral peoples of present-day Romania. One example is in the Geto-Dacians, within the period November-December when two *Old Saints* appear: Father Andrei (December 30) and Father Nicolae (December 6).

Some of the *Folk Almanac* traditions are to be found only in the academic studies of ethnographers while others are preserved only in the memories of old people. In both cases, their significance becomes clear when relating them to cosmic rhythms (equinoxes, solstices, moon phases) as well as to terrestrial ones (reproduction cycles of some plants and animals, or the dry and rainy season), and through a detailed interdisciplinary investigation, including correlations between both folk celebrations and customs and religious ones.

The pantheon of deities to emerge from what was an early "wood and clay" based civilization in this Carpato-Danubian geographic region is presented as an atypical mythical world. Though contrasting in many ways with the more widely explored and explained Greco-Roman pantheon, one can find some connections with the Greco-Roman one, as well as with those of Mesopotamia, of Sumer and of ancient India.

The intimate relationship between the Carpato-Danubian spiritual character and the ancient Indian one, in particular, fascinated some of the great contributors to Romanian and world culture such as the poet Mihai Eminescu, the sculptor Constantin Brancusi, and the philosopher-writer Mircea Eliade.

In Carpathian Mountain regions, some Gods bear Indian names and encompass the same domains as in ancient India: Shiva, the God of the Universe present in the Shiva Christmas carol; Rudra, the God of Rain, in the ritual of Paparuda; Yama, the God of Death. In some Romanian folk beliefs and expressions "to be struck by *iama*," for example used in reference to birds or cattle, means "to be struck by death."

The *Romanian Book of the Dead,* another landmark of spiritual culture of the Carpato-Danubian people, contains sacred texts initiating the soul of the dead into a mythical journey on the path separating this earthly world from the world beyond. These texts are sung by a women's choir at particular places and at significant moments of the funeral ceremony. The messages are addressed to *the dead*, to the *goddesses of destiny (Zorile)* and to the *surviving husband* (the fir-tree, the spear, the flag). The Goddess of Death appears in the shape of a bird of prey (the kite, the raven, the vulture) or as a goddess that looks human (the Old Fairy, the Virgin Mary, Mother Irodia). The texts to the songs contain, one by one, *providential guides* (the wolf, fox, or otter), *well intentioned customs*, as personified means of orientation (the willow tree in bud, the apple tree in blossom), *psychopomp characters* (the horse, the stag) and finally, in the world beyond, *the dead person's relatives.*

Funeral songs which, at the beginning of the twentieth century were concentrated in southwestern and the central Romanian counties of Gorj, Mehedinti, Caras-Severin, Timis, Bihor, and relatively concentrated in the south of Transylvanian counties of Alba, Hunedoara, Sibiu and Brasov, had strong ramifications to the north in Bistrita-Nasaud, Mures counties and in Moldavia's Suceava, Botosani, Iasi, Vaslui, Vrancea, Galati countries, as well as Romanian communities living in the Serbian-Banat and in the Timoc Valey.

In those areas where there was no evidence of funeral songs ("Zorile" - the Fir Tree, songs for the Death Watch), versified laments partially replaced their function. Hell, the realm of suffering after death, cultivated by both Indo-Europeans and Christian religions, is missing in the Edenscape described in the Romanian funeral songs. Funeral songs have not been found with peoples neighboring Romania and rarely with any other peoples in Europe. This led to Romanian funeral songs being wrongly included in the lament category until the great ethnomusicologist Constantin Brailoiu[1] demonstrated otherwise. Before his revealing work, the six-or-eight syllable lines, the six syllables once clearly predominant, were left merely as markings in 'stone' much as one observes verses carved on a sarcophagus. Yet he discovered that the sound of these melodies contrasts with the mournful despair of the real laments.

---

[1] Constantin Brailoiu, "Problems of Ethnomusicology," Cambridge University Press, Cambridge, 1984.

What do these findings suggest in terms of the origins of civilization? Research on three landmark legacies, the Folk Almanac, the Pantheon of Deities and the Romanian Book of the Dead, has served to confirm Marija Gimbuta's theory concerning the most Ancient Civilization of Europe. This she defined as a "cultural entity existing from 6500 to 3500 BC, based on a matriarchal, theocratic, peaceful society that lived and created art and that preceded the Indo-Europeanized societies..." And, she added: "We must give recognition to the achievements of our ancestors, the old Europeans, as they used to be: temple builders, producers of wonderfully painted pottery and of cult objects"[2].

During research on the Romanian left bank of the lower Danube River at Schela Cladovei, a new Neolithic culture was discovered pushing the European continent's documented human history two more millennia back in time. Using archaeological, paleoanthropological and paleolinguistic arguments, finds at Schela Cladovei demonstrated that within a geographic region occupied nowadays by Romania, Moldavia, western Ukraine, Hungary, the Czech Republic, Slovenia, Yugoslavia, Croatia, Macedonia, Bulgaria, Albania, Greece, including the Aegean Islands and South Eastern Italian peninsula, a large cultural and religious complex developed, that was dominated spiritually by the Mother Goddess[3]. This civilization preceded the Ancient Greco-Roman era as well as the biblical myth of paternal creation. Two to three millennia before the ancient Greco-Roman cultures blossomed, several splendid Neolithic cultures flourished in the lower basin of the Danube River and its broad delta including the Pre-Cucutenii, Cucutenii, Gumelnita, and Hamangia.

Their members belonged to agrarian communities, having no elaborated fortifications and no weapons. They were unsurpassed in their skill of processing clay and they were probably inclined towards meditation, a feature illustrated by the clay statuettes called 'The Thinker' from Hamangia. In these types of societies, women played a dominant role.

Ten millennia span the first Neolithic culture in the Balkans and in the lower Danube and the contemporary oral culture documented in the recently published volumes of the *Ethnographic Atlas of Romania*. Throughout this historical timeline, whose two extremes have been researched by both archeologists and ethnographers, there are a great number of cultural analogies. Some of them are illustrated in this volume such

---

[2] Gimbutas Marija, *"Culture and Civilization. Prehistorical Vestiges in South-Eastern Europe"*, translated by Sorin Paliga, preface and notes by Radu Florescu, printed by Meridiane, Bucharest, 1989, p. 49-50

[3] Gimbutas Marija, *"The Civilization of the Great Goddess and the Arrival of the Warrior Knights. The Origin and Development of the Oldest European Civilizations (around 7500 – 700 B.C.)"*, translated by Sorin Paliga, printed by Lucretius, Bucharest, 1997

as the kiss motif present in both Neolithic ceramics and in Constantin Brancusi's greatest sculptures.

The five-volume *Ethnographic Atlas of Romania* helps to cover this wide historical gap. Research for the Atlas, originated in the 1960s and of which I am currently the coordinator, is based on ethnographic material gathered from 18,000 subjects in 536 villages, using a survey with 1,200 questions. The answers received led to a drawing up of over 1,000 subject-specific maps, 600 of which were selected and organized into the five volumes, each containing about 120 maps. In parallel with the elaboration of the Atlas, the corpus of *Romanian Ethnographical Documents* is being published. This includes all the raw research material collected in the field, recorded as such from the questioned subjects.[4]

This 10,000 year period (8 millennium B.C. and 2 millennium A.D.) can be divided into three religious and cultural complexes: the first one dominated by the Neolithic Mother Goddess (8000 to 2500 B.C.); the second dominated by the Indo-European Father God (2500 B.C. to the year 0); and the third dominated by Jesus, the Son of God (year 0 to the present). As to how people imagined what their worshipped deity looked like, the early Europeans created two distinct archetypal worlds: a *geomorphic* one, of Neolithic origin, with the *egg* as a model of beauty and perfection, and later an anthropomorphic one, of Indo-European and Christian origin, with *man* as its model.

Unfortunately, a major spiritual crisis must have shattered the world at the turn from Neolithic to the following periods in history, determining two important effects: replacing the geomorphic maternal deity with the anthropomorphic and paternal one.

In reality, however, our world is a geomorphic one, from its absolutely smallest structures - the cell, the atom, the molecule, the sub-quantum units - to its absolutely largest ones - the planets, the stars, the galaxies, the galactic clusters and mega-clusters. But this world was subsequently 'redesigned' exclusively according to the beauty and perfection ideal of the anthropomorphic deity. This anthropomorphic environment, imposing its dominance heavy-handedly, has spawned widespread environmental dysfunctions felt from the Equator to the Pole and from the surface of the planet to the limits of the atmosphere. The two might still be reconciled – the *geomorphic* one, established experimentally by the Neolithic people, in harmony with the structure of the whole Universe, and the *anthropomorphic* one, imposed more arrogantly by man, the most powerful creature on the Planet. This theme is one developed in *"The Treasure of Romanian Villages"*.

From a reading of the many maps included in the *Ethnographic Atlas of Romania*, one can conclude that, during the time when the ethnographical

---

[4] *Ethnographic Atlas of Romania*, Coordinator I. Ghinoiu, Printed by the Academy, and the Official Monitor, Bucharest, Romania.

research was carried out between 1972 and 1983, modern-day Romanians preserved significant elements of the *wood and clay* civilization created by their ancestors, the Carpato-Danubian people, bearers of the first underpinnings of continental European civilization.

This civilization, persuasively if not definitively documented by Marija Gimbutas, is linked by its environment to 'running river waters' rather than to 'sea or ocean' settings. Considering that river environments provided the richest water and food supplies, it is not surprising that they became cradle regions of civilization. In this manner the Danube River was for the Carpato-Danubian people what the Nile was for the Egyptians, what the rivers Indus and Ganges were for the old India, what the rivers Tigris and Euphrates were for Sumer and Mesopotamia. This region shaped one of the great "Delta Civilizations" from which evolved modern day man. Namely this was the genesis of a great unheralded prehistoric civilization evidenced by the discovery of sophisticated Neolithic cultures of which living vestiges survive to the present-day in Romania especially in the day-to-day lives of its peasant culture. The Folk Almanac brings many of those beliefs and practices into focus.

Shepherd Family in Nucsoara with
the Almanac author I. Ghinoiu (center), Arges County
(AIEF Photo 1975 No. 75 788)

January
"Gerar"
The Frosty Month

1. The New Year
2. "Sorcova", Phytomorphic Deity
3. "Turca", Horn-Related Deity
4. The Old European Civilization
5. The Ritual Beat
6. Epiphany
7. "Iordanitul" or Women's Feast
8. Geomorphism and Anthropomorphism
9. Monday, the Day of the Moon
10. Tuesday, the Day of Mars and of the month of March
11. Wednesday, the Day of the God and Planet Mercury
12. Thursday, the Day of the God and Planet Jupiter
13. Friday, the Day of Venera and Planet Venus
14. Saturday, the Day of the God and Planet Saturn
15. Sunday - Circovii de Iarna
16. The Wolves' Saint Peter
17. Antanaziile
18. The Day
19. The Middle and the Borders of the Day
20. The Week
21. The Daily Meals
22. Sunday, the Day of the Holy Sun
23. Life
24. Afterlife
25. Pre-life
26. Folk Astronomy
27. Star Gazers
28. The Tale of the Hellebore
29. The Winter "Phillipies"
30. The Three Magi
31. Father Martin

January, the 11th month in the Roman almanac, in which the year started on March 1st, also the 1st month in the Julian and in the Gregorian almanac, keeps the memory of Ianus, the Roman god with two faces: one looking towards the year coming to an end (the Old Year), and the other looking towards the coming year (the New Year). *"Carindar"* or *"Calindar"* are folk names connected to the custom of making weather almanacs out of onion peels or nut-shells at New Year's night.

The Frosty Month, the name given to January, refers to the terrible frost of mid-winter, and the name *Snowy Month (Omatosul)* reflects the large amount of snow usually falling during this period. After Christmas and New Year, household activities are resumed, many of them performed in the evening sitting of village women, and after epiphany, an important wedding season starts. The folk holidays contain specific customs and practices for the beginning of the New Year, through which people try, by means of magic and the making of wishes, to obtain prosperity, health, peace and quiet in the months to come.

January 1
The New Year

The folk almanac starts on the day when the first deity of mankind was born, namely the year, a personification of the Sun. Anthropomorphically the sun is *Old* on December 31st and born again *New* on New Year's night.

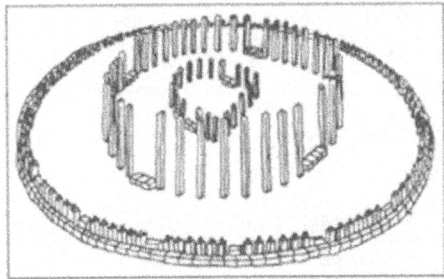 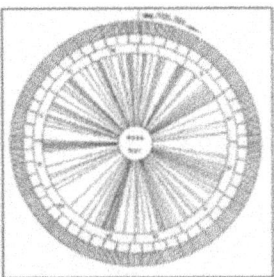

Left: Geto-Dacian Almanac (Circular Sanctuary) Sarmizegetusa (Micela & Florescu 1980)
Right: Popular Almanac 1921 (Ghinoiu 1997)

The Sun, star of the day, was associated with the most important gods of mankind: Zeus, Saturn, Shiva, Christmas, Mitra and many others. Starting with the birthday of the God year, the personified *time* begins to grow, to become mature, to age and to die, only to be reborn after 365 or 366 days.

The Saints in the *Folk Almanac* are metamorphoses of the same deity, can be younger or older depending on the distance in time (days) separating them from the death and the rebirth of the New Year: *Sanvasai* (Saint Basil), celebrated on the first day of the year, is a youthful partygoer, sitting on a barrel, who loves women and enjoys having a lot of fun; *Dragobete* (January 24th) son of Dochia is a god of love in the Carpathian Mountain lands; *Sangeorzul* (April 23rd) is a young warrior, riding a horse; *Santilie* (July 20) and *Samedru* (October 26) are grownups, followed by the generation of old age saints: *Father Andrei* (November 30), *Father Nicolae* (December 6), *Father Christmas* (December 25). In this manner is marked the death and the rebirth of the almanac cycle. The God Year is immortal through his perpetual death and rebirth rather than through the deluding wish of mortals for eternal life.

January 2
"Sorcova", a Phytomorphic Deity

Sorcova is a substitute of the phytomorphic deity invoked by children in the first day of the year in order to bring life, health and prosperity to the people on whom its ritual has been performed. Sorcova, as a ceremonial object, was made of one or several fruit-tree twigs from apple, pear, cherry or plum trees, or made from twigs of rose-tree cut and kept in the water to bud and bloom on the day of *Father Nicolae* Day on December 6 or on *Sântandrei* (Saint Andrew) on December 30.

"Sorcova", Museum of Wood of Câmpulung Moldovenesc (G. Habenicht, 1970)

In later times, the object used by children when performing the ritual was made of branches with twigs decorated with colored wool threads, with girdles and with a sweet basil blade on top. In Bucovina, Sorcova had a small bell attached to it, its metal tongue ringing to call the phytomorphic deity. Sorcova, a symbol of spring vegetation, is made in present times of colored paper and artificial flowers. After performing the "Sorciva" ritual on their parents and on their close relatives, children visit their neighbors, reciting the text in which they wish them to have a long and healthy life like the apple, the pear and the rose-trees and also to become as strong and sharp as iron and steel.

While reciting the text, they rhythmically touch the door or the window with the Sorcova if they are outside, or they touch the host-bodies if they are inside. Going around with Sorcova involves a ritual beat, a frequently found gesture in the almanac customs. such as beating the earth with a wooden hammer, beating the wooden or the metal plate to call people to church, and also in everyday life, such as patting someone on the shoulder. As observed in Muntenian, Oltenian, Dobrogean, and Moldavian regions, when the time for performing this ritual is over, the Sorcova object is kept throughout the year as a holy thing, hanging on the wall oriented towards East, placed close to an icon, or in a clean place in the house.

January 3
Turca, Horn-Related Deity

The role of the prehistoric zoomorphic deity is played, at Christmas and New Year, by one young man from a performing group who wears a horned mask called, according to the ethnographic zone to which it belongs, "Turca", "Boura", "Brezaie" meaning Bull, Stag or Goat.

"Turca", the corresponding feminine noun for "Bull", is symbolically born at the same time as the mask bearing its name is being made; it enjoys going to parties and having fun together with a group of young men, who are its divine company, and then dies symbolically, beaten with a cudgel, shot or drowned, later to be reborn together with the almanac year with which it merges.

The Turca costume consists of head, body and a stick (the leg) which supports it when standing on the ground. The head has two horns on it, which are decorated with ribbons, girdles, small bells, artificial flowers, and an indefinite animal mouth (wolf, horse, rabbit, goat) made of wood, which the one wearing the mask opens and shuts, clattering like a stork. The body is often made from a table cloth sewn like a sack, on which colored ribbons and scarves, rabbit skin tufts or bird feathers have been sewn and it has a tail at the back. The person wearing the Turca pulls it over his head, making his ankles visible and holds the supporting stick, carved in a phallus shape. In its totality, it looks like an odd four-legged creature in a bending position.

Goat Mask, Tudora, Botosani County
(N. Jula, V. Manastireanu, 1968)

Being a divine character, Turca acts according to its status. It performs independently from the other members of the group; it doe not obey the leader's orders; it takes pleasure in scaring women and children; it charges curious viewers who get close to the performers and demands a payment that it considers it is entitled to. Young men wearing the Turca mask are not allowed to speak, thus increasing the mystery surrounding him. Unlike Christmas practices, Turca never follows the members of the group who are going to church before performing, in order to be blessed, or to the priest's house to perform the actual ritual.

The Turca "Great Dance" performed alone in the middle of the village, with his simulated death followed by the burial ritual, and the young men's banquet are all reminiscent of the sacrifice to the King of Saturnalia, practiced in southeastern Europe fifteen centuries ago.

An anonymous martyr record from Moesia Inferior contained valuable information about selecting the King of Saturnalia and his faith. During yearly celebrations of Saturnalia, Roman soldiers in Durastorum (Moesia Inferior), would select a young man who they later dressed as a 'King' symbolizing Saturn by drawing names thirty days before the holiday. The young man was free to walk through the crowd and had total liberty to partake of any pleasure, even if that implied a degrading or shameful deed. However his happiness would not last long or happily, after a month when the holiday celebrating Saturn came, his throat would be cut on the altar of the substituted God.

In the year 303 A.D. Roman, soldiers of the legion in Durastarum town drew the name of a Christian, called Dasisus, to be the King of Saturnalia. He refused to play the role and spent the last days of his life in debauchery. Neither threats nor arguments from Bassus, his commander, could make him change his mind and consequently Dasisus was beheaded. His case was described in detail by the Christian martyrology, "recorded by soldier John, in Durastorum, on Friday, November 20, on the 24th day of the month, at 4 o'clock."[5]

---

[5] Frazer, 1980, IV, p. 243.

January 4
The Old European Civilizations

Rocking the Child in Camarzana an Echo of the Intra-Uterine Life (AIEF, Vol. I)

Spanning the Carpathians and Danube area, one finds Neolithic cultures from 8000 to 1000 B.C.[6] These were collectively labelled by the noted American anthropologist and archeologist, Marija Gimbutas as the *Old European Civilization*. Being contemporary with the Sumerian and Mesopotamian civilizations developed on the Tigris and the Euphrates and ancient Egyptian on the Nile, it preceded the Indo-Europeanized ones of the Bronze and Iron Ages, as well as the Ancient Greco-Roman one.

She described this civilization as "a cultural entity existing from 6500 to 3500 B.C. based on a matriarchal, theocratic, peaceful society. It was tremendously creative well before Indo-Europeanized societies." And she added, "We must pay tribute to the achievements of our ancestors, the Old Europeans, the way they were: temple builders, producers of wonderfully painted pottery and of cult objects."[7] Research situated at Schela Cladovei, on the Romanian left bank of the Danube River, uncovered a new Neolithic culture which pushed the known social history of the European continent two more millennia back in time.

The large cultural and religious complex that ensued was dominated by the Mother Goddess. Archeological, paleoanthropologic and paleolinguistic findings document its influence to have been widespread covering present-day Romania, Moldavia, Western Ukraine, Hungary, the Czech Republic, Slovenia, old-Yugoslavia, Croatia, Macedonia, Bulgaria,

---

[6] These cultures included: Schela Cladovei (8000-6500 B.C.), Vinca – Turdas (second half of the Fifth Millennium B.C.), Pre-Cucutenii (first half of the Fourth Millennium B.C.), Cucutenii (Fourth and Third Millennia B. C.), Gumelnita (second half of the first millennium – first part of the Third Millennium B.C.), Hamangia (Fourth Millennium - Second Millenium B.C.).

[7] Gimbutas, p. 49-50.

Albania, Greece, including the Aegean Islands and South Eastern Italian peninsula.

Most notable, according to Gimbutas, is that it preceded the Ancient Greek-Roman civilization as well as the Biblical myth of paternal creation. This meant that two-to-three millennia before the ancient Greek-Roman cultures blossomed, a splendid collection of Neolithic cultures - Precucutenii, Cucutenii, Gumelnita, Hamangia, and others - flourished in the lower basin of the river Danube and its broad Delta. In these societies, women played a dominant role. Their members belonging to agrarian communities had no elaborated fortifications and no weapons. They were unsurpassed in their skill of processing clay and they were probably inclined towards meditation, a quality illustrated by the clay statuette called *The Thinker from Hamangia*.

"The Thinker and Femal Figure - Hamangia, Cernavoda 5000-4500BC

January 5
The Ritual Beat

Called the *Ritual Beat*, this magical practice is based on a back-and-forth movement to bring health, to chase away evil spirits, to fertilize time and space, to induce friendship and solidarity among people like patting someone on the shoulder. Romanians associate the 'beat' with mating between living creatures. The ritual beat originates in this innate instinct of the setting up of the *The Child's House* through the nuptial act.[8]

Through the Ritual Beat, too, people ask for various things from the divinity they worship. They ask for health and prosperity for those on whom they performed the "Sorcova" ritual on New Year's Day. They want the heat to drive out the cold on the "Macinici" day by beating the ground with a wooden cudgel. Or on September 14, by beating a nut-tree with a wooden rod on the Day of the Cross, they ask for their trees to bear fruit in the following year.

A ritual Beat is also included as the main invocation in constructing a shelter or a settlement (house, village, state, grave). This is called *The Stake Beat* or *The Pale Beat*.

January 6
Epiphany

New Year's Day, the 6th of January is man's biblical creation and the time when one starts to count the days of the year. Based on this biblical myth of man having been created by God, the fathers of the Christian church merged the double birth of Jesus, the Holy Child: the physical and the spirit-

Christ's Baptism
(Olteanu, 2001)

ual one of his baptism. Putting together the two great Christian events in the same day, though logical from the new faith's standpoint, gradually became a source of misunderstanding and confusion for believers. Faced with that situation theologians came up with a compromise solution: they kept the 6th of January (Epiphany) for

---

[8] Ghinoiu, 2001, p. 14.

the Baptism of Jesus when the Magi visit the infant and they established the physical birth two weeks before, on the 25 of December, a day celebrating that traditionally celebrated the death and the birth of the Mesopotamian god, Mithra, and of the Carpato-Danubian God, **Christmas**. The transfer of the birth date of Jesus over the Roman New Year, celebrated at January *Calends* (January 1st), together with the overlapping of the Christian event, and the celebration of the mentioned gods, produced a confusion which makes it very difficult for us today to distinguish the Christian holidays and customs from the pre-Christian ones.

In the Folk Almanac, the epiphany period also contains behavior particular to both Christmas and New Year holidays: going from house to house singing Christmas carols; casting and binding magic spells and charms; finding out the predestinated husband; foreseeing the weather and how rich the new year will be. At this time, it is believed that the Heavens open and animals speak and that treasures burn. In reaction, prophylactic and purifying magic practices and rituals are predominant.

To the Christian rituals of hallowing the water (consecrated water), of going from house to house before epiphany, of the cross being thrown into the water by priests, people added new ones, such as: the ritual of washing or dipping people in the water of rivers or lakes; shooting, shouting and making noises ("Chiraleisa" in North-Eastern Transylvania); lighting fires ("Ardeasa" in Bucovina); spreading of bad-smelling substances; fumigating people, cattle and household outhouses; horse chasing. In their terrible fight against evil spirits people got help from the wolves, the only living creatures able to see the devils, chase them and tear them with their teeth.

Frightened by the wolves, the devils jumped into waters and those men who were brave enough jumped after them. Priests would hallow waters with consecrated water and would throw in the cross. An interesting practice for purification and for driving away the evil spirits is horse running or horse chasing. Once every year, at epiphany, the two almanac rivals: the Wolf and the Horse, the former being master over winter and the latter being master of summer, fight for a common cause, namely driving away the Devil. The typical ritual dishes for epiphany are pig's trotters and boiled wheat.

January 7
"Iordanitul" or Women's Feast

Iordanitul is a proverbial feast organized by wives during the day and the night of Saint John on January 7, a reminiscence of the Dionysiac manifestation. Women would get together in-groups and go to a hostess house where they would bring food - eggs, flour, meat - and drink for the feast.

They would eat and drink plentifully the whole night; they would sing, dance and cheer and say that they amused themselves. The following morning they would come out on the road, where they would take by force all the men passing by, pull them up and take them to a river, to the lake or to the well, threatening to throw them in unless they ransomed themselves with a gift, usually a pail of wine. They would also sit on a wooden harrow which they would drag like a sledge, or they would enter people's houses, sprinkling everybody with water. On that particular day, called *"Women's Feast"* all the good behavior norms of the traditional village were abolished, while excessive drinking and feasting beyond measure were tolerated.

Adam's Mistake, Original Sin of Humanity (Miniature 1843, Patrut, 1985)

Women considered themselves as being stronger and having more rights than men: they would go away from their houses, leaving their children in the care of their husbands or their mothers in law, they would drink and have fun, with no need to answer to anyone on that. In some villages, the young wives were integrated into the community of married women through a special ritual involving, among other things, sprinkling them with water at the river, at the lake or at the well.

This strange custom of fanatic dances and mystic ecstasy survived from its original ancient cult practices dedicated to Dionysus in antiquity in the ancient towns of Callatis, Histria and Tomis on the Black Sea's coast.

In the almanac of the ancient town of Callatis, on whose ruins today's town of Mangalia was built, one month of the year was dedicated to Dionysus, the god of vegetation, of wine and ritual drinking. Some specialists found the origin of this god in the Thracian world from the Iron and Bronze ages, others trace him further back to the micro-Asian and Aegean religions during the Neolithic Age.

Irrespective of the disputed geographical origin of the god, one can be certain of the fact that his cult, so well known in antiquity that it tended to become a universal religion. Seriously fought against by Christianity, it still survives among the Romanians, in the form of the custom called "Women's Feast". Record of the custom was given, until the 20th Century, in South-Eastern Romania, in the counties of Buzau, Ialomita, Tulcea, Constanta.[9]

January 8
Geomorphism and Anthropomorphism

According to the way in which people imagined their worshiped deity, the ancient Europeans created two distinct archetypal worlds: the *geomorphic* Neolithic one, having *the Egg* as its model, and the *anthropomorphic* Indo-European and Christian one, with *Man* as its model.

The ideal of beauty and harmony of the geomorphic shelter is based on the sphere, the perfect form centered at equal from all the points on its surface. We use the term *geomorphism*, from geoid, the typical form of the Earth. The geomorphic world is known to us to its projection into our time of the Neolithic archetypes: the egg and the pot, the clay and the dough, the womb and the vulva, by the mother deities such as the Forest Witch, Caloian's Mother, Rain's Mother, or the Holy Virgin.[10]

Ten millennia separate the first Neolithic cultures in the basin of the lower Danube and the contemporary oral culture documented in the *Ethnographic Atlas of Romania*. Between the two extremes of this long historical line, one researched by archeologists and the other by ethnologists, are a great number of cultural similarities, some of them illustrated in this volume, such as the simple practice of carrying heavy loads on the head by both Neolithic women and women from Oltenia, or the kiss motif present in both Neolithic ceramics and Constantin Brancusi's great sculptures.

---

[9] Fochi, 1984, p.147; Ghinoiu, 2001, p. 91.

[10] Ghinoiu, 2001, p. 91-92.

The archetypes of this 10,000–year span can be divided into three major cultural and religious complexes: the first one is dominated by the Neolithic Mother Goddess from 8,000 to 2,500 B.C, the second by the Indo-European Father God from 2,500 B.C. to the year 0, and the third by Jesus, God's son from year 0 to the present.

But a major spiritual crisis must have shattered the world during the transition from the Neolithic to the Bronze and Iron ages when the geomorphic maternal deity was replaced by the anthropomorphic and paternal one. The anthropomorphic world, organized according to the paternal deity prototype, is the world to which we now belong.

However, a most valuable concept is embodied in the geomorphic one whose prototype was the Mother Goddess, *Gaea*. This was the root from which the latter gods' genealogical branches emerged. Under the name of "Gaea", this Neolithic goddess still appears today in the funeral songs: "Gaea bird has sung/Taking away his soul…"; or in the curse: "May Gaea take you away" with Gaea meaning death; or in children's games: "Playing Mother Gaea"; and in some carols.

Given that our universe is geomorphic, from its smallest structures, the cell, the molecule, the atom, the subquantum units. to its largest ones, the planets, the stars, the galaxies, the galactic clusters and superclusters, its transformation into an anthropomorphic produced a serious rift that divided the natural world from the man-mastered one. But is still conceivable for the two models of life on earth can be reconciled: the geomorphic one introduced by the Neolithic people, in total harmony with the structure of the entire universe, and the anthropomorphic one, imposed with a certain arrogance by the most powerful creature on the planet, namely 'man'.

January 9
Day of the Moon
Luni (Monday)

Monday is the personification of the first day of the week, dedicated to the moon. In the Folk Almanac, this day's patron saints are Peter and Paul as found in the city of Iasi or the archangels Michael and Gabriel in Neamt. The day was believed to bring luck and to be favorable for beginning certain specific activities which were household productive, in particular long-lasting ones, such as weaving, sewing or embroidering peasant blouses and shirts.[11] At the same time on this day of the week, it

---

[11] Fochi 1976, p. 362-363.

was forbidden to trade, to give something on credit, to borrow material goods or to ask in marriage.

As a mythical character, Saint Mother Monday is invoked to help healing animals, especially those born on a Monday, who were also named after this day and named "Lunila" or "Lunaia". In order to gain St. Monday's benevolence, as she could bring health to children and prosperity to families, some women in Oltenia, Muntenia, Dobrogea, Moldavia, celebrate her by eating no food at all, which is even more severe than the fasting usually kept on Wednesdays and on Fridays. In some villages inhabited by cattlemen in Banat, women used to bake maize, flat cake, representing St. Mother Monday, meant to be ritually eaten by shepherds on the first Monday of Lent. By doing so, people believed that their sheep would be protected against wild beasts in the forest, mainly against wolves.

Those born on the Monday were thought to be ugly, but healthy and lucky. Monday is the only day of the week on which it is forbidden to bury the dead.

January 10
Day of the God and Planet Mars
Marți (Tuesday)

Tuesday is a personification of the second day of the week, dedicated by the Romans to God Mars and to the planet Mars, and by the Romanians to the souls which will be born, that is to souls in their pre-existence. Influenced by the Biblical myth, people in central Moldavia, Gorj, Hunedoara, believed that it was on a Tuesday when the world and the Earth were created and when Jesus was born. With strange malicious female representations as their patron, called *Martolea* or *Tuesday-Evening*, this day is a foreboding time, a bad day (Muntenia, Oltenia, Southern Moldavia), with no luck (Central Moldavia), during which there are three evil-chance moments and which brings misfortune (Oltenia, Muntenia, Moldavia), and unsuitable for beginning any major economic activities (plowing, sowing, building a house or a well.[12]

Mars, Bronze Statue
(Popa Lisseanu, 1928)

---

[12] Fochi, 1976, p. 363-364.

On this day of the week, weddings, engagements and proposals of marriage were forbidden. Unlike the other days of the week, Tuesday and Saturday were not considered holy days. In the Folk Almanac several Tuesdays held the equivalent of a holiday position: "Matcalaul", "Tuesday of the Dishes", "Tuesday of the Crows", "Tuesday of the Devil", "Crooked Tuesday", "Tuesday of the Thunder", "Woman Rain Maker", "Tuesday of the Griddle."[13] After Easter and sometimes after Pentecost follow cycles of three to six Tuesdays during which certain economic activities were forbidden.

January 11
Day of the God and Planet Mercury
Mercur (Wednesday)

Wednesday is the personification of the third day of the week, dedicated by the Romans to the god and the planet Mercury. In the Folk Almanac it is a female Saint, less important than Sunday and Friday, but more important than the others. The day was considered *carrier of waters, pitchfork of the Earth, Holy Mary's Day*. In Romanian beliefs and folklore she appears as an old-aged female saint (Neamt), skinny and miserable (Iasi), dressed in white (Vaslui) or, by contrary, undressed and disheveled (Suceava). She would dwell in Heaven (Falciu), in the desert (Tecuci), in the woods (Botosani, Vaslui), in cellars (Tudova, Botosani), or in big palaces (Neamt).

Wednesday looks after wild animals, protects and helps them to find their food. Animals born on a Wednesday are called *Miercan, Mierceaua*. When she appears in sick people's dreams, she cures them of their suffering (Vaslui). On these days, there were no weddings, no proposals of marriages, no parties or any other amusements. Instead, it was a favorable time for charms and for folk medicine practices.[14]

---

[13] Ghinoiu, 1987, p. 117-118.

[14] Fochi, 1976, p. 364-365.

January 12
Day of the God and Planet Jupiter
Joi (Thursday)

Jupiter and the Ligthning, Marble Statue, Drobeta (Miclea, Florescu, 1980)

Thursday is the personification of the fourth day of the week, dedicated by the Romans to the god and the planet Jupiter. According to folk beliefs Saint Thursday is a holy woman (Dorohoi), a beautiful maiden who protects people against heavy rain and hail (Iasi, Tutova), a well-meaning woman, sister to Sunday, Friday and Wednesday.

Thursday is the personification of the fourth day of the week, dedicated by the Romans to the god and the planet Jupiter. According to folk beliefs Saint Thursday. Dorohoi, is a holy woman, a beautiful maiden who protects people against heavy rain and hail (Iasi, Tutova), a well-meaning woman, sister to Sunday, Friday and Wednesday. Thursday lives among clouds, in Heaven (Constanta, Iasi, Olt), in unspoilt woods which are guarded by young maidens (Tutova), in places from which she exerts her magic power over crops, cattle, diseases.[15] In the Nineteenth Century, Thursday was observed as a holiday. In Maramures and Bucovina, social events were forbidden on Thursdays, but weddings or any general expression of love were allowed.

In the *Folk Almanac*, the customs belonging to this day confirm the assumption that Thursday functioned as a holiday, dedicated to worshipping and rest. A number of Thursdays were held as high days such as the Green Thursdays, the Precluded Thursdays, and the Mares' Thursdays.

Under Christian influence, the function of this day was transferred to Sunday which is the only day of the week having a Christian name, *Dies Dumini* or God's Day.

---

[15] Fochi, 1976, p. 365-366.

January 13
Day of The Goddess Venera and Planet Venus
Vineri (Friday)

Friday, the female personification of the fifth day of the week, was dedicated by the Romans to Goddess Venera and to the Planet Venus. Excepting Sunday, Friday was considered the most important day of the week. Venera also appears to be the oldest of all the days of the week. She helps those who take long journeys and those who fall sick by showing herself in their dreams and telling them how to cure themselves. She is patron over wild animals and birds which are her children. In the Folk Almanac she appears as a kind woman, living in reclusion, bearing scratch and blood marks because women work on her day. Saint Friday is the protector of married women whom she helps to deliver their babies and to get their daughters to be married.

An important day in the Folk Almanac, the 14th of October is called the Great Friday or the Sheep's Wedding. Saint Friday wears white or black clothes and dwells in the mountains (Arges, Suceava), in woods (Arges, Buzau, Neamt, Tecuci), in secluded places (Neamt, Iasi), in sea islets, in heaven and in the world beyond. She was invoked in prayers, in magic spells and charms for young girls to get married, for the growth of crops and cattle. Friday is also a day of serious fasting as a sign of respect.[16]

January 14
Day of the God and Planet Saturn
Sambata (Saturday)

Saturn (Popa-Liseanu, 1928)

Saturday is the personification of the last day of the week dedicated by the Romans to the God and to the Planet Saturn. It is an unfortunate time, with one or more evil chances for those living in this world. Instead, it is a favorable time for the

---

[16] Ovidiu Bârlea, 1976.

spirits of the dead in the other world beyond, to whom offerings (alms) are given on Saturdays, especially on the Dead's Saturdays. When practicing magic spells and charms, people frequently invoked Saturdays. Also Saturdays were not thought to be favorable for initiating any important kind of work which took several days, nor for starting a long journey. Children born on a Saturday would have a humorous way of speaking, while cattle delivered on that day would be called "Sambotin" or "Sambotina".[17]

January 15
Seasonal Deities

The middle of the Shepherd's winter, a six months season starting at Saint Demeter (Samedru) on October 26 and ending at Saint George (Sangiorz) on April 23rd, is marked by a three-day holiday between January 15 and 17, is dedicated to several fearful weather deities called *Winter Trials*. They are supposed to be responsible for all the violent manifestations of nature (blizzards, whirlwinds, hail, thunder, etc.) and for all damages brought by wolves and bears to the cattle herds. Together with their brothers, the *Summer Trials*, celebrated six months later in the middle of the Shepherd's summer from July 15 to 17, they divide the cattlemen's year into two symmetrical seasons: winter and summer. They can also cause a neurosis or disease known as *Struck by Trials*. In order to court the favors of these devilish forces, people would show respect toward them by strictly forbidding work.[18]

January 16
"Sanpetru" – The Wolves of Saint Peter

In the night of the 15th to the 16th of January, during Winter's Trials, wolves gather in packs at *howling places* where they start singing to call their great divinity, *Saint Peter* ("Sanpetru"), to distribute their share of prey to which they are entitled for a whole year. Their god arrives at midnight on a white horse and allots each wolf its prey: a lamb, a sheep, a deer, or a human. The wolves would spare no morsel of the shares

---

[17] Fochi, 1976, p. 368-369.

[18] Ghinoiu, 1997, p. 45.

promised by their master, but as obedient subjects they would not touch any other prey.

A Pack of Wolves Invoking the Winter Saint Peter, to Share Their Prey for One ("Jurnalul National", No. 13, 2005)

The story is told of a shepherd being curious to see how wolves meet their divinity. To find out he climbed up to a howling place in broad daylight, and hid himself among the branches of a high fir-tree. After the wolves had gathered and howled their calling, Saint Peter arrived on a white horse. Quietly he distributed the prey to each of his subjects. But before the end of the meeting, a lame wolf came limping. Seeing him, Saint Peter barked at him: "Since you didn't come on time, you should eat that human over there, hiding in the fir-tree." Within a year's time, the story goes, the curious shepherd was eaten by the lame wolf.

January 17
The Anastasia Celebration

The *Anastasia*, Romanian mythical representations celebrated at mid-Shepherd's Winter (16-17 January), bears the combined names of Saint Antonie the Great and Saint Atanasie in the Orthodox Almanac. In the Folk Almanac, the two Saints, also called Anton and Tanase, protectors against the pest, are invoked for bringing health and for curing serious diseases. (Banat, South-Western Oltenia)

January 18
The Day

The first unit of measure for time offered by the cosmos to humans was the solar day, divided into day and night. The time flow during the day was estimated, without using a clock, according to the position of the Sun in the sky: morning, dawn, daybreak, early in the morning were used for the time at sunrise or immediately after it; early midday or little noon was called the moment when the Sun has traveled one third of its ascent; noon or "high noon" were the names for the time when the Sun had traveled half of its ascent, at about nine or ten; "under-noon" represented about 11 o'clock; "at noon", "noon at the cross", "at the crossing in the sky" were names given to the moment when the Sun ends its ascent; finally there were "afternoon:, "small dinner", "at supper", "at vesper bell", "at sunset".

God said: This is the day and this is the night." (Gromovnic, 1993)

In some ethnographical regions, the day was divided into three parts (morning, noon and evening), or into four parts (morning, noon, afternoon and evening). The night in its turn was also divided into three parts (evening, midnight and morning), or into four parts (evening, midnight, rooster's crow, and morning).

As with other unit measures of time, the solar day became anthropomorphic: "In the beginning, days were viewed as humans who were walking around on the Earth. But now there is no more of this, because people have become so sinful." Some days became male (Monday, Tuesday and Thursday), others were females (Wednesday, Friday, Saturday and Sunday). In many cases days turned into mythical representations (St. Friday, St. Sunday), or received a patron Saint ("Sântilie" or "Sântion" - "Saint John" for Thursday, Holy Mary for Wednesday, Saint Nicolae for Thursday and Saint Lazarus for Saturday).[19] (Niculita-Voronca, 1903, p. 261)

---

[19] Niculita-Voronca, 1903, p. 338.

January 19
The Midpoints and the Borders of the Day

The solar day has two midpoints (one in the daytime and the other in the night) and two borders (sunrise and sunset). According to folk belief the two midpoints in the time of the day were critical moments for man's life development and accomplishment. At midnight a fierce confrontation between good and evil forces took place. Gradually the space and the time of the night purified themselves and the good forces reached maximum power at dawn. Midnight and sunrise were opposing moments for the fulfillment or the annihilation of magical acts. However, the midpoints of the day and of the night had also a positive function. They were resting moments for the immortal stars, the Sun and the Moon, as well as for humans on Earth. "Only at midday does the sun straightforwardly take a rest, just an eye's wink long. There is no more resting for it and then it travels on and on, all day and all night long... Therefore when the Sun is right up at noon, Man must also rest, which means that working is a sin".

January 20
The Week

The time unit equal with the number of nights passing between two successive phases of the moon is called a *week*. The old lunar almanacs divided time into lunar months, each month starting when the New Moon appeared, and into weeks, each week having seven days. In a solar year with 365 days there are 13 lunar months or lunar periods and 52 weeks or moon phases. The days of the week bear the names of stars visible with the naked eye from the Earth: The Moon, Mars, Mercury, Jupiter, Venus and Saturn. Regionally, those weeks are dedicated to some terrible mythical representations (Saint Toader's Horses, Philippies, Epihany) have 8 days and are manifest in the most important ritual knot-shaped pieces of bread, which are sacrificed at Macinici celebration and are shaped in the figure eight.

A seven-day week was for a long time not known to the Romans. They used an eight days sequence called *nundinae*, in which the days were marked with letters from "A" to "H". Every end of a almanac period (day, week, month, season, and year) was considered of an ill-fated nature.

The ritual of the end and of the beginning of the week comprised 3 days: Saturday whose baleful nature was revealed by its three 'evil-chance' moments, Sunday, which celebrated the victory of the good forces over the evil ones accumulated in the previous week and Monday which marked the beginning of the week under the most favorable signs for human activities. The time span of a week was born on Sunday, it became nature on Thursday and then it got old, which was an indispensable condition for its weekly rebirth.

With the spread of the Christian religion, the first day of the week, the Roman Sunday became *God's Day,* a reality preserved throughout the Medieval Chronology. It was Constantin the Great who set up Sunday (Dies Domini Dominica) as the beginning of the week, in the year 321 A.D.

For Romanians and for other South-Eastern European people the week starts with Monday, as it did in the past and as it does at present.[20]

January 21
The Daily Meals

Lunch with the granparents

The determined moments in which people living in the countryside interrupted their work in order to eat and rest are called the *daily meals.* There are two factors which indicate the number of meals and the time length from one meal to the other: an astronomical one, namely the height reached by the Sun in the sky, and another one pertaining to human psychology, namely feeling hungry. According to the meals criterion, the day was divided into three uneven parts: lunch, dinner and evening meal. In summer days, one more meal was added: "the small dinner" ("chindia"). A synonym for "chindia" is the term

---

[20] Ghinoiu, 1988, p. 60-62.

"ojina" used in Transylvania to describe the time between lunch and sunset.

January 22
Sunday, the Day of the Holy Sun
Duminica (Sunday)

Sunday, the only day of the week bearing a Christian name (Dies Dominiu Dominica- God's Day), is dedicated to the Sun, the 'star' which humans love most. In Romanian beliefs and folklore, Sunday orders each day of the week what tasks to perform, eats once every seventh day and spends all the time praying. It is a benevolent mythical character: a holy woman (Covurlui, Iasi, Vaslui, Dolj); a human being (Neamt, Caras-Severin); the greatest Holy Mother (Tutova, Botosani); a nun (Iasi, Salaj); a great lady whose subjects are all the other days of the week and who gives orders to every one of them

The Sun with a Human Face Dressed in Traditional Clothes
(Sucevita Monastery Fresco, N. Dimancescu 2006)

telling them what to do (Falciu); a live goddess (Tecuci); the other days' eldest sister (Iasi, Neamt, Vaslui). Holy Sunday would seemingly live on the other side of Saturday's Waters, in golden palaces (Neamt), in woods where humans never set foot (Botosani, Vaslui) and she wears white garments. She appears in people's dreams or in reality to teach them how to get rid of diseases and to prevent damage (Vaslui). But she may also appear with a woman's face, with hen's legs if people eat meat on fast days (Neamt), she may be scratched and be bleeding if women have washed the laundry, have spun or have sewn on her day (Romanati). Sunday celebrates herself by not working (Fagaras), she prays and eats once every seven days (Tecuci), she can make miracles, bringing only good things to people. Often she appears in the form of a river surrounding Heaven, unlike "Saturday's Waters" which surrounds Hell. On Sundays magic charms are forbidden, excepting love spells and spells for finding a pre-destined partner or guessing one's fate (Oltenia, Muntenia, Dobrogea, Southern and Central Moldavia). Cattle born on a Sunday bear the names *Duman* or *Dumaia*.[21]

January 23
Life

Man's existence on Earth spans two major biological landmarks: birth and death. At his arrival from another world, from his pre-existence, the newly born is a stranger here, lacking any identity. Throughout subsequent integrative stages experienced by each individual from pre-existence, then as a newborn and until his departure into post-existence, help is provided by intermediaries, namely the grandparents, the godparents, the parents, the priest and by some institutions such as the family, the community, the young lads' and maidens' troops, the church.

Prehistoric Couple, Gulmenita Culture Mil. IV-III B.C.
(I. Miclea, R. Florescu, 1980)

Immediately after birth, the baby the baby is laid on the ground, a gesture symbolizing his coming into *this world*. In time, other integrative rites follow in stages over a lifetime: into the *family* (paternal recognition of the child, a custom called "paying the switch" in Moldavia); into *the faith community* (baptism, crossing the baby in front of icons, the ritual bathe after baptism,

---

[21] Ovidiu Bîrlea, 1976, p. 452.

christening feast); into the *sex group* (the custom of trimming the forelock for the boys and breaking the flat cake for the girls); into *age and spiritual kinship groups* (rituals of young people: they called or behaved themselves as sisters, cousins, close friends or blood brothers) into *pre-marriage social groups* (the young boys' troop, the maidens' sitting, the village ring dance ("hora"); into *the group of married people* (asking in marriage, engagement and wedding ceremonies); into the *householders' group* and then into the *old folks group*.

Preparation for other important passages, over the threshold of death, became a priority in one's old-age. This meant gathering all the necessary things for burial, sharing confidences with one's children and grand children, asking for forgiveness from those to whom one had done wrong, bequeathing one's possessions on one's deathbed or by will.

Throughout the integrative stages experienced by each human since, from pre-existence, to birth, and until his departure into post-existence, help is provided by intermediaries. These are the grandparents, old men, parents, priests, or social groups such as the extended family, the wider community, young men and maiden groups, or the church.[22]

January 24
After-life

The transformation from one form of being into another, from the laws ruling over life into the laws ruling over death, have in all times, caused humans to fear. After-life or *post-existence* is the life of the soul after death, in the beyond. The colloquial expression *time has come* refers to what must necessarily happen at a certain moment, including death. In an unspoken way, people accept their mortality and submit to the windmill of time. Paradoxically, in nature death generates life. If every living thing on Earth became immortal and if the living creatures' tendency to breed endlessly was maintained, our planet would turn into a wasteland after the resources generated by the living creatures' death have been quickly consumed.

Fortunately post-existence, or the world beyond, is hospitable and infinitely roomy. The only unnatural events are those happening before or after the destined point, for example the death of an unmarried young person or of the *unwed* who haven't known *the way of the world*; getting over the passing of the right time of marriage, as in the case of *spinsters* and *old bachelors*.

In order to regain balance and to correct natural or social errors, people resorted to rituals and to myths, thus using unnatural methods for

---

[22] Ghinoiu, 2001, p. 70.

unnatural happenings. But while every individual can decide to marry or not, to have children or not, none can decide not to die.

Confronted but such irreversible dilemmas, people formulate optimistic explications: death is not an ultimate extinction but only a departure into post-existence. The belief of the traditional Romanian village was that when a man dies, he only changes his shelter and moves from his house, as a young girl does when she gets married.

January 25
Pre-Life

Pre-life or pre-existence, the soul's life within the uterus, starts with the nuptial act and ends with the child's birth. The soul in this form of existence passes through an extremely condensed time from the egg-cell stage into a human creature. The life inside the uterus is a time of rapid changes in which ontogeny repeats phylogeny. The placenta, also called *little shelter* or *the child's house*, insures the embryo and the fetus protection against the aggression of infections, germs and toxins, against blows, noise or disturbing light. Truly miraculous are the first 40 days when the embryo lives according to the paleontological time of its ancestors. The latter are grouped by biologist into two categories: invertebrates and chordates (fish, amphibians, reptiles, birds, mammals). After 6 weeks the conceived being takes human shape. During the second month of its intra-uterus life, it rapidly develops its cephalic end and its face is also being formed. The evolution is quite amazing. Within the first days of its existence, its volume grows 8,000 times and it's diameter about 20 times.

Man comes into being through a biological explosion in the same way in which the Universe was born through a cosmic explosion (The Big Bang). The first part of a human's intra-uterus time, of about 40 days, equates in years to the components of his entire social life (the young married couple's first visit to church, the confinement period at death) as well as of his religious one (the main-fasting periods over the year, the number of days between Christmas and the Day of Welcoming the Virgin Mary, and also between Easter and Ascension).[23]

---

[23] Ghinoiu, 2001, p. 154

January 26
Folk Astronomy

Social life order was achieved by observing repetitive moving phenomena observed in the in the Sky (sunrise and sunset, equinoxes and solstices) and the Earth (succession of cold or warm seasons, of rainy and dry ones, plant life cycles and animal reproduction cycles). The part of the folk science containing observations and representations about stars, empirically obtained and transmitted through folk channels, is called *Folk Astronomy*. This astronomical knowledge, based on a practical need for time orientation and for planning human activities over seasons, months, weeks and days, developed an efficient chronometrical system on which the Folk Almanac was grounded.

According to some folk beliefs, the myriad stars in the sky would represent the number of humans born after Adam, while, according to others, stars are born, and die together with the people to whom they are dedicated. Therefore, stars and people make up two parallel worlds having an equal number of inhabitants: one in the Sky and the other on Earth. Based on this belief, charms were performed using, for example, a sick person's star to make him well, or using an unmarried girl's star to find out her destined future husband and to hasten her marriage.

January 27
Star Gazers

The sky with its huge star family has always helped people to orient themselves in time and space. It offered meteorological and climatic information, marked the beginning and end of the day, and determined seasonal or yearly activities. Those stars (the planets, the comets) visible to the naked eye were given names relative to people's material and spiritual environment on Earth.

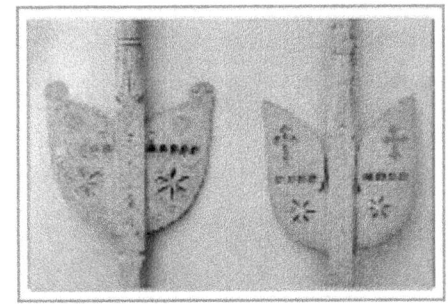

Solar symbols on distaffs from Valea Sebesului
(Gh. Pavelescu, 2004)

Romanian folk ways built up a parallel world out of stars, similar to the one they were living in on Earth: *household and rural site elements* (the House and its Grounds, the Hut, the Well at the Crossroads, the Girl with the Yoke, the Maiden in the Ring Dance, the Pit, the Ring Dance, the Well, the Well with the Trough, the Pen, the Wooden Bell Board, the Stake), *occupations* (Fiddler, Cowherd, Coachman, Swineherd, Archer, Warrior), *domestic animals and birds* (Ram, Ox, Dog, Whelp, Clucking Hen, Shepherd's Dog, Little Dog, Hen, Kids, Pigs, Sow, Boar), *wild animals and birds, fish, snakes* (Raven, Carps, A Pack of Wolves, Wolf, the Home of Wolves, Hares, Black Bird, Fish, Crab, Scorpion, Thrush, Snake, the Big Bear, The Small Bear), *means of transport* (the Big Cart, the Small Cart, the Shepherd's Yoke, Path, Carriage, the Slaves' Road), *agricultural and handicraft tools* (Drill, Scythe, Rake, Plough, Little Plough, Butting Plough, Sickle, Terrier, Ground Auger, Gimlet, the Big Auger), *household inventory pieces* (Scales, Balance, Alarm Clock), *cult, biblical elements* (Monastery, the Cross, Midnight's Cross, the Small Cross, the Friend's Cross, the Cross of God's Chair, the Holy Mary, the Virgin, Virgin Mary, Abraham), *heroes or characters from fairytales* (the Crab's Cart, God's Cart, Treasure, the King's Daughter with Yoke, the Three Kids, King, Queen of the Stars, Dragon, the Foe, the Dawn).[24]

The people in the Carpato-Danubian region, who could not read and write, but who knew a lot about the stars were the descendents of a marvelous oral civilization, which survived in part as of the Folk Almanac, the Pantheon and the Romanian Book of the Dead.

January 28
The Tale of the Helleborus

As the story goes, the hellebore plant, whose roots can heal cattle from anthrax and from bleeding, had a wicked stepmother. Wanting to get rid of him sooner, she woke him up one night in the Frosty Month, and said to him hoping he would sprout in the midwinter with snow over his head: "Wake up, Hellebore, wake up, for all the flowers have waken, they might also have already blossomed!" God who sees and knows everything bestowed him with the gift to cure illnesses. Since then it is said that the hellebore root, a plant which springs in winter, can save from death all those suffering from anthrax. The ritual requires that the plant be pulled out from the ground by a naked man during the Pentecost Week.[25]

---

[24] Pamfile, 1915, p. 48-49.

[25] *Legends of the Flora*, 1994, p.204.

January 29
The Winter "Phillipies"

The Winter Phillipies are divinities who protect wolves and they are celebrated by shepherds at the end of January and the beginning of February. In the "Folk Almanac" *The Winter Phillipies* mark the end of a long mating period for wolves, having started about eighty days before at the *Autumn Phillipies*.

January 30
The Three Magi

Trisfetitele or the *Three Magi* is the folk name given to the holiday dedicated to the three hierarchs (saints), Vasile, Grigorie and Ioan, celebrated on January 30 in the Orthodox Almanac. They are recognized as the great scholars of Christianity, who studied science and the philosophy of their time. But to put an end to the misunderstandings and to the discord that had appeared among the Christian believers, it was established for the sake of conciliation, that the three saints be celebrated on the same day. Thus, by celebrating them together, the Orthodox Church jointly acknowledged and praised their righteous faith in Jesus Christ as well as their wisdom and their struggle against the heretics. In their honor, Moldavia's ruler, Vasile Lupu built in Iasi the Three Saints' Church. People associate them with doctors who performed miracles and with healers of human diseases. Locally, for fear of being punished with fire, diseases or loss, people celebrated the Three Saints by prohibiting work in various ways. To them were also dedicated the group of stars in the middle of the constellation of Orion, called the *Three Magi*, the *Magi from Sunrise*, the *King's Belt*.

Together with other neighboring stars, the Three Saints form "Rarita" (Plough or Rake), The Gimlet or the Big Anger (Moldavia and the Western Carpathians). In Mehedinti this star group, in the constellation of Orion, is called The Staves.

January 31
Father Martin

Father Martin is a personification of the bear in the Carpathian Pantheon. He is celebrated during the Macavei days on August 1, the Autumn Martin between November 12 and 14, the Winter Martin between February 1 and 3, the Bear's Day on February 2), and on the Bear's Saturday one week before the Saturday before Palm Sunday. On these particular days, people avoid using the word "bear", or, when necessary, they use other names, such as Father Martin, the Old One, the Old Father.

Bear Costume
(N. Jula, V. Mănăstireanu, 1968)

In some shepherd communities, the bear used to receive on its day a veal leg (Tara Hategului). The characteristics that raised the bear to rank of god were its force, its seeming resemblance to humans and its capacity of walking on two legs. At the geographical latitude where Romania is situated bears usually pair at the end of the summer and beginning of autumn, period in which they produce a lot of damage to the sheep herds, to the orchards and to the bee hives. The day opening the reproduction cycle of the bear is called in the Folk Almanac The Bears' Cub Making or The Bears' Macavei on August 1. After a pregnancy period of 7-8 months the female gives birth in difficult conditions at the beginning of February. The Romanians marked this event in the Folk Almanac by a three-day holiday called The Winter Martin on February 1 to 3.

In the Romanian tradition, Father Martin is rather more useful than harmful to humans. He can have a good influence over the Fates when a child is born; the new born, who is oiled with bear grease, will grow up strong and healthy (Luncani, Tara Mosilor); the one who is smoked with bear hair can be cured from fright; men who were stepped on by bears in spring would get rid of backache during the summer; the bear masks meet dead people's disoriented souls in the death watch nights (Vrancea). Children named Bear (Urs) were believed to be spared from diseases or the diseases could be traced away by charms when the name Bear was invoked:

Get away, you ill-health,
You weakling,
For a big bear will come after you,
He will crush you,
He will scrape you with his claws,
He will eat you up with his mouth ...

Often, Father Martin's teeth would be worn as a talisman.

FEBRUARY
"FAURAR"
IRONSMITH

1	Trifon of the Vineyards
2	Arezan of the Vineyards
3	The Meteorologist Bear
4	February, the Naughty Kid
5	The Devil ("Dracul")
6	Three Types of Plum Brandy: "Drachiu", "Dracila" and "Tuica"
7	"Paca" – The Witch Mother of Smoking
8	"Child Born of Flowers" - Illegitimate Child
9	Wedding Customs Related to the Folk Almanac
10	Haralambie, the Patron Saint of the Plague
11	Vlasie
12	Superstitions
13	Thirteen, the Unlucky Number?
14	The Ironware's Weed
15	Folk Units for Measuring Time
16	The Spell and the Greeting
17	Shelters of the Soul
18	Entrances and Exits of the Soul
19	The Charm
20	The Technique of the Charm
21	Number and Order of the Months in the Almanac
22	The Snowdrop
23	"The Stormy One"
24	Dragobete
25	The Ritual Pot Breaking
26	Shrovetide for Meat
27	The Goblin
28	The Fools' Week
29	The Legend of the Leap Year

February

The name *Faur* given to the month is connected to ironsmiths, handicraft men who processed iron into work tools and who sharpened or produced iron bars and plough knives before the farming season began. As a personification of the shortest month of the year, 28 days normally, 29 days in leap years, Faur is the youngest of his 11 brothers. The Macedo-Romanians in Bulgaria from the village of Pestera, meaning 'the cave', use the name *"Scurtul,"* the Short One, for the month of February.

The changing weather during the month of February reflects the child Faur's whims. When the child laughs and smiles it is fine weather, when he cries it is a snowstorm, when he is angry it is bitter cold. He gets into conflict with March who refuses to give back the cold days he has borrowed because he wanted to spoil brother Prier's flowers which explains the changing weather from the beginning of March, when the two brothers allegedly fight over the borrowed days.

By recounting such tales, old people would explain to their children and grandchildren why the month of February contains fewer days than the other months of the year. During the month, it is said that peace and quiet are brought into a village by Santoader's Horses. This is symbolized by strong and handsome young men wearing horsetails inside their trousers and hooves in their peasant sandals. They enter a home at evening sitting-time when girls meet boys and take the girls to dance. They fly with them high up into the sky where they then let them fall back on the earth.

During February, village evening events when young people enjoying amusements during the long winter nights. With the farming season drawing nearer, economic preoccupations took precedence. This meant attending to animals used for work, repairing tools, and preparing seeds for sowing.

February 1
Trifon of the Vineyards

Trifon of the Vineyards, celebrated on February 1, is a mythical representation ruling over caterpillars, grasshoppers, worms and beetles. In the Muscel area of Wallachia, on this particular day, called *Trifon of the Worms*, water was consecrated in church and then sprinkled over the orchards.[26]

Hearts's Tongue - symbolic of true love (Parvu, 2000)

Celebrated one day before the Christian holiday called Welcoming our Lord (February 2nd), Trifon of the Vineyards is also called *The Stormy Young Man*. He was a handsome young man fallen from the sky who would come in the way of young girls and young wives. When he came into a village "every female would come out of her senses and would walk around dizzy and confused." The Stormy Young Man is said even to have scared Holy Mary when, 40 days after birth, she was taking the baby to church for purification. For his disrespectful behavior Virgin Mary turned him from a handsome young man into a love plant, casting a spell on him:

Stormy as you are, may you be stormy;
Live as you live among love weeds,
May you become a love weed forever!

That day was also favorable for performing charms or spells which would cause loss and damage to one's enemies.

February 2
Arezan of the Vineyards

In some parts in the South of Romania, the night of February 1 to 2, a Bachic ceremony of Thracian origin was performed, which was called *Arezan* or *Gurban of the Vineyards*. During the morning, men would ride into the vine plantations, usually in horse-drawn sledges. Before leaving the village they would call out: "Come, let us go to Gurbanu!" Once

---

[26] Bratiloveanu-Popilian, 2001, p. 34-36.

they arrived at the vineyard, each owner took a couple of vine shoots and put them around their waist. Then they would dig out the bottle of wine which had been buried the previous autumn and get together on a hill around a burning fire. There, around the flames, the men ate, drank, danced, jumped over the fire and sprinkled wine over the hot glow. In the evening they returned home with burning torches in their hands and continued to feast in family groups. Judging from the name of the custom, it is possible that in old times, an animal (sheep or ram) was sacrificed there and the participants ate it.

February 3
The Meteorologist Bear

The first three days in February are dedicated to a prehistoric deity called The Winter Martin, patron of the bears.

Carpathian Bear (Zoologica Atlas, 1983)

The strongest and the most dangerous of them, the Great Martin, is celebrated on February 2, a day also called *Stretenia* or The Bear's Day. This period is considered a favorable for making weather and astronomical observations and also for predicting how rich the vine and the fruit-tree production will be. According to traditional beliefs, the bear comes out of its den on this particular day to see its shadow cast on the snow. If it is a cold and foggy day and it cannot see its own shadow, it destroys its den, dances frantically, goes to the river, drinks some water and attends to its duties in the woods. Instead, if there is nice and sunny weather and it can see its shadow, it goes back into its den as the winter will last for another 40 days.

In folk beliefs, fairy tales and legends, the bear appears as a mysterious creature of the woods. His cubs are born in winter, whereas other animals wait for warmer seasons. If the weather is fine, he goes into his shelter; if the weather is bad he starts up his activities in the woods. When he finds a bridge over a river he destroys it; when he does not find one, he fells a tree and lays it across the river. People associate this unusual behavior with the changing weather conditions at the end of the winter and the beginning of spring.

Father Martin used to be a human, perhaps a miller or a shepherd in his village. But as legend has it, he became a bear though continuing to have human qualities. He fell in love with a woman whom he stole and took to his house (den) in the forest, building a shelter for wintertime, forecasting the cold and the warm weather over the coming year. But there was one thing he could not do. He could not make fire.

There is a unique connection between the vine whose patron is Trifon of the Vineyards and the bears whose patron is Winter Martin. This is expressed by the phrase: *A good wine has the power of a bear.* The common celebrations of the bear and the vine in the beginning of February overlap two biorhythms in nature. When bears bring forth their cubs in the forest, sap starts to run through the vines and through the trunks of fruit-trees.

February 4

February, the Naughty Child

As with measures of time, days, weeks, seasons, and years, months are personified. They can be old or young, good or bad. One story is told as follows:

"The Year was an old man who had 12 sons, named like the months: January, February and so on. His only possession was a vineyard. With God's will, the man and his sons managed to harvest the grapes. They made wine, which they stored in one single barrel and they agreed not to drink of it before the beginning of the year. So far so good!

"After that, to avoid causing any misunderstanding, each of them set his own tap in the barrel, which was quite sensible of them. February, the youngest of them, placed his tap lowest of all, close to the stave. That was how things used to work in those days, namely the youngest one would always chose last. Each of the twelve brothers wished to keep the wine in the barrel and not drink of it, only to show off and make the others envious, except for February who started to drink of his wine little by little. That made him cheerful and talkative. He kept babbling and whistling all the time. The others were laughing at him and thinking for themselves: 'He's going to finish the wine pretty soon and then we'll see if he will be so happy any longer.'

"One day, January felt like tasting his wine. He turned on the tap, but not drop of wine came out. The others also tried but found, too, that there was no wine left. Only at the lowest part of the barrel, close to the stave, which was February's share there was some wine still pouring out. Angered, all the brothers rushed to get February and gave him a thrashing for what he had done to them. As then ran after him, February cried loudly; but when they let him be, he would laugh like a child.

"That is why, from that time on, the month of February is a changing one. Sometimes it is warm, sometimes it snows, and other times it freezes – in the same way as it was when February's brothers were chasing him."[27]

February 5
The Devil (Dracul)

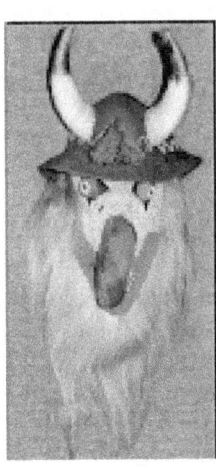 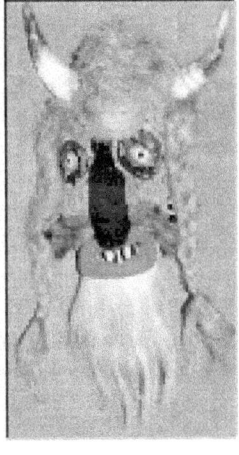

The Devil and His Spouse: Terrible Couple

The Devil is the most dangerous demon of the Romanian Pantheon, a great Indo-European godlike spirit usurped by Christianity. Actually in certain expressions and sayings people see the Devil as being less repellent. For instance, the phrase *a devil of a girl* refers to a young, smart and quick-minded girl; *turning the devil ten times around* means that a person succeeds or achieves something in life.

The Devil has a mother (the Devil's Mother), a father (Scaraoschi, Satan, the Fiend) and younger brothers (Aghiuta). There are two kinds of devils: *visible* ones with horns, a long tail and long claws, and *invisible* ones who were originally angels that were banished from Heaven by God. Their residence is Hell or the wasteland, which is often mentioned in charms.

Sometimes the Devil is named after the place where he stays more often. *May he vanish in the wasteland. The one in the marsh. The marsh dweller.* The fact that he comes from under the Earth is confirmed by his physical

---

[27] *Legends of the cosmos*, 1994, p. 212-213.

appearance and by his behavior. He is black and ugly (The Dark One); he is handicapped (The Lame One or The Hideous One); he has a tail (The Tailed One) and horns (The One With Horns); he is wicked and dishonest to God (The Un-brotherly One); he wears a skullcap which can make him invisible (Little Skull Cap or The One With the Red Cap); he is repulsive (The Monster, Filthy Monster, Wild Beast); and he can metamorphosize into animals, birds and dragons.

But though transformed into certain creatures or objects existing on Earth, he cannot become a sheep, bee, lamb, pigeon or donkey. He can be driven away by making the sign of the cross with the hand on the body or with the tongue in the mouth, by consecrated water, by the smell of frankincense, by the sound of church bells, or by the beat of the wooden bell-board used to call people to church. This explains the origin of some euphemistic names attributed to him: Cross-May-Kill-Him, Cross-May-Beat-Him, Church-Toll-May-Kill-Him.

Being ingenious and impatient, he can invent various things, plants and animals on Earth, in a playful way, by accident, on his own initiative or at he suggestion of God, his Brother. He is invoked by those who perform witchcraft, but driven away by those who perform charms.[28] Using well-known curses invoking the Devil, people send him all kinds of objects or creatures on Earth. Initially, having been God's brother, he contributed to the Earth and the world creation.

But though powerful, he is less intelligent than God. Whatever he makes remains unfinished, or either he doesn't know how to use his creations, or he uses them for destructive purposes. He builds a house with no windows. He invents the sieve for carrying water or struggles to put both feet in the same boot. Some of his creations are taken over by God who gives them an appropriate use by making a pot for carrying water, a house for living in it, a boot for being put on someone's foot.

God and the Devil often compete with each other. Thus arose popular dichotomies: the Devil creates the goat, God creates the sheep; the Devil builds the pub, God builds the church; the Devil invents tobacco and plum brandy while God invents frankincense and wine.

---

[28] Candrea, 1999, p. 143-146.

February 6

Types of Plum Brandy: "Drachiu", "Dracila" and "Tuica"

Unlike wine, which was created by God, plum brandy was invented by the Devil. Folk accounts from the Bucovina region describe it this way:

"Once there was a man who made *mamaliga*, unsalted cornmeal mush, by mistake. The Devil, who only eats unsalted food, found some and ate it. In the evening, when all the devils gathered in front of their chief, they told him what they had done in that day. The one who had eaten the unsalted cornmeal mush, confessed about it. 'Well,' said the oldest and chief, 'I'm afraid you didn't do the right thing, so you must go and do some work for that man in exchange for the food you have eaten.' The Devil had no choice but to become that man's servant.

"The devil sent the man to his landowner to bale all the wheat in the field until the next morning and the only food he would get was what his boys could carry on their backs. The Devil together with his demons worked all night and finished all the work by morning. They worked in the same way for several landowners. 'What shall we do now? With all this bread that is left?' asked the man. 'Don't worry, I'll teach you,' said the Devil. 'Make a still!' So he taught the man how to make one.

"When the still was ready, the devils gathered to decide over the name of the drink that they were going to make. The older devils decided that, in their name, the drink should be called "drachiu". 'How about in our name?' argued the middle-aged ones. And what about us said the youngest?' That was how they established the name "drachiu" for the strongest plum brandy, the name "dracila" for the medium-strong one, and the name "tuica" for the weak one".

February 7

Paca – The Witch Mother of Smoking

Ever since its introduction into the Romanian provinces, smoking was considered a vice and traditional means were used to fight against it. The mythical folk representation invoked for every man who smoked was called *Paca* in Alba, Hunedoara and other Transylvania counties; in Vâlcea, it was called *Pafa*. The malefic character Paca or Pafa is identified as the Devil's Mother, creator of the Devils of tobacco and smoking habits. In folk representations Pâca resembles an old hag, ugly and as dark as Hell, with horns on her head, with a long hooked nose, with swollen eyes like a drowned goat, with fangs like a wild boar's, with claws like sickles, with a tail like a beast's, with a long pipe in her mouth, with flames coming out of her nose and stinking of tobacco from her mouth. For the memory of their Mother, the story goes, the Devils managed to drop a seed in the earth from which "Devils' weed or tobacco came up. The Devils gave this weed to Man so that he could draw smoke in his throat and when the smoke came out it would sound like Pfff! In that way they would remember Pafa, their Mother."

Masks for Death Watch made by PavelTertiu from Nereju, Vrancea County (AIEF Photo by C. Eretescu)

Another legend explains the creation of frankincense and tobacco. "When our Lord Jesus Christ died and was buried in the earth, frankincense grew on his tomb. On the Devil's tomb grew the Devil's incense, tobacco. Then the Devil said to God: 'Let's see now what would most people run for: the incense or the tobacco?' When people came, most of them ran to tobacco on the Devil's tomb. Seeing that so many people came for tobacco, the Devil said: 'Lord, give me all those who will smoke tobacco!' And God said: 'They shall all be yours!'"[29] The connection between the Devil and tobacco is often mentioned in extemporaneous songs:

> *So many girls have gathered here,*
> *All have pipes in their mouths,*
> *The Devil comes out from the precipice,*
> *And lights them!*

February 8
"Child Born of Flowers" - Illegitimate Child

A child born of flowers is the expression used for a child who is born outside marriage. It refers to the legend of the virgin girl who got pregnant while smelling a flower. Used in situations that violate the norm,

---

[29] *The Legends of the flora*, 1994, p. 213.-244.

namely a woman giving birth to a child before getting married, the expression has a wide range of regional synonyms.

The terms used can be euphemistic and metaphorical child born of 'flowers', or of a 'leaf', or in the 'field', or as harmful and insulting as a child born of 'pity', 'bastard', a 'slut's child', a 'foundling', or an 'outcast'. Linguists consider that the ancient term used for a child born of an unwed woman, prior to the separation of the South-Danubian dialects from the North-Danubian ones, would have been *copil*, found with both Romanians and Megelno-romanians. Even today in some villages in Banat, girls who have illegitimate children are referred to with the same word (*se copilesc*).

Illegitimate childbirth had negative consequences. The most rejected person was the mother. By giving birth to a child before getting married, she became an undesirable member of the wives' community. "A girl with a begging child," it was said, "is a shame in front of everybody. Even if she sometimes cast away the child or tries to hide, people would find out about her. She would stay unmarried, or in case she manage to get a man, he had to be a widower, or divorced, anyway, quite worthless". (Suslanesti, jud. Arges).

As for the child's father, if known, he would be blamed and people would speak badly about him for some time, but he wouldn't suffer any other consequences. People used to say about him "He puts his hands in his pockets and carries on as before", or "When a man's hat falls on the ground, he picks it up, shakes off the dust and keeps walking."

Children born outside marriage were considered innocent and definitely not to be blamed for not being born within a real family. They are said to be luckier, more beautiful and cleverer than legitimate children. However, in the case of an illegitimate girl, she could face difficulties in marrying, because in the partner selection the image of her mother counted. This is suggestively expressed by the saying: "The she-goat jumped over the table, but the kid can jump over the house!" or "High as the she-goat can jump, the kid can jump ever higher."[30]

February 9
Wedding Customs Related to the Folk Almanac

Planning for a wedding required time and a proper psychological preparation. A folk saying remarks that :

---

[30] Trebici, Ghinoiu, 1986, p. 214.

*When it's time to marry,
it's no time for working,
for if you go to work then
your heart feels heavy and in pain!*

The reproduction cycles of plants and animals and rules subsequently imposed by the Church established two major wedding seasons: the autumn season until Shrovetide before Christmas in predominantly farming villages; and the winter season, between the January Epiphany and the day before of the beginning of Easter period of Lent in pasture land villages. During the summer season some preferred days for having weddings are influenced by country feasts held at *Dragaica*, (on the 24th of June) and at *Santilie* on the 20th of July.

*Breaking the Bride's Knot-Shaped Bread
(AIEF photo by Maria Constantin)*

Marriages and conjugal relations were forbidden by the Church during fasting days of the week, during the periods of Lent throughout the year and during fasting periods. Thursdays and Sundays were considered the most favorable days of the week for asking in marriage, engagements, "giving away", and the actual religious service. As for the other days, the mythical personification of Wednesday is a lonely widow, ill-fated in not marrying. And for Saturday and Tuesday, each has three evil moments. This is reflected in various sayings: "Everything is upside down and the wedding is on a Tuesday"; "Not only are they no longer young, but they also got engaged on a Friday!" Until the Nineteenth Century, Thursday was considered a holiday, a custom also preserved in other cultures. In Maramures and in Bucovina people were free to have weddings and to make love in general on Thursdays. To the present in some villages in Maramures, weddings are held on Thursdays and not on Sundays. Ethnographic evidence support of the theory that Thursday used to be a day dedicated to a domestic cult and to resting. This changed under Christian influence when the functions of that day were transferred to Sunday.[31]

---

[31] Trebici, Ghinoiu, 1986, p. 269-276.

February 10
Haralambie, the Patron Saint of the Plague

Haralambie, the martyr Saint celebrated by the Orthodox Church, is considered a great protector against diseases. He allegedly keeps them tied up with chains and releases them whenever humans ignore his power. As a secular character, Haralambie was said to have been a shepherd, one reason why he was chosen to be the patron saint of domestic animals. In that capacity he protects people and cattle from becoming ill and also from attack by wild beasts. In order to gain his benevolence on his day people fast, sprinkle consecrated water over cattle and fruit trees, perform charms and forbid any household activities connected with wool or animal hide processing. Customs and beliefs about Haralambie have been recorded in Bucovina, Maramures, Moldavia and in Wallachia.

Haralmabie
(Irimie, Focsa, 1968)

February 11
Vlasie

The martyr Saint Vlasie, celebrated on February 11, is the protector of forest birds and of pregnant women. On that day non-migratory birds, including those that spend the winter in the Carpato-Danubian area, are said to start singing. This holiday is observed by farmers in order to prevent damages brought to their crops by birds in the forest. It is also celebrated by pregnant women wanting to give birth to a healthy child (Bucovina, Moldavia).

Two weeks following Vlasie Day comes *Dragobete* on February 24, when birds pair up and begin to build their nests, and other celebrations such as *The Birds' Constandinu* on May 21, when they teach their nestlings to fly, *The Birds' Storage* on September 1st, when they prepare their winter supplies, or *The Crows' Tuesday* the first week during the Easter period of Lent. The migratory birds are celebrated on some special days like *Cuckoo's Hush* on June 24, when it stops singing, and *The Storks' Day* at the first snowfall after the Forty Martyrs' Day.

February 12
Superstitions

While few would argue that superstitions should be rehabilitated, neither should one conclude that any human belief for which there is no immediate explanation be labeled a prejudice or a superstition.

One example is the superstition according to which the baby who cries before being born becomes a ghost or a werewolf. Behind this belief lies a partial truth. Only a few decades ago, western doctors and psychologist discovered that in the 24th week from conception, the foetus emits certain sounds. This phenomenon called call *vagitus utteterinus* or *fetus cry*,[32] is known as the *cry before birth* by Carpato-Danubians. The cry of the child may anticipate being expelled from its intra-uterus Paradise where he receives food, oxygen, a constant temperature, and protection. Believing in ghosts and werewolves, the child's cry while in his mother womb, or the unlucky number '13', were all seen as superstitions. They were based on people's incapacity at a certain time to find out the truth that lies behind certain natural manifestations.

The criterion distinguishing superstitions from non-superstitions is, naturally, the truth born from real observation. During the Middle Ages, belief in the spherical shape of the Earth and its revolving around the Sun caused people to be burned at the stake. At the same time, throughout history so many truths thought to be unerring finally proved erroneous.

Traian Herseni, a noted Twentieth Century Romanian sociologist, argued that a population with beliefs, convictions, conceptions about life, although seemingly false, was superior to a population that might retain all truths in the world, but not believe them. Over time, people have fought, suffered and died for their misconceptions. We can only start talking about a lie after recognizing the truth and then deliberately refuse to acknowledge to it.

February 13
Thirteen, the Unlucky Number?

Bad luck, a manifestation of evil, announces its arrival through various signs: a hare crosses your way, a woman who comes your way carrying an empty bucket, one eyelid that flickers. But the harbinger of bad-luck most widely known in Romania - indeed in many other places in the world - is the number '13'. The contemporary belief about the bad luck

---

[32] Schiopu, Verza, 1997, p. 68

that the number 13 might is common the educated urban class in large parts of the worldwide. Many buildings in some countries exclude the floor #13 number on elevators or addresses.[33]

This worldwide superstition has a singular origin. It comes from the number of lunar months in a Solar year which corresponds exactly to the number of the constellations in the Zodiac: Pisces, Aries, Taurus, Gemini, Cancer, Leo, Libra, Scorpio, Ophicus which belongs to the ecliptic by approximately by 15 degrees, Sagittarius, Capricorn, Virgo, and the thirteenth which is Aquarius.

The personified year is born on the first of January, grows from a child into a young man and then a mature man throughout the twelve constellations and lunar phases of the Zodiac, after which he becomes old and degraded and finally dies in the 13th one. The number 13, announced the death and rebirth of the worshiped divinity in the structure of the ancient Dacian Almanac in Sarmizegetusa Regia, the Aztec Almanac, and the Ancient Mexicans' Almanac. Because at the end of the year, marked by the 13th lunar phase and by the 13th constellation of the Zodiac, time and divinity died symbolically, this number received the malefic and an ill-fated connotation.

Peasants mark the dark side of the end of the year with specific customs and by magic practices without consciously associating them with 13th lunar month.

February 14
The Ironware's Weed

The *iron's weed* or the *ironware's weed*, even called the *robber's weed*, is an imaginary plant invoked by villains to soften metal and to open iron padlocks. It is said to grow in places which are difficult to reach, and also in places which are often struck by fires. At night it shines like the sun, "like gold, like a burning candle", while by day it is sad and covered with dew. It is difficult to find because it hides in the earth whenever it sees people around. In the morning, at sunrise, drops of blood fall from it leaving red spots on the ground.

According to peasant lore, the weed can be discovered by various means. A rope with several iron padlocks attached to it is drawn in the grass, and if the padlocks unlock themselves it means that they have touched the Ironware's Weed. Another method is to tie up the legs of a horse with iron chains and a padlock and when the horse gets untied, one must pick up the plant, which untied the horse. Another trick is to catch a hedgehog cub and lock it up in a cage; its mother, who knows what the

---

[33] Ghinoiu, 1997, p. 204

Ironware's Weed looks like and where to find it, comes running with it in its mouth and opens the padlock with it; after that one can take it from her mouth.[34] The miraculous plant can also be discovered with the help of other animals (polecats) and of birds (woodpeckers, orioles). Swallows also know where to find it since they take it to their nest in order to be protected by it.

People who manage to posses the weed receive miraculous powers. They can open padlocks, are not harmed by arrows or bullets, also they understand the language of animals and plants. It was believed that in all times, some famous thieves and outlaws, some famed ones in Romanian included Tunsul, Marcul, Pintea the Brave, Fulga, possessed the weed.

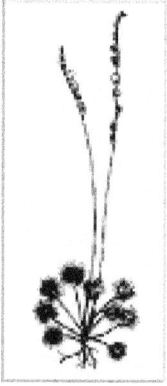

Dog's Bane (Parvu, 2000)

The real *Ironware's Weed* (Cynachum Vincetoxicum L.) belonging to the Asclepiadaceae family usually grows in orchards, in forests, bushes, stony places and was used in folk medicine for healing cuts, wounds, foot pains and it was also used in charms and spells against fright. The plant is collected at night on the eve of some great almanac holiday such as Saint George, Baptist's Day (Sanziene), Holy Mary's Entering the Church, also known as Ovidenie on the 21st of November.

February 15.
Folk Units for Measuring Time

For peasants the Sun was the primary cosmic guide for judging the time of day. *Dawn,* the starting morning moment for determining time; *Sunrise* marking the beginning of the day with the appearance of the Sun at the horizon; *Early Midday,* synonymous with *Little Noon,* indicates during the summer the time between 8 and 9 hours. At Early Midday the Sun has risen as high as the lances in the sky, which represents one third of its ascent; *Great Noon,* synonymous with *Under-noon,* marks approximately 11 o'clock; *Noon,* a moment when the sun reaches its highest point also synonymous with good noon, noon at the cross, the crossing in the sky indicates 12 o'clock. According to folk tradition, at noon the Sun which is at the peak of its ascent rests for a moment, drinks a glass of wine, and eats a piece of communion bread before starting its descent.

---

[34] Euseev, 1997, p. 178.

Like the Sun, the peasant who tills the land stops working and rests; *Vesper Church Bell* ringing is determined by the Sun approaching the horizon alerting people to stop working in the field. *Sunset* is synonymous with the sinking of the Sun.

A sub-unit of time equivalent to about half-an-hour is called *The Lance in the Sky*. It is used for measuring the ascent and the descent of the sun in the sky. A summer day is 18 lances long including nine from sunrise till noon. Dawn is one lance; early midday is three lances and nine from noon till sunset.

February 16
The Spell and the Greeting

The custom of sending greetings and wishes of long life, happiness, good health and prosperity at Christmas and New Year time is meant to induce a favorable course of future events.

Horse and Horse-rider depicted on a Cheese Mold. Vrancea (Cherciu, 2003)

The common greetings "May you live long", "Merry Christmas", "Happy Anniversary," which we so often offer at various occasions and celebrations, used to play the role of a spell in old times. They would convey good health, prosperity, happiness, or long life, by means of the magic power of the word. The direct utterance of the wish, or externalizing the wish in an imperative form, affirmed a person's desired goal (long life, health, happiness, wealth) through the word designating it. That was the origin of the total trust in the power of the *word* which once pronounced *can* cause the appearance or the fulfillment of the goal embodied in the word.[35]

Wishes and curses addressed to a person are based on the same psychological expectation. It is only the type of desire that differentiate

---

[35] Caraman, 1983, p. 361.

them: a positive one in the case of wishes and a negative one in the case of curses.

Throughout centuries and millennia the direct assertion of wishes has been used in charms, spells, witchcraft. Wishes usually contain something that is wanted and the time for it to be accomplished in the present or near future. It can be time specific (Good morning! Good day! Good evening! Good night!), or at beginning of an activity (Good luck!), or when parting for a period of time (Have a good trip!, See you soon!, Goodbye!).

February 17
Shelters of the Soul

As every particular thing in the Universe has its own shelter, the soul irrespective of how it is defined by theologians, philosophers, or biologists, must also posses a home of its own. The way in which one learns about a person by investigating the home in which that person dwells is illustrated by the folk proverbs and sayings: "A man's looks is the mirror of his soul." "The face shows one's soul." "A man's heart is displayed on his face." "You can tell a tree from its bark and a man from its coat."

Heaven and Hell in the View of a Peasant
(Miniature 1844 - Picu Patrut, 1985)

By observing the shelter of one's soul from the outside (one's body, clothes, or home), Romanians get a first impression of whatever lies inside. A similar method is also used by a doctor when he determines a first diagnoses of some internal dysfunctions of a patient from the aspect and the color of the patient's face, feeling the temperature of the body, or considering the way the patient expresses his thoughts, speaks or acts. This same method can be used to study the traits of the soul by where it *exists* (the body, the house, the village, the state, our world), in its *post-existence* (the coffin, the grave, the cemetery, the world beyond) and in its *pre-existence* (the uterus, the placenta or the baby's house, the womb). The shelters of the soul can be infinitely small such as sub-quantum particles, or infinitely large such as the galaxies, the galactic clusters and mega-clusters, each engulfs the other according to the principle of "the big fish swallowing the small fish".

February 18
Entrances and Exits of the Soul

The Romanian language distinguishes between shelters of the soul situated above ground which one can enter or exit through a gate or door of a house, church, or fort, and shelters situated inside the earth or inside the living creatures' wombs in which the entrance and the exit is made through the *mouth*. This could be "the mouth" of a cellar, of a cave or of the underground, through the entrance of a pit house or through the genitals. There are also popular expressions in the language such as: "With the soul on the lips" meaning to be very keen on doing something or "With the soul on the mouth" meaning to be exhausted.

The ethnographer's interpretation of the soul as an affectionate meeting of two souls reaching as far as the mouth – further than the mouth implying death – leads into a pandora's box of psychoanalytic interpretations.[36]

February 19
The Charm

Many healing methods were contained in the therapy of the *charm*, a prehistoric technique which has been widely misinterpreted as witchcraft or as some supernatural manipulation. The charm was based on applying various therapies according to the particular case. Illnesses were considered personifications of the evil that could penetrate the human body sent there by people who used witchcraft, by curses from enemies, or by God, or the by The Holy Mary, Saint Friday, as a punishment. As an antidote to

---

[36] Ghinoiu, 2004, p. 87-90.

all kinds of witchcraft practices, the use of charms preserved valuable knowledge and observations about causes, manifestations and empirical cures for diseases. Psychotherapy, music, water, and chiropractic therapy are modern manifestations of ancient curative techniques using healing herbs, mineral water, bio-energy, or massage that moves bones.

Fright Charm in Poiana Village from The Timoc Valley (AIEF, no 18,000)

Charmers were women with strong personalities, able to provoke and master certain psychic processes. They had knowledge of human anatomy, healing herbs and could use techniques for curing or alleviating sufferings. The so-called "punctured clay puppets," discovered by archaeologists on some sites and by ethnographers in their research in the field, are evidence of the fact that acupuncture was used in the Carpato-Danubian space. Some charmer women, especially those whose main technique was moving bones, used bio-energy in treating diseases. The number of words or lines which made up a charm could vary from a few words to dozens of lines and was transmitted orally like any other folklore communication of knowledge. Being secret, the texts and the techniques of the charms were learned stealthily, as were other traditional crafts, or they were passed on to the descendants in great secrecy, sometimes before dying.

February 20
The Technique of the Charm

Excepting the *charm* against the evil eye, which was performed at any time of the day or night especially on children who suffered some ailment, the perfect time for the curing incantation varied according to the type of illness and the skill of the charmer. Charms were performed at the New Moon or at the Old Moon, in the morning or at sunset, on an empty stomach or after eating. The remedies used in charm techniques were so varied that it is difficult to make a complete inventory. Commonly the charmers used healing plants, various kinds of foods and drinks, mineral water and organic substances. The effect of the treatment depended on the knowledge, the experience and the skill of the charmer in combining and applying the healing techniques.

The Evil Eye Charm, Dragus, Brasov County (Golopentia, 2004)

An atmosphere of mystery, favorable to suggestive psychotherapy, was created by the appropriate time for reciting the charm. This could involve singing the charm, or by the archaic pentatonic melody, or by rapid rhythms with a low tone and a soft recitation, by dramatizing a dialogue between the charmer and the evil spirit or the disease itself. After identifying and pronouncing the name of the one that had sent and caused the disease, he was then threatened, cursed, taken out from the body and cast-away. By using words, gestures and tough actions, the malefactor was sent into places where he could no longer get in contact with the sick person: in Hell, in the Black Sea, to a place 'where the Sun does not rise,' where man does not set his foot, in the 'horns of the stags,' or in the 'head of the wolf.'

To cure a particular disease, the sick person was cared for with a massage and a poultice of various remedies made of fresh vegetables, dried ones, or prepared substances (tea, concoctions, inhaling substances, juices, ointments, liquids), mineral or organic substances.

February 21
Number and order of the months in the almanac

Names of the present-day almanac months remind us that the ancient Roman almanac started in the 1st of March. September was the seventh month (*Sept* meaning '7'), October was the eighth month (*Oct* meaning '8"), November was the ninth (*Nov* meaning '9) and December was the tenth (*Dec* meaning '10'. These designations only have meaning, if it is remembered that March was once the first month and not January.

Unlike the civil and the religious almanac years whose months bear the names of Gods (Ianus - January, Mars - March) and of famous personalities of the Roman history (Iulius Caesar - July, Augustus - August), the months in the *Folk Almanac* are connected with people's day-to-day lives and with phenomena taking place on the earth.

"Carindar" is the month of January during which there was the custom of making the weather almanac out of onion peels and of nutshells; "Faurar" or the month of February is when ironsmiths make or repair their farming tools; "Florar", the months of May, is also called the month of flowers; "Ciresar", the month of June, is when cherries ripen; "Cuptor" (Oven), the month of July, is the hottest period of the year; "Brumarel" (Little White Frost), the month of October is when the first white frost appears; "Brumar" (White Frost), the month of November, is when thick white frost falls.

These old almanacs, made up at Christmas or at New Year, were meant both to reflect the weather over the whole year, specifying which months would be rainy and which ones would be dry and to measure passing time.

February 22
The Snow Drop

Snowdrop
(Parvu, 2000)

The best-known symbol of springtime in Romanian flora is the *snowdrop* (*Galanthus Nivalis* L.).

Another legend refers to the white color of the snowdrops: "When God created all the things on earth, including grass, herbs and flowers, He gave beautiful colors to them. When he created the snow, He said to it: 'As you go around to all places, you may choose the color that you like best.' The snow asked the grass first: 'Would you give me some of your nice, green color?' But the grass refused. Then it asked the rose for its red color, the bluebell for its blue color and the sunflower for its yellow color, but none of them would give their colors. The snow, sad and disappointed, went to the snowdrop and described its dilemma: 'None would give me their color. They all send me away and mock me!' Feeling sorry for the snow, the snowdrop said: 'If you like my white color, I would be glad to share it with you.' The snow was happy to receive the gift from the snowdrop and that, it is said, was how it got the white color which it has worn ever since. In order to show its gratitude to the snowdrop, the snow always allows the snowdrop to pull out its head as soon as the first signs of spring begin to show."[37]

According to a more obscure legend, the flower was once a man who became a widower with eight children, four boys and four girls. But when he remarried, the new stepmother rejected his children and they turned into eight different species of flowers. Their father, looking for them everywhere but not finding out what had become of them, also turned into a flower with the name of Snow Drop.

February 23
"The Stormy One"

The Stormy One is a fern species also called "The Stag's Tongue" (*Scolopendrium Vulgarae*), usually growing in forests and on cliffs with big leaves pointed like a spear. It is invoked by witches when performing a love spell. The plant is also used in folk medicine in preparing certain remedies for curing wounds, ruptures, coughs, or tuberculosis.

When picking the plants in order to perform a love charm, a series of ritual steps are followed. The first step is to seek out the place where the plant grows, then prostrating and making the sign of the cross, after which one lays offerings of salt, bread, and sugar at the root of the plant and recites a request in a whispering voice or silently in one's mind.

> *You, Stormy One,*
> *You, glorious king,*
> *As you developed and grew more than any other plant on earth,*
> *As you grew more than the flowers,*
> *So should people rush to Maria, who has bought you.*

The next step is to pull up the plant with its roots which are to be kept in safe place, worn in one's bosom, or put in bathing water. In Moldavia, old women, who performed love spells would conduct a prenuptial ceremony on the 15th of August, on Holy Mary's Day.

"At dawn, an old woman accompanied by young boys and girls would go into the forest. Those who found the beautiful and powerful plant (The Stormy One) would shout happily in louder and louder voices. It was not right, it was said, for a sad person to go into the forest searching for the Stormy One. Everybody should be happy and in high spirits. The young people carried sugar in their hands and the old woman dressed in a white clean blouse said: 'Let love storm into my house/ In the same way as people storm to get sugar!'"

---

[37] *The Legends of the Flora*, 1994, p. 182.

If the fern was picked for evil purposes such as separating people who loved each other, then it was done at midnight by a witch with no clothes on and her hair undone who would make contorted facial expressions in front of the plants.

February 24
"Dragobete"

True love that young people feel for each other is associated in Romanian tradition with the twitter of the birds when they are mating in the forest. The patron of the birds is a favorite mythical representation called *Dragobete*, or *Spring Start*, still widely celebrated in present times on February 24. Dragobete, initiator of love and creator of good moods is identified with Cupid, the Roman god of love, with Eros, the Greek god of love, and with the *Stormy One*, the personification of passionate love, in the Romanian mythology.

According to the folk tradition, on Dragobete day the birds gather in flocks, twitter, couple and start building their nests in which they will raise their chicks. That is why in some parts of northern Oltenia the day is called *Engagement Day* or *Birds' Coupling Day*. The legend says that those birds not mating on that day will be lonely and will have no chicks until the Dragobete Day of the next year.

Boys and girls must also meet to celebrate Dragobete. In Gorj it is said that it is enough for a girl to touch a man with her hand or in Mehedinti for a girl to slightly step on a man's foot in order that they be loved for the rest of the year. On that day, young girls and boys go into the forest in order to pick up the first flowers that come out in spring, snow drops and spring crocuses. One can hear everywhere that "Dragobete kisses the girls!"

The Kiss: Neolithic Figurine made of Burnt Clay - Vinca Turdas Culture, V. Millennium B.C. (Miclea, Florscu, 1980) and modern Constantin Brancusi sculpture (Comanescu, 1972)

Like birds, girls *fly around*, which is akin to a ritual running around, and end-up being caught and kissed by boys. Not only forest birds fly around, but also domestic ones (hens, ducks, geese) that, before mating, rush around, fly, chase each other, strike at each other with their wings.[38] Traditionally at Dragobete. swings would be hung on tree branches for young people who share loving words, make love vows, and kiss each other.

The name Dragobete is given both to those boys who are touched by the thrill of love and to the buds that the girls pick up from trees and they wear them around their ears as they do with cherries in May. Dragobete boys compete in taking girls in their arms and swirling around. Girls and young wives would save water from un-melted snow to wash themselves on certain days of the year to keep their skin looking fresh. Nobody dared to work on Dragobete day, for fear they would be punished to chirp like birds for the rest of their lives.[39] Also on this day, in some villages old women would pull out the *helleborus* root which was used in folk medicine practices.

In recent years, a new imported holiday, Valentine's Day, has started to compete with the Romanian Dragobete. Only the future can tell which one will win, but Dragobete may have the better chance as it bears the name of love, it is a mythical representation intimately connected with the cycles of nature, with blossoming of plants and mating of birds. If it weren't for the intense commercial promotion and advertising, Valentine's Day would have the lesser chance of being adopted.

February 25
The Ritual Pot Breaking

In magic practices the clay pot is used ritualistically by a witch, a midwife, a grandmother, or the head of a group of "Calusari" dancers. When thrown into a well or a river in hot summer days, it becomes a person's messenger sent to the divinity which discharges rain. When broken on the first bathing of a baby, the midwife performs a magic transfer of health and of the pleasant smell of the baked clay into the newly born baby; by braking a new, unused pot, the godmother repairs the mistake made by a girl who was not a virgin when she got married.

The pot can also contain evil spirits. That is the reason why pots are turned upside down to prevent unwanted spirits from hiding in the house during the confinement period after a child is born or during the time when a dead man is being watched in the house, or while spells and charms are being performed to discard evil spirits. In many villages, after a dead person has been carried out of the house, a close member of the family breaks an empty pot or a pot filled with ashes in the place where

---

[38] Ghinoiu, 1997, p. 65-66.

[39] Pop Ilian, 2001, p. 38-39.

death has occurred or on the threshold of the house, or on the grave. Based on this custom comes the expression: "They broke his pot," meaning *he died*.

February 26
Shrovetide for Meat

Shrovetide for meat is a night holiday with a moveable date. During that night, during the period of lent, neither meat, nor lard is to be eaten by Christians (Transylvania, Banat).

February 27.
The Goblin

The *goblin* is a mythic with a human or dragon face that into houses at night. There, it torments girls and mothers during their sleep causing tiredness and restlessness. When having a human face, the goblin represents lonely persopns unfulfilled in love or those who visit a loved one married by her parents to another. Driven by desire, the goblin enters through a chimney, keyhole, or crack in the door into a room where a girl sleeps. He kisses, hugs and makes love to her after which, at daybreak, he turns himself into a flame and flies out of the chimney. Such nocturnal visits cause loss of appetite and weariness that could be cured with a weed named 'goblin' or by charms against the goblin or by leaping of the Calusari dancers over sick ones during Whitsuntide.

February 28.
The Fool's Week

Parade in the Villageof Prajesti, Bacau County (Ciubotaru, 2002)

The *Fool's Week* in the *Folk Almanac*, is referred to as the White Week or The Cheese Week in the Christian Orthodox Almanac.

After an important wedding season, starting immediately after Epiphany and ending at

Shrovetide, Romanian allowed one more week for marriage to those with smaller chances of marital selection, such as disabled people, widowed ones, or girls with children born outside marriage. In the Cheese Week, groups of men dressed up in women's clothes, would go around to evening gatherings of village women and start dancing or improvising games and having fun with the girls and married women present there. During daytime, the men would gather round in the village, playing "foolish, crazy jokes."[40]

In some villages in the Banat region on the Day of the Shrovetide, a wedding parody of those unfortunate people would take place. After dressing up as bride, groom, priest, psalm reader, godparents and wedding party, everybody would walk the village roads, with the bride and the groom leading the procession. As they passed on the road, they would kiss the girls and young wives they met and would scare children. The mock marriage ceremony took place in front of a tree from which a bell hung. From the marriage tree the procession went to the river where the *newly wed* couple washed their hands with water poured from a pail. Then the party went house to house in the village and received tuica (brandy) as the custom is at real wedding parties.

...and every four years

February 29
The Legend of the Leap Year

The exact duration of the tropic year is 365 days, 5 hours, 48 minutes, 45 seconds or 365.242217 days. To round it off to a whole number, a solar year of 365 days was adopted. The problem was to find a way to add a day so that the succession of years would reproduce the succession of tropic years.[41] In response, a tale was created to explain the changing month of February from 28 days in normal years to 29 days in a leap year.

"Once Saint Cassian, who is celebrated on the 29th of February in leap years, complained to God that people don't celebrate him properly as they do with the other saints. God asked him if he had done any good on earth like the other saints, who were celebrated on a particular day of the year. God had hardly finished his words, when Saint Nicolae appeared soaking wet. God asked him why he was so wet. Saint Nicolae said: 'Well, there was a storm on the sea and it almost sank a ship. So I threw myself

---

[40] Marian, 1898, p. 14-15.

[41] Teodorescu, Chia, 1982, p. 24.

into the sea and saved both the ship and the people on it.' Then God turned to Saint Cassian and said: 'You heard the good deeds made by those who are celebrated! Go away now and only come back every four years.' From that day on the month of February is 29 days long every four years."[42]

---

[42] Pamfile, 1914, p. 172

MARCH

"MARTISOR"

1. "Martisor"
2. Dochia
3. The Old Woman's Days
4. Winter Fathers
5. "Cucii"
6. "Jujeul" or the Dog Chase
7. The Week of Sântoader's Horses
8. Martyrs' Day
9. The Fires On Martyrs' Day
10. Ritual Bathing
11. Anthropomorphic Offerings
12. The Kiss Fair & Newlyweds
13. Banishing the Cold
14. The Crocus
15. The Belladonna
16. The Origin of Prostitution
17. Father "Alexe"
18. The Stork
19. The Fish's Day
20. Father Noah and Odd Things on Earth
21. Weather Predictions at the Vernal Equinox
22. Stima, The Mistress of the Waters and Her Daughters
23. New Moon
24. The Cuckoo's Day
25. Annunciation
26. Customs and Beliefs at Sowing Time
27. The Cock
28. The Grapevine – A Strength Bearing Shrub
29. "Tarnoasele" – The Midpoint of the Easter Period of Lent
30. The Forbidden Thursdays
31. The Home Industry Almanac

March,

the first month in the Roman Almanac starting on March 1, is the third month in the Julian and Gregorian almanacs that start on January 1. It is dedicated to Mars, the God of War. The regional names of the month usually maintain the stem of the original word (Mart, Martisor, Martiu), or use expressions related to the awakening to life in nature and the sprouting of the sown seeds (Germinar, Germinariu). Because of a very strict period of fasting before Easter, when fruit, greens or vegetables are not yet available, the month was called "Empty Bag." Macedo-Romanians called it "Martul" and Megleno-Romanians called it "Marta."[43]

During March peasants start to plough and to sow, to take the beehives out from the winter shelters, to clean the orchards and to trim the honeycombs. Holidays with a fixed date or variable dates, mainly "Macinicii" or the "Martyrs," involved some very special old customs.

---

[43] MALR, 1967, Map 599.

March 1

"Martisor"

Martisor is given as a gift on the First of March, the ancient date marking the beginning of the Farming Year. Its entwined white and red thread symbolizes the winter and the summer binding the 365 days of the year together. At some point an amulet was added. Those who receive a "martisor" believe that they will not be sunburned in the summer, that they will be healthy, beautiful like the flowers, kind, pleasant and loving, rich and lucky and that they will not be affected by illness and by the evil eye.

At the beginning of the Twentieth Century, a "martisor" with a silver or a gold coin attached was given before sunrise as a gift to young boys and girls. Nowadays, it is a popular gift from a man to a woman. The thread can be worn tied around the wrist, around the neck, or fastened on clothes. Kept until a particular spring holiday such as "Macinici" (Palm Sunday), Easter, "Armindeu", or until the blossoming of certain fruit-trees and shrubs (wild rose, sloe tree, rose tree, hawthorn, cherry tree), it is then hung on the blossoming tree branches.

Martisor token gift (red and white)

In earlier times, the "martisor" was made from two twisted woolen threads, black and white or white and blue, when the New Moon appeared in the sky. Macedo-Romanians celebrated Martisor on the eve of the First of March, that is in the evening of the 28th or 29th of February. Both the celebrations on the eve of the holiday and the measuring of time in relation to a certain phase of the moon are typical to more ancient lunar almanacs than the contemporary solar ones.

In the Carpathian Mountain regions, the tradition of "Martisor" is tightly linked to Dochia, the Christian saint who usurped the power of a lunar and equinoctial goddess. The legend says that the "Martisor" thread was spun by an old woman called Dochia while she took her sheep up on the mountains. The spinning of the thread represented the endless flowing of time. When a child is born, the Fates spin the life thread of that person and Dochia spins the thread of the year at the beginning of spring. The custom was recorded in all the territories inhabited by the Romanians, both in the North and in the South of the Danube. Over extended areas in Transylvania, Banat, Maramures, Central Wallachia, Western Oltenia, and Southern Dobrogea, the opening of the vernal equinox and of the Farming New Year was called "Martisor."

March 2
Dochia

The name *Dochia* in the Carpathian Mountains region is similar to Saint Endochia, the Samaritan born in Lebanon. He lived during the rule of the Roman Emperor Trajan who crossed the Danube River in 110 A.D. to invade and conquer Dacia. Dochia was a rich and beautiful woman who lived dissolute in her youth. When she got old she did penance and was baptized by Archbishop Theodot. She donated her wealth as charity to the poor and withdrew to a monastery where she was said to perform many miracles. The Church canonized her a saint, Saint or Martyr Endochia, and allotted a celebratory day on March 1. This was the same day celebrating the death and the rebirth of a great agrarian goddess. In this way, a minor Christian character became an important holiday in the *Folk Almanac* by overlapping the date of her celebration with that of a farmer's divinity.

The legends of Dochia recall the atmosphere of old Romanian villages. The inevitable tensions between the mother-in-law and the daughter-in-law are cleverly used to mirror the opposition between the Old Year (Old Dochia) and the New Year, the one that is being born, between winter and summer. Not influenced by other shepherds the old woman persists in taking her sheep up to mountain pastures at the end the February and the beginning of March. To make sure that summer has come, she sends her daughter-in-law to bring her ripe wild strawberries. With the help of God disguised as an old man, the young woman finds ripe wild strawberries and brings them to her mother-in-law in a small jar. When Dochia sees the ripe wild strawberries symbolizing summer, she starts preparing her herds for the slow climb up to the mountain pastures.

Cloaked in nine sheep-skins, a number equal to the ancient number of months of the year, or even twelve in some variants form Moldavia and Bucovina, she set off towards the mountain often accompanied by her son, Dragobete. Unfortunately, it started raining for nine days and nine nights. As the woolen skins got wet and increasingly heavy on her back, she took them off one by one until she had only her blouse left. On the ninth or the twelfth day, she and her sheep succumbed to a terrible frost. Their bodies, turned into stone, appear today as names of places in Ceahlau, Vama Buzaului, Caraiman, Izvorul Raului Doamnei,

Semenic and in other Carpathian Mountains locations.[44] Dochia's, death on the 9th of March, the vernal equinox in the old almanac, was followed by the birth of the *Newborn Dochia*.

Starting with Dochia's Day, the female deities of the *Folk Almanac* are grouped into three generations: *maiden goddesses* (Floriile, Sanzienele, Dragaicele, Lazariaele and Ielele), *mother goddesses* (The Virgin Mary, The Holy Virgin, The Woods Mother, The Caloian's Mother) and *old goddesses* (Saint Friday, Saint Varvara, Dochia).

March 3
The Old Woman's Days

The *Old Woman's Days* is a ritual time which lasts for nine or twelve days in the beginning of March, a period corresponding to the time spent by Dochia to drive her sheep up the mountain. The numbered days are divided among the female members of the family, neighborhood, or work group. The days were divided according to the age of the participants. This is done in order to foretell their well-being over the year.

Spring by Peasant Miniaturist Picu Patrut -1851

Given that the weather at the beginning of March is quite variable, actual conditions on the given day would determine the person's soul and nature: sunny or dark, good or bad. The cold days following the 9th of March are called *borrowed days*, a name generally given to changing weather with snow, sleet and wind. Those days are dedicated to birds and their names always contain the word *snow* (the Storks' Snow, the Heron's Snow, the Swallow's Snow); they are also dedicated to lambs (the Lamb's Snow) and to shrubs of strong essence (The Cornel Tree's Snow). According to the weather conditions during the month of March, the number of cold 'borrowed days' vary from year to year. In some areas, people believed that when the Old Woman's Days from the 10th until the 17th of March

---

[44] Adrian Fochi, 1976, p. 23-29.

were over, nine more Old Man's Days followed which were warmer.[45] In some villages in Moldavia, it is said that if it does not snow when the Cornel trees should blossom, it will not bear its cherry fruit.

March 4
Winter Fathers

Saturday before Whitsuntide, which precedes the Shrovetide for meat, is called *Winter Fathers* and is dedicated to the dead. For the celebration of the Winter Fathers, it is customary that women distribute alms in remembrance of the dead. This includes food (pie, dairy products, pigs' feet) and sometimes bowls filled with cooked food or with water. Together with another celebration of the dead in the *Folk Almanac* called Fathers from Samedru, they make up the Great Fathers celebrated over the year.

March 5
"Cucii"

"Cucii" are masked men who, through ritual acts and magic practices performed in the first day after Shrovetide, fertilize and purify time and space when spring begins. As performed in the Nineteenth Century, the spring ritual of the "Cucii" for purification was recorded only in Wallachia and Dobrogea. Wearing skirts like women, with a hood over their head, a stick in their hands and a big bell on their back, "Cucii" run after children, girls or other people whom they touch and often push down to the ground. Towards midday they tie-up a peasant's shoe to a rod and continue to chase and to hit on the back curious people who come in their way. In the evening, they gather and go from house to house, where they perform a circular dance in the owner's yard. With very few variations, it is still performed in localities such as Independenta, Braneati in Calarasi county.

Related to this custom are numerous folk beliefs: "The ones who become 'Cucii' must do this for the following three or nine years, otherwise they would turn into a Devil at death." "Women use feathers taken from the hood worn by 'Cucii' to burn and make smoke that helps those who suffer from fright." "The one who is not roughed-up or hit by the 'Cucii' on this day will not enjoy good health over that year." [46]

---

[45] Ghinoiu, 2003, p.230.

[46] Marian, 1898, p. 248.

March 6
"Jujeul" or the Dog Chase

A custom practiced on the 1st day after Shrovetide called *"Jujeul"* or *The Dog Chase* is a magic practice of driving away the wolf that ruled over the cold season. It is symbolically driven away through its domestic relative, the dog. In villages from southern Romania where this custom was practiced, "dogs are driven away from the village. The older ones have an instinct about this day, and for this reason early at dawn they come out freely. Nobody chases them away and one may see packs of dogs that start howling when they see a man. They gather in the fields, where they hide in places where people cannot find them."[47] In the this manner the 'wolf' is symbolically driven away.

March 7.
The Week of Santoader's Horses

Unlike the wolf that devours the stars as evidenced in solar and moon eclipses, the horse is a devoted friend of the Sun. It draws the solar cart on its way from the winter solstice to the summer solstice. Actually the saints of the warm season ride on horseback (Santoader, Saint George, Saint Dumitru) or travel in heavenly carts drawn by horses (Santilie).

Thracian King Killing Wild Boar (Scortan, 1967) and
Saint Geogre Killing the Dragon (Irimie, Focsa, 1968)

---

[47] Marian, 1898, p. 112.

The eight-day period, which starts Tuesday after Shrovetide and ends the following Tuesday, was called *Santoader's Horses*. The practice carried out during this week is intended to dampen pleasures from the period when there was no fasting. Because people need to start sowing and plowing at winter's end, life needs to take a normal course as soon as possible. Order is established with the help of some mythical representations, Santoader's Horses, a powerful group of eight horses disguised as strong young men, dressed in festive clothes. They distinguish themselves from other young men in the village by hooves in their peasant shoes and by horsetails hidden in their trousers. Every day of this week is dedicated to a horse belonging to the divine herd. The most feared of them all is their leader The Great Santoader. the Limping Santoader is celebrated on Friday (*Santoader's Friday*).

Santoader the Great with the Face of Michael the Brave on Glass Icon from Nicula
(Irimie, Focsa, 1968)

During the week bearing their name, the horses go to places where village gatherings are held, take girls to dance with them, and fly up high into the sky with them only to drop them back down to earth and kick them with their hooves. Beliefs in Santoader's Horses, half gods that who put an end to feasts during the winter, reflected a practical necessity. During springtime, when farm work starts, the young people had to sleep and rest during nights that were getting shorter. Village girls are so afraid that they do not leave their homes for normal evening gatherings.

March 8

Martyrs' Day

All the customs on the Martyrs' Day make up a ritual scenario typical for the New Year preparing ritual food called Saints, Little Saints or "Bradoai". It includes ritual drinking when tradition claims that on this day it is good to down forty or more wine glasses. Others include opening of graves and Heaven's gates for the dead people's souls to come out and be with the living ones; lighting fires in the yards, in the gardens, in front of the houses and in the fields; purifying people and cattle by sprinkling them with consecrated water; providing a magic protection of homes and household annexes by spreading ashes around them from the burnt-out fires.

Martyrs' Day is considered as a favorable time to make weather observations and predictions, and for fortune-telling in the New Year by preparing a flat cake. People believe that on this day, more than on any other, charms and spells more easily produce their effects, that all kinds of diseases can be cured with honey and that cutting vines shoots will ensure rich fruit.

March 9
The Fires On Martyrs' Day

Celebrated at the vernal equinox, *Martyrs' Day* preserves a lot of rituals of the agrarian year. On that day two celebrations overlap: a pre-Christian one, the last day of Dochia when the old woman dies and turns into a stone statue, and a Christian one, the first day of Martyrs who were sacrificed and burnt to ashes at the stake for their religious fate.

The most spectacular magic practice, at Martyrs' Day on March 9, is the lighting of fires in yards and gardens at dawn. Chairs are placed by the fires, so that the dead people's souls coming to celebrate the New Year can sit, rest and eat. On that day, villages in the south of the country are enveloped by huge clouds of smoke. The fires made from waste in the yards, gardens and out-buildings had a practical cleansing value and also a ritual significance. It helps the Sun to get over the equilibrium point reached at the vernal equinox. As the fire intensifies, young people jump over the flames to let the smoke penetrate their clothes thoroughly.

The Fires' at Martyrs' Day are recorded in Wallachian, Oltenian, Banat and Transylvanian villages. In Transylvania, "on The Eve of The Forty Martyrs' Day, people burn heaps of straw and they jump over the flames one after the other."[48] In Banat "people poke the fire with their boots to make the weather warmer sooner."[49]

---

[48] Francu, Candrea, 1988, p. 129.

[49] Marian, 1898, p. 170.

March 10
Ritual Bathing

Ritual Bathing, Dragus, Brasov County - 1938
(Golopentia, 2004)

People believed that the elecampane (called *homan*) protected their house from dangers and protected humans and animals from diseases. Still the most important function of the plant was for the *ritual bathing* of girls and young wives. The ritual bathing on the Friday of Santoader was practiced both in villages and in towns. In the beginning of the Twentieth Century, homan was still sold in Bucharest market places and advertised like any other merchandise: "We sell nice smelling homan for washing!"

This is why the rhizome of that plant pulled out from the earth was kept houses hanging from beams throughout the year. It was also worn by men tied to their woolen caps and tied by girls and wives to their head scarves. The plant was also used to 'smoke' sick children, the household and the out buildings in order to drive away evil spirits.

The *elecampane (Inula Helenium)* plant is used on Friday after Shrovetide to bring beauty and thick hair to the girls and to the wives. Early in the morning, before sunrise, girls search for and pull up its roots. With salt and bread, they pay homage to the earth where the plant grew and then address the Great Santoader:

> *Toader, Santoader*
> *Give fine hair to the girl*
> *Like the mares' tail!" or "Toader, Santoader,*
> *Give fine hair to the mares,*
> *So that the girls would grow it too,*
> *Long like a thread,*
> *Soft like silk!*

In Southern Transylvania some girls pick the leaves of another plant for a ritual bathing. The plant is called "Popelnicul" and they call upon its powers like a divinity:[50]

---

[50] Apolzan, 1983, p. 703.

Popelnic, Popelnic,
I will give you bread and salt,
You will give me long hair!

In the villages of the Western Carpathian Mountains region, girls from the age of 14 washed their hair in the evening of Santoader until the cuckoo starts to sing with a lye wash prepared with a plant called "parlagina" which had a pleasant smell. The plant was also worn by girls and mothers on their bosom. Washing and combing the hair in a certain way marked reaching an age of puberty, 14 years old, that meant entering the group of girls who could get married.[51]

March 11
Anthropomorphic Offerings

In many areas there is a tradition on the 9th of March of making dough in the form of humans, bees, birds, rings or knots. There is no other holiday in the almanac when women make so many anthropomorphic shapes from dough as they do on the Martyrs' Day. Often they look like dolls that children play with, they have a head, eyes, nose, mouth, arms and legs and are made from wheat flour, honey and nuts"[52] They also resemble figurines shaped like humans found by archeologists at ancient dig sites.

In the South of Romania, anthropomorphic dough shaped as the figure '8' were dried and then boiled and sugar and nuts added. Irrespective of their name and of their form, this dough was usually given as alms to relatives and to neighbors in remembrance of the dead. Cooked beans, nuts, fruit and peanuts could also be given away for the dead. In some villages in Wallachia, a bigger knot-bread was made shaped like a human with mouth, ears, nose but no eyes, called The Forgotten One. It was made in remembrance of all the dead that had been forgotten in that year and therefore had not been honored. Children would make a fire in the yard and then dance with the Forgotten One after which they spreading honey on it and ate it." (Marian, 1898, p.166)

Offerings such as these carried out on New Year's Day with figure '8' shapes for the Indo-European anthropomorphic god. And human-shaped knot-bread represented the Neolithic mother goddess. Both are reminiscent of human sacrifices practiced at the New Year's ceremonies in pre-historic times.

---

[51] Marian, 1898, p. 65.

[52] Marian, 1898, p. 162.

March 12
The Kiss Fair & Newlyweds

On fair-day in the Tara Zarandului region, a post-marital custom called for young wives to kiss all the men that came their way on Santoader's Day. Symbolizing a farewell sign to all the fun and liberties allowed before marriage, it was called *The Kiss Fair*. Those young women who had become wives during the prior year, accompanied by their mothers-in-law and sometimes even by they husbands, dressed up as brides, offered a drink of brandy from a jug to the men whom they knew and also kissed them after which the men had to give them a gift.

A distinction between being a maid or a lad and being a wife or a married man was made through special rituals carried out during the wedding or immediately after it. The most well known custom, called "Calea-Valea", required young married couples to pay a short visit to the wives parents one week after the wedding. Another custom was "Tearing the Cat." In front of the bride and the entire wedding party, the groom sacrificed a cat by holding it from its front legs and hind legs. Although it was believed that it meant a way of the husband to scare his wife and show her that he was the master, it is actually a reminiscence of the ritual sacrifice given in ancient times to Juno or Vesta, the goddess protecting the family.

March 13
Banishing the Cold

One of the magic practices carried out by children on the Martyrs' Day, is to beat the ground in order to banish the cold and bring out the warmth. While beating the earth with sticks and cudgels, the children call out all:

Cold get in an warmth come out!
Come, good weather, In our yard!
(Muntenia, Oltenia)

Over quite extended areas of the country, people believed that the earth was beaten with some huge wooden hammers, with staves and bludgeons or with clubs by the spirits of their ancestors. These were identified in the Christian Orthodox Almanac with the Forty Saint Martyrs from the city of Sevastia. While hitting the ground, children in Moldavia encouraged each other, calling out loud altogether:

Forty brave saints,
Beat the earth with your clubs,
For the cold to get in,
For the heat to come out!

March 14

The Crocus

The beginning and the end of the vegetable cycle are designated by two plant species: the spring crocus (*crocus heuffelions Herb*) and the autumn crocus (*colchicum autumnale L.*) or *Crow's Onion*. The former blooms in spring and announces the end of winter, and the latter blooms in autumn and announces the beginning of winter. The only resemblance between these two flowers is the violet color. The determinants *spring* and *autumn* used before the name of the flower indicate the *incipit* and the *desinit* of summer and winter, two major seasons of the year.

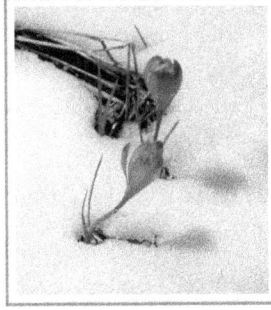

Spring Crocus

The earth's stepmother is responsible for the blooming of the spring crocus even before the snow melts when she maliciously forces it to come out and bloom. In Bucovina there is a saying about mothers with stepchildren: "Don't be so heartless like the earth's step mother." The name crocus is also given to some of the anthropomorphic knot-bread made and given away as alms in the Banat region on the Martyrs' Day.

People distinguish the spring crocus, which is a flower of the living ones, and the autumn crocus which is the flower of the dead. "The autumn crocus is the joy of the dead. In the same way as we are happy the spring crocus when it comes out, so are the dead when the autumn crocus comes out. It is a sin to pick it up."[53]

---

[53] Butura, 1979, p. 48.

March 15
"Matraguna," The Belladonna

Matraguna, or Belladonna, is the personification of a magic plant used from ancient time to the present by traditional medicine practitioners. Local names used for it are: *Wolf's Cherry, Great Lady, Empress of the Herbs*. As a mythical representation it is invoked for love, marriage, wealth, happiness or even quite the opposite. It can be invoked for separating people who are in love, causing hatred, feuds, poverty and death. Picking it up and using it is done according to a strict ritual.

Belladonna
(Parvu, 2000)

The female spellbinder, entirely clean physically and spiritually, goes into the forest far away from the village, where "no cocks sing and no cats mew." She looks for the belladonna, stares at it and marks it with a red thread. Returning to the village, she waits for the most favorable time, usually on a Tuesday, when she goes alone or accompanied by unmarried women or married women who were not loved by their husbands. All needing help from the belladonna, they leave their homes quietly before dawn on an empty stomach and go to the place where a belladonna plant was marked. Once there, they greet it respectfully: *"Good morning, Great Lady!"* and then undress, undo their hair, genuflect and move around it in a ritual manner. Female couples would hold each other, caressing each other and miming a sexual act, while the spellbinder recited softly:

> *Belladonna, Kind Lady*
> *I do not pick you to drive anyone mad,*
> *I pick you to make someone fall in love ...*[54]

The spell was different when used for girls who had not been asked to dance by any young lad, or for causing dispute among people. When the plant was called upon to help young couples to marry, the spellbinders mimed being joyful and in high spirits, whereas when used to make people hate each other and separate, the spellbinders mimed sadness and quarrel.

---

[54] Nitu, 1999, p. 135-136.

March 16
The Origin of Prostitution

According to certain folk beliefs, Noah saved the living creatures from the deluge and was involved in many other activities that were to take place on earth later on. One of them was prostitution: "Noah lived for 260 years and had 12 sons and 13 daughters. Noah's sons and daughters married each other, except for one daughter who remained single. "What will become of me?" asked the girl. "You will be a servant for the others," answered Father Noah. "No, she won't," said God. "She will be for the soldiers!" And that is how prostitutes existed ever since.

March 17
"Mos Alexe," Father Alexe

March 17 is *Father Alexe* or *Alex the Warm One* day. He is a servant of God and a saint who made miracles on waters also known as *Alexe The Pious* in the Orthodox almanac. He is the patron of living creatures that spend the winter under the earth, in hollows, under the bark of the trees, under stones or water. On this day, he warms-up and opens the Earth in order to let out creatures that spent the winter in the earth. After six months on September 14, the *Day of The Cross* around the autumn equinox, Alexe locks the Earth. This is why unlike other saints who wear only one key tied to their waist to open up one season (*Sangiorz* opens the summer and *Samedru* opens the winter), Alexe wears two keys. One unlocks the summer season and the other unlocks the winter season.

In some legends he is severely punished by God for disobedience. It was said that, because insects caused a lot of trouble to man, God gathered them all on September 14, locked them up in a wooden coffin and called Alexe to throw it in the sea. When he reached the seashore Alexe opened it as he was curious to see what he had been carrying on his back. Instantly, the bugs, the grasshoppers and all the other insects in the coffin quickly dispersed into the sea, onto herbs, plants, and trees. From then on "not only the earth, but also the sea water is full of all sorts of awful small creatures and insects. As for Alexe, who disobeyed God, he was turned into a stork which would collect all the insects during the time between March 17 and September 14."[55]

---

[55] Pamfile, 1914, p. 51.

March 18

"Barza," The Stork

The Stork is the substitute of the Neolithic life-generating Bird Goddess who brings brothers and sisters to small children by dropping them on the chimneys. A welcome guest, expected to arrive in spring from the countries where it spends winter, the stork predicts the *weather* "If the stork leaves early, it means that the winter will be long and frosty; if they leave late, the winter will be short and warm."

The Stork Symbolizing Fertility
(AIEF Photo Radu Maier, 1975)

"If a man sees many storks in spring, he will harvest a lot of corn.

"It is believed that there will be a lot of good luck in the house on which the stork builds its nest."

"It is believed that people who see only one stork will remain alone, especially the young men and women will remain unmarried."

"It is said to be a sign of death for the one who is first to see a single stork in spring."

"If there is a house on fire somewhere, the stork warns people about it by knocking loudly with its beak."[56]

Its divine sound is reproduced by a rhythmic beat with two, wooden hammers on a wooden bell board, or, when hearing bad news by knocking on wood with the finger and uttering the words "God forbid!" The ritual beat from knocking the board or ringing the church bell has been magic practice since ancient times.

March 19

The Fish's Day

Warming weather around the time of the vernal equinox brings insects to life, allows reptiles to revive, lets pikes toss about in the water announcing the reproduction period, and drives bees out of the hive to look for food. On that *Fish's Day*, when *the fish are tossed in the water* before

---

[56] "The Evening Sitting", VIII, 1904, p. 51-55.

spawning for reproduction, fishermen do not go fishing, instead, they abstain from food, or catch a small fish over which they recited an incantation and then eat it raw This is practiced in regions near the Delta of the Danube River.

The Day of Alexe was also called in some localities the *Serpent's Day* or the *Cutting off of the Hives*, meaning that the honey which has not been consumed during winter is taken out of the hive.

March 20
Father Noah and Odd Things on Earth

Attempting to explain natural curiosities, illiterate Romanians created all kinds of quaint stories. One of these stories explained why, unlike the crow and the salamander that can walk by stepping, the frog and the sparrow hop when they are walking. "While Noah was in his ark, having in it a pair from all the living creatures on earth, the water became shallow and the ark stopped on the Ararat Mountain. Seeing that, Noah undid their bonds and set all the animals free. But he forgot about the frog and the swallow and they remained with their feet tied up. When they realized that they were the only creatures with their feet tied up, the frog lay flat on the sea allowing the sparrow to stand on his back. That is how they saved themselves from drowning as there was still some water left. Since then, the frog and the sparrow have been hopping with their feet tied up."

March 21
Weather Predictions and the Vernal Equinox

Early in March, the ancient beginning of the agrarian year, weather predictions are made. During this period farmers ritually take out their ploughs and place them in the fields. The timing of the tradition varies according to the geographic location: on Martyrs' Day (March 9) in the flat plains of the South; on Alexe Day (March 17) and on Annunciation Day (March 25) in the centre and in some Southern parts of the country.

"If around the Martyrs' Day the earth gets frozen, there will not be any white frost in autumn and peasants will be able to sow corn and they will still get fine crops."

"The weather over the whole spring will be similar to the weather on the Martyrs' Day."[57]

The belief that starting an economic activity on the agrarian New Year brings prosperity is well illustrated by the custom of taking the plough out in the field and drawing the first furrow. A few days before March 9, the blades of the plough are straightened and sharpened; all the other parts of the plough are checked and repaired, oxen or horses that will draw the plough are well fed, and because wooden plough are drawn by 2-3 pairs of oxen agreements among farmers are made to help each other with the plowing.

Most practices performed on the morning of March 9 have a purifying role and the time to start plowing will be in physical and spiritual cleanliness. The Oxen yoked to the plough and the farmers who will start plowing are smoked with frankincense and sprinkled with water. And a fertilizing ceremony is carried out when the housewife throws an egg in front of the plough.

March 22

"Stima," the Mistress of the Waters and Her Daughters

The mythical female representation of the mistress of the waters, who can be seen and felt only in the night, is called *Stima of the Water*. She is a cold woman who lives in water and can take the shape of a mermaid. She has enormous breasts which she throws over her back. In bad weather and on moonlit nights she comes up to the surface of the water, she bathes, shakes off the water and strolls through the village like a cloud. Of her it is said: "If you leave her alone, she doesn't do you any harm, but if you don't she will make you dumb and mutilate you." She is said to walk until the cock starts to crow at midnight and can lure people to drown by saying: "The time has come. The man hasn't come!" (Moldavia, Bucovina).

Ruling over still and running waters, Stima has several daughters called *The Water Girls*. They are half women with their hair undone and half fish. Unsurpassed in their beauty with white wings instead of arms, The Water Girls are the creators of songs. Before they start singing, water waves rise as if swept by the wind. Coming to the surface on the crests of waves, The Water Girls play, sing and slash each other. As soon as the waves break, they begin to sing in a divine voice, softly at first and then louder and louder. When they finish the song, they go underwater and rise

---

[57] Marian, 1899, p. 154-156.

again to play and sing other songs. If a young lad sees them, he is bewitched by their beautiful bodies and songs. Trying to touch them, they might quickly dive deep into the waters or they might drown him. (Bucovina)

March 23
New Moon

The first face of the Moon, when the Moon is not visible with the naked eye, is called *New Moon*, Young Moon, Moon in Two Horns or New Prince. After two or three moonless nights, in the direction where the Sun sets, a thin and shiny sickle appears which grows more and more every night until it reaches the Full Moon phase. In the lunar almanac the days are counted by the nights, starting with the night when New Moon appears in the sky.

Young Sunday, a reminiscence of an ancient lunar almanac, is the first Sunday in a month with New Moon. When it was new moon, people sowed those plants that grow and bear fruit *upwards* at the surface of the earth (rye, wheat, corn). They performed spell and charms and invoked the New Moon by reciting lines that would bring bread, health, a wife:

> *New Prince, New Prince,*
> *You found me healthy,*
> *You should leave me healthy!*
> *You found me without a wife,*
> *You should leave me with a wife!*

> *New Moon, New Moon,*
> *Cut the bread in two:*
> *Half for you,*
> *Health for me!*[58]

March 24
The Cuckoo's Day

Of all the birds that must face the winter difficulties of the temperate continental climate, or that arrive in our land only to spend the summer, the cuckoo enjoys a privileged position.

---

[58] Ghinoiu, 1988, p. 62-63.

The Cuckoo
(*Zoological Atlas, 1983*)

There is no other bird in the Romanian ornithology to which the people have dedicated so many legends, stories, songs and proverbs. The cuckoo is not a singing bird and its feathered appearance not particularly charming. It looks more like a miniature hawk. Its contribution to pest destruction is negligible. The cuckoo doesn't build a nest, nor does it hatch its eggs or feed its chicks. It lays its eggs in the nests of other birds and its chicks and, being stronger, pushes out their step-brothers over the edge of the nest in order to benefit from more food and to develop more rapidly.

As the cuckoo is the symbol of spring, of fine weather and of passionate love, people forgive its sins. There are some wonderful stories in which the cuckoo is endowed with human roles, such as farm hand, servant, robber, outlaw, parent, husband, or lover. As an endless source of inspiration for melancholic and sad songs, the cuckoo increases the feeling of alienation and of loneliness.

This bird would be less known in the Romanian folklore were it not for marking, through its behavior, two important astronomic phenomena from the vernal equinox until the summer solstice. Through its song, it announces the coming of spring and it also predicts man's fate. That is why, when the cuckoo started singing, everybody wishes to be cheerful, nicely dressed, well fed and to have money in their pockets.

"As soon as the cuckoo arrives, it clears its throat, it starts singing immediately and it goes on singing from Annunciation until Sanziene or until Saint Peter's Day."[59]

On June 24 at "Sanziene" or "Dragaica", the cuckoo chokes with barley and unable to sing turns into a hawk until the next spring, at Annunciation.

---

[59] Marian, 1901, p. 22-29.

March 25
Annunciation (Blagovestenia)

Annunciation on the Church Altar from Salt Valley (Cherciu, 2003)

Annunciation or *Blagovestenia* is the day when the Christian Church celebrates the announcement made by the Angel Gabriel to Holy Mary that she would give birth to a Son. This holiday, being celebrated very closely to the vernal equinox when the swallows arrive and the cuckoo starts to sing, is called *Cuckoo's Day* in the Folk Almanac.

On this occasion, home spaces are purified and snakes driven away from around the house as well as insects and caterpillars from the orchards by smoking the buildings, the yards and the cattle with burning frankincense and rags (Transylvania, Banat); or by making noise that scares away the evil spirits by dragging a small bell tied to the ankle (Transylvania); or by hitting iron objects (Banat); or making fires in gardens and orchards; or taking clothes and fabrics out of the chests and hanging them outside to be refreshed.

Fertility for the new year was invoked by sprinkling plum brandy over the roots of the plum trees and by threatening the fruit trees to be cut with an axe if they do not bear fruit.

Annunciation, the day of divine fertility, was not considered favorable for the fertility of birds, animals and plants. If brooding hens did not sit over their eggs, it was believed that no chicks would come out of the eggs laid on that day; cows were not taken to the bull; corn was not sowed (Moldavia, Bucovina). In all the regions of the country that day was a favorable time for telling fortunes, anticipating the fertility of fruit-trees and for making predictions about the weather.

March 26
Customs and Belief at Sowing Time

In old times, people used to choose the right time for sowing in relation to favorable climatic conditions and to a certain phase of the moon, an ascending or a descending one. "That which grows in the earth like potatoes must be sown at Old Moon (full moon); while that which grows above the earth, like cereal plants, must be sown at New Moon."

"The Moon influences the seed planted in the ground, its growth and its bearing fruit. Therefore, you must sow the hard seed (rye, wheat, corn) in dry ground, when the moon is ascending; otherwise you stand a good chance to get a bad crop. The soft seeds (flax, hemp, oat) must be sown in wet soil when the moon is descending."

"The Moon makes the wheat seeds spring," and "The Sun makes the grains grow and ripen."[60]

This ethnographic information pertains to a powerful lunar cult. In folk beliefs, direct relationships were established by analogy between burial of the dead in graveyards and burial of the seeds in the fields. Both the plant seeds and the dead body of a human being, after having been put in the ground, germinate and thus return to life.

By repeatedly experiencing success and failure, man learned how to detect certain reference moments which would point out the most appropriate time for sowing plant seeds: corn should be sown "from Annunciation till Ascension or Armindeni"; the autumn sowing of the wheat should be done "between the two celebrations of Holy Mary" running from August 15 to September 8. Hence, the saying: "You should sow in dust in autumn and in mud in spring", which means that wheat, rye and barley should be sown early;[61] in Banat, the best time for sowing beans was at Ascension; in Bucovina, horse bean was sown until "Sangiorz"; autumn garlic was sown until "Santandrei" (Saint Andrew); hemp at the end of April and at the beginning of May; cucumbers at Ascension; pumpkin was sown one-hundred days after Christmas, sweet basil was sown when the frogs started to sing; millet when the sloe tree blossomed.

In this manner, dates for sowing were indicated by the almanac holidays, by the arrival of the migratory birds, and by the sound of the insects. All these were correlated with the local climate and soil conditions, with the geographical altitude and latitude and with the plant species. Until the beginning of the 20th century, the *Folk Almanac*, in which both the holidays and the types of work were indicated, was akin to an agronomy handbook of the Romanian farmer.[62]

---

[60] Pamfile, 1915, p. 83.

[61] Garofild, 1943, p. 74.

[62] Much like the Farmer's Almanac in the United States

March 27
The Cockerel

In order to determine specific times of day or night, people observed the Sun, the Moon, the Stars and the planets in the sky. When the sky is covered with clouds the estimation of their position with the naked eye is an approximate one.

To designate time during the night, people needed a terrestrial clock that was closer to them and easier to observe. Before inventing a device to measure time, man observed nature's creatures, as close as possible to his home and household, to inform him at various intervals about the passing of time.

Thousands of years ago, people in different parts of the world surprisingly chose the same clock: the *cockrel* (rooster). Plinius believed that "our night watchers were created by nature to wake the mortals for going to work and to interrupt their sleep. They go to sleep with the Sun and at the fourth watch they call us to attend to our duties at work. They cannot bear that the sunrise should catch us unprepared: they announce the coming day through their song and the song through the flutter of its wings."[63]

In ancient times and in the Middle Ages, armies kept cockerels with them to signal the changing of the guard during the night. A similar task was carried out by the rooster, which Romanian shepherds brought, together with some hens, up to their sheepfolds in the Carpathian Mountains. As it was endowed with the gift of crowing around midnight, a moment of balance when the good spirits were thought to confront with the evil ones, people placed the cockerel as a reliable guardian of transitional time. After the rooster's crow, the evil spirits lost their power, hid themselves and were only able to get into action again the following night.

Although today there are clocks and watches in peasants' houses from the most remote small villages, people still continue to orientate themselves in time by the cock's crow. It signals to them at least three major moments of the night: *midnight* at the first crow, *three hours before daybreak* at the second crow and *the daybreak* when it crows several times (in the sky the Pleiades go down and the Morning Star rises).

---

[63] Marian, 1883, p. 239.

March 28
The Grapevine - A Strengthening Shrub

As the story is told, there was a king who, while traveling through his kingdom, saw that much trouble by wine causing people to lose their heads. As a remedy, he decided to destroy the cursed grapevines. When the king died, others took over his throne. Once, a prince from that country went out hunting wild beasts in the woods.

Horse Skull Protector of the Vineyards, Campofeni, Gorj County
(AIEF Film No. 19)

"While hunting, he came across a bear. He started chasing it until he reached a hermitage, where an old monk had lived since Noah's time. When the monk heard the noise, he came out from his cell and saw the bear and the people who were chasing it. He took off his monk clothes, he rolled up his sleeves, went up to the huge animal, and grabbed it by the ears so hard that it started trembling like a lamb. Amazed, the prince asked him how he became so strong. The monk told him that it was from a grapevine, a strength-bearing shrub which makes grapes in the autumn. Gathering plenty, he stored them to enjoy throughout the year. Returning home, the prince came back and ordered: "From now on the grapevine can be freely grown all over the kingdom and anyone can enjoy the power of its fruit, but not more than needed to be strong enough to grab a bear by the ears."[64]

March 29
"Tarnoasele," The Midpoint of the Easter Period of Lent

The midpoint of the Easter period of Lent on a Wednesday is called *Tarnoasele*, The Eggs' Holiday or The Mid-Paresimilor in the Folk Almanac. On that day, housewives check the eggs by looking at them

---

[64] Butura, 1979, p. 250.

through a candle light, in order to separate the good, fertile ones from the non-fertile ones which are then painted and decorated for Easter. The eggs chicken sit on starting that day will hatch after three weeks right on Easter Day (Banat).

In this manner, Easter-Day hatched eggs are broken open naturally by chicks in order to come out of the shells, while the painted or the decorated eggs are broken to symbolize the resurrection of Jesus Christ.

March 30
The Forbidden Thursdays

The *Forbidden Thursdays* are the cycle of nine Thursdays within the period between Easter and the second week after Pentecost when certain household, farming and grazing activities were prohibited.

Early in the Twentieth Century the number of Thursdays which were observed varied from region to region: three, nine and only rarely one, two or four. The Forbidden Thursdays, also called The Green Thursdays in the South, and The *Remembered Thursdays* in the East, were considered hostile. They brought rainfalls with hail, storms and strong winds, thunder and fires, white frost and late frosts. Hoping for good influences, people introduced work interdictions on those occasions in the Folk Almanac described as The Forbidden Thursdays. These Thursdays were reminders also of ancient times when the day of the week dedicated to cult and resting was Thursday, which was later on replaced by the Christian Sunday.

March 31
The Home Industry almanac

The Great Thursday of the Trials Week before Easter, a day for commemoration of the dead, was the last day when the women and particularly the young women could spin wool. On Great Thursday, the weaving of hemp threads was stopped, as that household activity could be carried out with the best results only in certain humidity and temperature conditions.

The spinning of threads was done by old and young women particularly during evening sittings starting in mid-autumn and finishing at the end of the winter and beginning of springtime. Spinning was an activity carried out by groups of women and girls who enjoyed telling stories, singing, joking and laughing.

On the other hand, weaving was an activity that could not be done by group sittings and it started after Shrovetide and went on until

The Great Thursday. The maidens, especially those who were to join the round dance at Easter for the first time, had to finish sewing a new blouse for themselves, which was another activity that did not take place in the evening sittings. Those who had not sewn themselves a new blouse for Easter were to be punished by the spirit of that day called *The Wicked Woman of Thursday* or *Joimarita*.[65]

Spinning in Rogoz Village,
Maramures County
(AIEF Photo by Hertea, No. 52.293)

The ornamental motifs, the choice and the combination of colors that were used would be kept secret, thus every house was turned into an individual creation workshop, after the period of the evening sittings. The young women fit for getting married would display their hard work, their talent and their good taste in their newly-sewn clothes, worn only when joining the first ring dance in the village which was allowed only after the Easter period of Lent. On that occasion, the young men and their mothers had an opportunity to appreciate the young women's artistic work.

---

[65] Marian, 1899, p. 267-268.

APRIL

"PRIER"

1	The Bear's Massage
2	The Flute
3	Guessing a Young Woman's Predestined Husband
4	The Bell Board
5	The Bell King
6	The Maidens' Solemn Sworn Unity
7	The Forgiven Woman
8	The Soul
9	The Soul Bird
10	Death – Goddess and Biological Phenomena
11	The God "Iama"
12	The Death Messengers
13	Empirical Knowledge About Equinoxes and Solstices
14	An Incantation for Charming the Cuckoo
15	Lazarus
16	Palm Sunday
17	The Shepherds' Partnership
18	Adorning Eggs
19	When Heaven and the Graves Open
20	"Joimarita"
21	"Sangiorz Vacilor" - Cows' Saint George
22	"Sângiorz" - Saint George
23	Easter. Knocking the Eggs
24	Dance on the Graves
25	Marcus, the Bulls' Master
26	Death Tools: the Sickle and the Scythe
27	Tools of the Death of the Wheat: the Grinding Mill
28	Breaking the Pot
29	Bequest on the Deathbed
30	Easter of the Clement Ones

April

is the second month in the ancient Roman Almanac and the fourth month in the Gregorian and Julian Almanacs beginning January 1. The folk name of the month, *"Prier,"* means good weather, favorable for crops and for cattle. In the northwestern part of Transylvania, April was also called the *Bull's Month*.[66] In Transylvanian and Bistrita-Nasaud localities it was called "Florar," the month of the flowers. When the weather is unstable, with cold and dry days considered bad for sowing, April foretells poverty and is called "Empty Bag." This first day of the month is also called *The Fool's Day* in Maramures when people play practical jokes on one another. During the month of April the spring plowing and sowing take place, fields for random grazing are enclosed, cattle herds are gathered, and both shepherds and cowmen are hired. Before being driven up to mountain pastures, sheep are sheared and cattle folds built or repaired. Among the most important holidays with a fixed or variable date is Easter, the central holiday of the festive Christian almanac coinciding with "Sângiorzul" that marks the ancient beginning of the agrarian year.

Knocking Eggs at Easter, Babeni, Valcea County (Noi Media Print 1998)

---

[66] MALR, 1967, Map Nr. 600.

April 1
The Bear's Massage

This custom, a chiropractic and psychotherapudic practice, consisted of massaging men's backs by a trained bear in April or May at the inception of the Agrarian Year. Bear leaders walked through villages, going from house to house with a bear tied by a chain. First the bear would dance in the yard of somebody's house to the rhythm of a drum and to the sound of an incantation.

Dance well, Father Martin,
And you will be rewarded with bread and olives!

After which, the man who was the head of the family for whom the ceremony was performed would lie flat on the ground to be stepped on his back by the bear. The bear leader would order the bear to step heavier or lighter, or to sit on the "patient."

Those men who were stepped on their backs by the bear were firmly convinced that they would be stronger and safe from backache throughout the year. On that occasion the women would, if they managed to, pluck out hairs from the bear's fur, which they would use to cure those children who had been frightened by "smoking" them.[67] This is done by burning the hair of a bear and then blowing the smoke over the face of the child.

April 2
The Flute

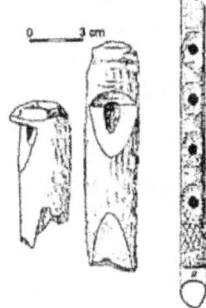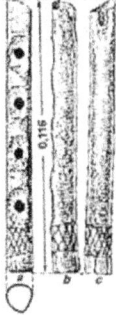

Bone Flutes from Dacian Site at Sprancenata, Olt County and from Early Feudal Site at Dinogetia (Preda, 2000)

Romania's oldest and best known musical instrument is *the flute*, a cult object through which people's souls on the earth communicated with the spirits from the beyond. Ethnographical, linguistic and archaeological studies confirm the hypothesis according that

---

[67] Ghinoiu, 2000, p. 97.

flutes used to be made from a bone of an ancestor, hence the Romanian word for shinbone – "the leg's flute." Later on the human bone was replaced with that of a bird (the crane) and also with wood from sacred trees as mentioned in some lines of the famous "Miorita" ballad:

> *Flute of bone,*
> *Sweet sound!*
> *Flute of elder,*
> *Passionate sound!*
> *Flute of beech,*
> *Dear sound!*

Legends say that the first flute was made by God at the time when He used to be a shepherd living on Earth. He placed flutes in the sheep's wool where they were found by shepherds during springtime shearing. According to other legends, God gave the flute, which was kept in an honored place in Heaven, to Peter as a reward for the fact that the smoke of frankincense from the Earth reached the sky. Even today a real shepherd is buried holding his flute in his hands. Indeed, in shepherd communities one could not become a shepherd unless able to play the flute. The flute was also a sacred instrument used for casting away the evil spirits ("Iele") at Pentecost, the ghosts and the witches at Saint George ("Sângiorz").[68]

April 3
Guessing a Young Woman's Predestined Husband

Every New Year starts with unknowns and mysteries. That is why people using various methods try to find out as much as possible about their future. Will they will be healthy or sick, rich or poor and will there be peace or war.

A favored custom for this purpose was the young women's ritual guessing of their predestined husband ("Vergelatul"), usually performed in the evenings or the nights of the most important holidays throughout the year. Young women would meet, usually at the house where normal evening gatherings were held. After locking the doors, covering the windows, they perform by candlelight the ritual of *vergelatul* conducted by the hostess also called "Fate" in Moldavia.

After placing on a table several objects with symbolic and mat-

---

[68] Ghinoiu, 2004, p. 141-142.

rimonial value - knife, salt, charcoal, comb, ring, stone - and a corresponding number of clay containers - bowls, pots, plates, the Fate invites one of the young women to go out of the room. In her absence the containers are turned upside down and the prophetic objects were put under them. Once returned into the room, the young woman lifts one of the pots and the Fate reads her fortune by interpreting the significance of the found object: *the knife* meant a severe man, with a sharp tongue like the knife, that hurts his wife's feelings; *salt* meant a good man, like salt in the food when used in moderate amounts; *charcoal* meant a dark, tall and healthy man who should not be "lit", for it can only be put out by his wife's tears; *a comb* meant a strong and determined man, but kindhearted; *the ring* meant a good-looking man, who could be "drawn through a ring"; *a stone* meant that the young woman would remain unmarried in her home.

A young women's predestined husband could also be foretold in other ways: taking lead and bee-wax, melting them on the fire and then throwing them into cold water, or with the white of an egg dropped into a whole glass of water, also with pig hairs burnt on the stove, or burning candles reflected in the water of a well, with salted little flat-cakes given to cats to eat, or by counting the stakes of the fence and marking one of them in the dark and then seeing in the daylight what the future husband would be like, or by waking up cows by kicking them, or by listening to barking dogs and thus finding the direction where the future husband would come from.[69]

April 4
The Bell Board

The ritual practice through which the voice of the phytomorphic deity is obtained by rhythmically hitting a sycamore plate with two wooden hammers is known as the *Wooden Bell Board* ("toaca") or the *Wooden Plate Carroll*. The wooden bell board whose name suggests the sound produced during the beat, is also found in the sacred toponymy of the northern Carpathians ("La toaca" in the Ceahlau Mountains) and in folk expressions and tales.

Calling Parishioners to Church by Beating the "Toaca", Calinesti, Maramures County

---

[69] Ghinoiu, 1997, p. 214-215.

In northwestern Transylvania young men and children beat the wooden board to call the spirits of the dead that were leaving their graves during the Great Thursday in order to celebrate the holidays of the vernal equinox, along with the living. In other parts of the country the sound of the bell board was used to cast away clouds that bring hail and storm in the summer time.

Using its unique sound, the Eastern Christian Church soothes and calls its believers to prayer and announces the beginning of every ritual day as well as the main liturgical moments. Similar to the resonant plates used by the Buddhists and the Shinto from the Far East, the ritual beat of the wooden bell board is practiced today by Romanians, Greeks, Armenians, Bulgarians, Latvians, Russians, Serbs, Croatians and Estonians. The bell board certainly belongs to the pre-Christian proto-history. As a magic practice of invoking the phytomorphic deity with her own voice, the bell board beat ritual is far older than the ritual beat of the drums or the bell toll, whose beginnings can be traced back at the Indo-European agrarian populations during the Bronze Age and the Iron Age.[70]

April 5
The Bell Ring

The brass bell personifies the voice of the divinity; it soothes and it calls the believers to pray; it also casts away and removes the evil spirits of nature. Unlike the wooden plate, a symbol of Neolithic wood culture, the bell is the emblem of the Indo European solar deities dating to the Bronze Age and the Iron Age and that of the subsequent Christian God.

The sound produced by the small bells which were tied up around the waists or the legs of the "Calusul" dancers at the Penticost ("Rusalii"), as well as by the bells attached to masks worn at Christmas and Easter ("Goat," "Brezaia," "Turca,") were meant to cast away evil spirits and to purify a specific place. The cattlemen would hang bells around the cattle's necks to protect them from the witches who could come and steal their milk during the night.

Similarly to the wooden plate, the bell was taken over by the Christian church from the pre-Christian cultures. Nowadays, by means of the bell ring, the farmers continue to announce somebody's death, to invoke the rain in times of draught and to cast away the storms and the clouds threatening to bring hail. The bell is hung differently, according to the message it sends, and every soul in the village listens to it carefully. In

---

[70] Ghinoiu, 1999, p. 16.

order not to mistake a death announcement for a holiday announcement, the bell is rung using a special technique ("pulled by the rope") in the case of a death message, by which a specific sound is produced. In those villages where there are several bells, it is also possible to announce the approximate age of the dead person. "If the dead person was old or in the prime of life, then all the bells were rung, that is every bell in the church was rung, whereas if a child died, only the small bell rang."[71]

April 6
The Maiden's Solemn Sworn Unity

The solemn sworn unity promised until death between several maidens is called "Matcutatul" in Banat after the folk deity Matcalau. The ceremony is held in the house, around a table, or in the garden, around a fruit-tree, usually an apple tree in blossom. When the ritual takes place in a house, it follows several steps. First, the maidens who decide to become "sisters" or "matcute" must come to an agreement; then, a "clean" maiden or "forgiven woman" who can no longer have children prepares a flat cake of wheat flower. A hostess is then chosen to lead the whole ceremony; the baked flat cake is sprinkled with salt and placed on a table around which sit the maidens; a piece in the shape of a cross is cut from the flat cake and on it are poured a number of drops of wine, equal to the number of maidens who will become sisters ("matcute"); using a silver coin, the cross is cut in as many pieces as the number of maidens who wish to become sisters; then each girl eats a piece of the sacred flat cake. Folk deity are also invoked:

> *Matcalau, Matcalau!*
> *Pray to God*
> *To keep us away from evil,*
> *For we shall honor you*
> *All through the year*
> *We shall bring you flowers*
> *On every Holiday!*
> *We shall honor and remember you*
> *As long as we live*
> *As long as we shall be sisters!*

After hugging and kissing each other, the maidens conclude the ceremony with a party at which their parents and closest relatives participate. Each of them receive one silver piece which they are to protect until

---

[71] Marian, 1892, p. 95.

they die. At death, the silver piece will be placed in their bosom for burial so that the sisters might recognize each other in the world beyond. During their lifetime the sisters pay each other a visit on the day of "Matcalau" holiday. On that occasion, they offer each other gifts and bunches of spring flowers called "matcute."

In some parts of the country on the same day ("Matcalau"), a similar sworn unity among young men takes place, following the same ceremony.[72]

April 7
The Forgiven Woman

Forgiven Women, Runcu, Gorj County

A woman at menopause who has not been married or who has become a widow is called in some rural communities a *forgiven woman*. She holds a special position in the community, which allows her to perform a lot of rituals at the borderline between the sacred and the profane. They are comparable with ancient priestesses. Her sins are forgiven, and given her age is respected for her knowledge of customs, rules for preparing the ritual foods such as knot-shaped bread, boiled wheat given as alms, "mucenici", communion bread, Easter cheese cake, the healing plants, and invoking charms and spells.

April 8
The Soul

The *soul* is the immortal, invisible and intangible vital essence, which is sheltered in its *pre-existence* in the maternal womb and in its *existence in* the placenta. It is sheltered in the body, the house, the village of the World about us. And in its *post-existence*, it is sheltered by the coffin, the grave, the cemetery, and the Beyond. The soul becomes vulnerable when it must leave its shelter which is destined itself to be destroyed. It cannot

---

[72] Evseev, 1997, p. 264-265.

both enter and come out through the same entrance of each shelter in the great passage moments from pre-existence into existence (birth) and from existence into post-existence (death).

That is why certain things with no exit such as the egg, or with only one exit like a clay pot, are meant to be violently broken: the custom of breaking the egg at Easter, for releasing God, or the custom of breaking the clay pot at a person's burial for releasing the individual. In certain idioms, the verb "to break" has the meaning of *to die*, in some contexts.

The exhalation that comes out of people's mouths, or the vapor released through the skin of tired animals is sometimes associated with the soul. *Vapor* is the name given to cooked food offered as alms after the funeral (in Dâmbovita and Buzau counties) or on other occasions to celebrate the dead (Muntenia, Dobrogea).

April 9
The Soul Bird

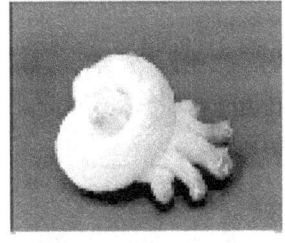

Bird Made of Dough for Funerals, Seaca Valley, Suceava County
(AIEF Photo by Alina Ciobanel, 1998)

The *soul bird* is an artistic representation of the dead man's soul found on poles and on crosses in some cemeteries. The bird is rendered in its whole shape or partially through carving, fretwork or painting. In the region at the junction of the Jiu River and the Danube, a bird carved or painted on the cross is rendered in a descendent flight, oriented towards the core of the Earth where lives the Neolithic mother goddess. However, in most cemeteries from Oltenia and from other parts of Romania, two wooden boards together with the pole itself, make up an arrow-like shape oriented towards the sky. Seen from above, the arrow-shaped crosses in the cemeteries look like flocks of birds grouped in families in the same way in which people are grouped and related in the precincts of a village. Unlike the soul bird rendered in ascendant or descendent flight, which is found in the cemeteries from the South of the Carpathians, in some villages in Southern Transylvania there are one or two birds, painted in black or in blue, that are resting on top of the cross, or in its arms, or on a wooden board, fastened vertically on the grave fir tree which is placed besides the cross. (Pavelescu, 1998, p.231-240)

The soul bird, a common archetype in folk art, appears carved in wood, painted on pottery, drawn on eggs, or sewn on woven materials.[73]

April 10
Death-Goddess and Biological Phenomena

In Romanian the notion of *death* has two meanings. One is the biological phenomenon characterized by ceasing of the vital functions and the other is a personification that takes people's souls. The more positive image of the Neolithic goddess of regeneration, able to cure illnesses and to bring peace, also called the *White Goddess* by archaeologists, was replaced with a terrifying mythical representation by the Indo-European peoples, including the Christian ones.

Death in Double Stage by Miniaturist Picu Patrut, 1844 (Patrut, 1985)

Because the Neolithic goddess of death and regeneration was viewed as undermining the authority of the deities that took her place - Zeus, God, The Son of God - she was condemned by Indo-Europeans and Christians. As a consequence, the face of death was changed into that of an ugly old woman.

The inanimate body, free from all sufferings which provoked its death, acquires a total serenity, immediately after passing away, which is in contrast to the preceding moments of agony. Sometimes at funerals, people can talk about the dead person's *good looks* and his/her *smile*. However, the common image of death is that of a hideous skinny old woman, with sunken eyes, a scythe in her hand for taking people's lives, or a glass of some bitter drink - the death water – to be given to humans when the time comes. That representation is totally different from the one that the ancient Indo-Europeans must have had of death.

---

[73] Pavelescu, 1998, p.231.

In the texts sung at funerals in many villages in Oltenia, Banat and in Southern Transylvania, death has an anthropomorphic appearance, the prototype of the Indo-European cultural complex, and it also looks like a bird of prey, typical for the Neolithic Age. In the anthropomorphic state, named *Death* or the *Old Fairy*, she takes out the soul from a dead body, transports it on an animal's back (horse, stag) into the world beyond, writes his name on the list of the dead ones, and so on. In the bird state, named *Gaia*, the Raven takes the soul from a dying man's body and transports in on its wings into the world beyond.[74]

April 11
The God "Iama"

In the Romanian pantheon *Iama* is a mythical representation, identified with Yama, the Indian god of the dead. In the south of Romania, the expression *"to be chased by Iama"* used about birds, animals and even about harvests, means *to die*. The difference between the Carpato-Danubian god and the Indian one is minor. Indians believe that the god takes the humans' souls, while the Romanian belief is that the god takes the life of plants and animals.

Kite Bird of Prey Associated with Death (Bogoescu, 1983)

Ancient Indians believed that, after the burial or after the dead bodies had been thrown into running waters, the souls left to meet with their parents who had gone to the underworld realm of the god Yama. Later on the home of the god Yama was transferred from deep under the Earth to high up in the sky. Yama is not the only god that is common to the Indians and the Romanians: the Indian god of rain, Rudra, is invoked by the groups of children who, in the dry summer days, follow a strange phytomorphic mask, "Paparuda"; a carol sung on Christmas day is dedicated to the Indian god Shiva, the carol being called Siva, or Vasilica, under the influence of the Christian Saint Vasile.[75]

---

[74] Ghinoiu, 1988, p. 123.

[75] Ghinoiu, 2001, p. 88, 143-144, 175.

April 12
The Death Messengers

In its personified state, Death will not arrive unannounced. Its messengers can be certain domestic animals (the dog, the ox, the horse), or wild animals (the wolf, the bear), some birds of prey (the little owl, the great owl), or even domestic birds (the hen). They send the death message through the sounds they produce. The dog and the wolf do it by howling, the hen sings like a cock and the owl hoots. In some folk legends and beliefs, the howling of the wolves is associated with the prayers which they address to lycomorphical deities like The Winter Saint Peter (January, 16), The Great Philippy (November 20), and Saint Andrew (November, 30). Similarly, the religious man sings songs dedicated to the god that he worships, in the church, in the temple, in the synagogue or in the mosque. In a beautiful folk poem from Oltenia, the man's song is compared to the howl of the wolf:

> *I am alone with my song,*
> *Like a wolf howling to itself.*

The death messengers of the god Yama from the Indian Pantheon are the owl and the dog, the same as the ones that announce Death from the Romanian Pantheon.

April 13
Empirical Knowledge about Equinoxes and Solstices

"Push forward-Pull back" is the folk expression defining the vernal and the autumn equinox, when day becomes equal with night. Such phenomena are made known to Romanians through various biological signs. The most evident is the first song of the cuckoo (the day of the vernal equinox when the cuckoo starts singing), another is the return of migratory birds.

People used to say that, starting from the equinox day (*"Push forward-Pull back"*), the day became longer or shorter, little by little, the length by which it was modified being equal to the jump of a hen from the door's threshold.

The *solstice* was determined by people with the help of other terrestrial signs such as the cuckoo's silencing (the day when the cuckoo stopped singing), the appearance of glow worms in the forests, or the blooming of the plant called Our Lady's Bedstraw. ("Sânziana" or "Dragaica")

April 14
"Cucu-rascucu" Incantation for Charming the Cuckoo

Cucu-rascucu is the name of a magic practice, performed at "Sângiorz" (April, 23), which was meant to annihilate the power of the cuckoo to take away the manna (the plenty) of the sheep during the summer season. This custom takes place according to a ritual scenario made up of several significant parts. A big knot-shaped piece of bread is baked with a hole in the middle, called the "Sângiorz knot-shaped bread"; then, the bread is placed over the container used for milking the sheep, which has been decorated with willow boughs, lovage-plant leaves and various wild flowers; then the sheep are milked through the hole in the bread; afterwards two children break the bread into two pieces; the two children, usually a boy and a girl, while pulling the bread in opposite directions, say the magic incantation three times: "Cucu-rascucu"; those pieces of bread are then eaten by the sheep owners and by the other participants at the ritual; one piece of the same bread is kneaded and mixed with salt in order to be used as remedy for the sheep.

The same magic practice was performed for milk cows, especially for those who had their calves in spring, after the arrival of the cuckoo. There is evidence of the Cucu-rascucu ceremonial, in several regional variants, in Banat, Oltenia and Bistrita-Nasaud.

The cuckoo-bird is secretly related to a ploughman's life, as it signals to him the vernal equinox and the summer solstice. The place from where a person hears its song coming for the first time (from behind, in front, from the left, or from the right), the place where the cuckoo stands when it sings (on a dry branch, on a hillock or on a garbage heap), or the repetition of its song, etc. are all interpreted as good or bad signs for the man and his animals. The cuckoo can forecast good-luck, good health, marriage, disease, separation, or death.

April 15
"Lazarelul" - Lazarus

Biblical Myth of Lazarus' Resurrection by Miniaturist Picu Patrut (Patrut, 1985)

In Southern Romanian villages, the Saturday before Palm Sunday, a complex ceremonial was practiced, dedicated to a pre-historic goddess of vegetation, and structured by the model of the carols. Under the influence of Christianity, it was called *Lazarus* or *"Lazarelul"*, or even *"Lazarica"*. One of the caroling young girls, called Lazarica dressed up as a bride, goes round the villagers' houses, together with her friends. She walks slowly to and fro in a circle formed by her friends who, in a simple melody, tell the dramatic story of the vegetation hero, Lazarus or Lazarica: he left home with his sheep; he climbed up a tree to get some leaves to feed his cattle; he fell and he died unexpectedly; the girls searched him for a long time and finally found his lifeless body; they brought him home and gave the body the ritual bath in milk; then they covered the body with nut-tree leaves and threw away the bath liquid under some nut-trees.

In a variant from Dobrogea, the funeral scenario is completed with Lazarus coming back to life and turning into flowers, which becomes the climax of the ceremonial, marked by the girls cheerfully dancing a ring dance. Two mythical representations: Lazarus and Flora, the former Thracian origin, which took over the evangelist Luke's name and the latter, the Roman goddess Flora, are both celebrated in The Folk Almanac, one after the other: on Lazarus' Saturday and on Palm Sunday.

April 16
"Floriile"
Palm Sunday

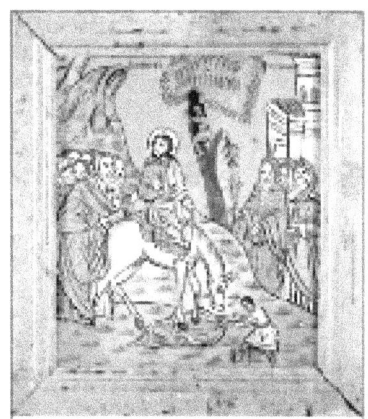

Christ's Triumphal Arrival in Jerusalem by an Icon Painter in Laz, Sebes valley (Irimie, Focsa, 1968)

Floriile are personifications of the flowers celebrated on the Saturday b earing their name: The Sunday of the Flowers (Palm Sunday). On the same day, the Christian church overlapped the celebration of Christ's entrance into Jerusalem. As a mythical representations, Floriile are identified with the Roman Goddess Flora who was frequently identified by the archaeologists in Roman-Era Dacia sites.

When all of nature comes to life, when all the plants, willow and fruit-tree blossom, new meanings are added mainly connected with the descendants' cult. On that day, it is customary to give alms, to clean the graves and the graveyards, to stick willow boughs in the ground over the graves, and to invoke the dead peoples' spirits.

The willow bough, hallowed in the Church, is a symbol of chastity and of annual revival of the vegetation. It was with palm boughs, which Christians identify with willow bows, that the Jews greeted Jesus Christ on His triumphant entrance into Jerusalem. The willow boughs in blossom that have been hallowed in the Church on Palm Sunday are used for various purposes: to decorate the grave crosses, the graves, the roadside crucifixes, the doors and the gates of the houses; to ensure magic protection and to cast away the evil spirits; to give them to the cattle to eat in order to help them breed; to be stuck in the field ground, or to be hung in the fruit-trees or in the vines to help them produce rich crops and be fruitful; to be worn around men and women's waists in order to prevent them from having backache during harvest time; to stop the storms and the hail in the summer; to help spellbounds and charms work, etc.

On Palm Sunday (Florii), in some villages from Oltenia, children would sing carols with green willow boughs, while women would make a ring of willow boughs for sick people to go through, for becoming well again, at Circovii Marinei (July, 16-18). Wreaths made of willow boughs were sacred objects through which girls used to kiss each other before getting married, or they were being worn on the head of the girl performing the "Paparuda" ritual. Locally, on that day people would hang the "Martisor" amulet that they had received as a present in a wild rose tree or in a tree in blossom. In those villages where they believed that nettles bloom on Palm Sunday, people would no longer eat them and the day was called *"The Nettles' Wedding"*.

April 17
The Shepherds' Partnership

Shepherd's Partnership Celebration, Sarbi, Maramures County (AIEF Photo by C. Popescu, Nr. 60.353)

The first milking of all the sheep from a herd is usually followed by a beautiful village feast, called The Shepherds' Partnership or The Shepherds' Shares, which takes place on the day of *Sângiorz* or on any other day from the end of April and the beginning of May. On that day the shepherds measure the milk obtained from the number of sheep owned by each partner, the quantity is marked on a wooden plate, and then the corresponding amount of cheese that every shepherd had the right to is also measured. They get their share of cheese when the herd is dispersed.

In order to get as much milk as possible for themselves, the sheep owners prefer to graze, to guard and to milk the sheep themselves. Out of the very first milk obtained from the sheep, the owners usually prepare a kind of whey cheese which they then partition among themselves.

All the practical and the legal activities connected with sheep raising are accompanied by numerous ritual acts, meant to protect the sheepfold and the shepherds from the evil forces during the summer: the lighting of The Live Fire; the smoking of the shepherds and of the sheep; casting away, with loud cries and noises, the witches who steal plenty of the milk; destroying the cuckoo's power to take away or spoil the milk, through the magic practice called "Cucu-rascucu!"; the purification of the sheep and of their owners by sprinkling them with consecrated water; the ritual bathing in clean river water, or washing oneself with dew water; preparing certain ritual meals; sacrificing the lamb; uttering some magic incantations.

At the village feast, people eat special dishes ("balmos", corn meal boiled in milk to which butter is added, lamb roasted on spit in the outlaws' manner, knot-shaped bread, whey cheese made from the first milking). They sing and dance to shepherd songs. With its local variants and its various stages of evolution, this custom is known to all shepherds.

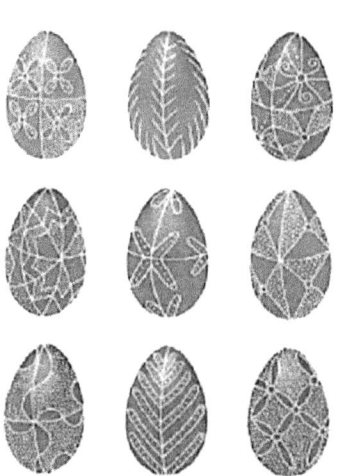

April 18
Adorning Eggs

Decorated Easter Eggs
(Ciobotaru, 2002)

Decorating the egg is a technique meant to make the sacrificed (broken) egg at Easter more beautiful, using anthropomorphic, zoomorphic and phytomorphic motifs, the egg being a symbol of the divinity which dies and comes back to life every year. The folk technique by which the egg becomes both a divine substitute and a work of art has several stages: selecting the fresh hen or duck eggs by putting them in a bowl with water (the fresh eggs fall on the bottom, while the old ones raise to the surface); choosing the nice, big ones with a thick and smooth shell; then the eggs are carefully washed in warm water to which a little vinegar has been added, to remove the fat and to obtain an even coloring; the eggs are placed horizontally in a bowl with water so that the air bubble should come on the side, and not at the edges; the eggs are cooked gently so that they do not break; painting colors are prepared from plants or from chemical products (for each paint a clean bowl must be used); decorating tools are made and prepared (the oldest pens were: the candle, whose heated tip was used to draw certain signs, and the quill, that was used in the same way as the horn tip to decorate pottery); the bee wax is melted, to which some crushed coal is added; eggs are actually decorated with ornamental motifs. The egg is dipped in the bowl with paint of the desired foundation color, taken out of the paint, and wax traces wiped out, leaving in their places the white decoration against the colored background. A one-colored egg is achieved in this manner.

In order to obtain multi-colored decorated eggs, the previously procedure must be repeated for each color. Locally, some stages of the procedure are reversed, or some modern decoration methods are used, that are more or less related to genuine egg decoration with wax (e.g. the eggs can be painted, carved in relief, decorated with plant leaves or with small pearls, also wooden or plastic eggs which are decorated or painted).

April 19
When Heaven and the Graves Open

Thursday from the Passion Week bears several regional names: *Great Thursday*, *Trials Thursday*, or *Black Thursday*. A great number of traditional practices underscore the religious importance of this day. According to what villagers from Muntenia and Oltenia believe: "Every year, on that particular day, the dead return to their former houses, where they stay until Saturday before Whitsuntide, that is until Sunday before Pentecost or before the Great Sunday, when alms are distributed for the parting of the souls, which means that knot-shaped bread and pots are given as pittances and the dead leave each with the bread and the pot they have received."[76] In other parts of the country, the dead are expected to arrive in the yard, where people place chairs for the dead to rest and they light fires for the dead to get warm. The dead people's souls can also come and rest in other places, like the eaves or on the roof of the house.

---

[76] Marian, 1899, p. 270.

In Banat, on Christmas Eve and on Great Thursday, women would incense the graves and on their way out from the cemetery, would call out their dead:[77]

*Get up, get up
And come home!*

It is believed that, at Great Thursday, not only the graves, but also the sky, Heaven and Hell open "for the souls to return home and spend time there" (Mangiuca, 1883, p.137-138) Great Thursday is probably the most important day in the Folk Almanac dedicated to the dead and to the forefathers. In some villages in Banat and Muntenia, knot-shaped bread and pots filled with wine or with water were given as alms for the dead, while in Nasaud area, people would lay out tables with food and drink in the cemetery.

April 20
"Joimarita"

In the Romanian pantheon of deities, *Joimarita* is a human representation of the goddess of death. In folk imagery she appears frightening with a huge head, long and undone hair, wide teeth and a gaping mouth.

Dwelling in some deserted forests, or deep inside some high mountains, she is usually associated with a dragon-like old hag, or a ghost, or an evil spirit, and seldom appears as a Saint. A small pail or clay pot with embers, and a fire hook are carried with her as fire-related tools for punishing and torturing. Being related to cult of the dead, Joimarita appears in places where people lit fires in the night of the Great Thursday during the Trials Week. Like funeral pyres for all the dead, the fires were set on the clay floor of the house, in the yard or garden, on graves or beside them, in the cemetery or churchyard.

*Mourning at Costesti Cemetery, Arges County
(AIEF Photo Nr. 1938)*

---

[77] Marian, 1899, p. 275.

From being a goddess of death, related to the funeral burning ritual specific to the Geto-Dacian population before the Christian burial custom came into being, Joimarita became a redeeming character who, at the beginning of the 20th century, controlled and punished lazy young women and married women, particularly those who failed to finish spinning hemp, flax and wool prior to the Great Thursday.[78] Merciless, Joimarita used terrible torture methods. She burned the lazy women's fingers, hands, nails, hair or she burned the hemp, tow or the bundles which had remained unspun.

The important role that Joimarita used to play in the Romanian folk beliefs is confirmed by her frequent presence in lots of customs and sayings from Oltenia, Muntenia, Banat, Dobrogea, Moldavia and Southern Transylvania.[79]

April 21
"Sângiorz Vacilor" – Cows' Saint George

On the 22nd of April, when "Mânecatoarea", Saint George's sister in the Romanian Pantheon, was celebrated, people believed that some ghosts ("strigoi") and some witches came to steal the milk from cows, the fruit from the field, the dream from the girls and the good-luck from the boys. On the night of the 22-23rd April, the living ghosts (strigoi), who leave their bodies without their knowledge, gather, riding on swindles in deserted houses, at crossroads and at village borders. After trying to prove their force by fighting with swindle wings until midnight, they return to the village, enter the bodies which they have left and go to get the manna from the milk cattle. The women witches also went round through villages' pastures, hayfields and cornfields, until dawn, dragging a sieve made of thin cloth, called "sidila", tied to their feet. The sidila got soaked with dew water, which was then squeezed out in a bewitched wooden container (a pail) and given to their own cattle to drink. That was how the *manna* or the plenty of the milk was transferred by magic practices from the neighbors' cattle to the witches' and the live ghosts' (strigoi) cattle.

Other times, the manna and particularly the fertility of the cattle were stolen by other methods: a salt ball was buried under the path on which cattle usually passed, then it was dug out and given to the breeding cattle to eat (Bucovina).

---

[78] Marian, 1899, p. 267-268.

[79] Muslea, 1972, p. 235-237.

People's belief that cattle could actually lose their milk, or that they might not be able to breed was so strong, that the entire village was deeply concerned with finding the most efficient ways or magic practices of fighting against witches: hiding the wings of the swindle from the live ghosts; smearing the swindles, the gates, the doors, the thresholds, the windows, the cattle and the people with garlic or garlic sauce; using charms and putting the mystical plants (wormwood, valerian, common celandines, lovage*, dwarf elder) in the stable or in the shed. Over large areas, people would hang wild rose and blackberry boughs at the gates, at the doors and at the windows; they would hang green breech, oak or willow twigs at the house pole or the gate pole; they would shout and blow their open horns to drive away the witches; they would carefully watch their cattle while grazing; they would smoke the cattle and the cattlemen; and they would light the "live" fire.

* Lovage is a well known plant used in soups such as bortsch and in charms against human and animal diseases.

April 22
"Sângiorz" - Saint George

The Christian religion superposed Saint George the Great Martyr, over a god of vegetation, protector of the horses, of the milk cattle and of the sown fields, identified in the Romanian Pantheon with the Thracian Knight, who is celebrated on the 23rd of April. This mythical representation is called *Sângiorz* in Transylvania and in Banat and *Saint George* in Moldavia, Muntenia and Oltenia.

Together with "Sâmedru" (October 26) Sângiorz divide the rural (pastoral) year into two symmetrical seasons: summer-time, which lasts from Sângiorz to Sâmedru and winter-time from Sâmedru to Sângiorz. Tied to their waist belts, they carry the keys of the year which Sângiorz uses to lock winter and unlock summer on the 23rd of April, and Sâmedru locks summer and unlocks winter on the 26th of October. One of the two saints makes the forest come into leaf and the other makes it lose its leaves. They put their lives at stake on a bet: if the trees have not come into leaf before the 23rd of April, Sâmedru will kill Sângiorz.

In the Folk Almanac, the two saints are rural (pastoral) divinities of Indo-European origin and bear obvious likeness with The Great Sântoader, celebrated on the Saturday of The Sântoader's Horses Week. In the Romanian beliefs, folklore and iconography, Sângiorz and Sântoader have common features with the Thracian Knight: they are young, hypomorphical divinities, carried on horseback (Sângiorz), or having horse hooves themselves (Sântoader's Horses); they purify the space of evil forces, they kill the dragon, they lock the winter and unlock the summer.

April 23.
Easter – Knocking the Eggs

No Romanian can conceive celebrating *Easter*, the central festive holiday of the Christian Almanac, without the *ritual knocking of breaking the eggs*.

As the ritual substitute for the primordial divinity, the egg is skillfully adorned by being painted and decorated with beautiful patterns, during the Passion Week, in order to be sacrificed mercilessly by being hit on the head after the service on Easter evening for Christ's Resurrection.

In the beginning, the eggs were colored with vegetal plants, in yellow, which is the color that the Sun has when it is high up in the Sky, and in red, the color that the Sun has at dawn and at dusk. Later on, the eggs were decorated with Christ's image, with angels, with a lamb, and then with various artistic motifs. (Ghinoiu, 2001, p.47) Without being aware of it, the Third Millennium man practices a prehistoric cult solemnly carried out according to a predetermined traditional ritual: the older person, usually the man, powerfully hits with the head of his egg the head of his partner's egg, while uttering the recognized phrase:

- *Christ is resurrected!*
- Hristos a Inviat
- *He is truly resurrected!*
- Adevarat a Inviat

Decorated Eggs
(Ciobotaru, 2002)

The colored and decorated egg is the symbol of The Savior who leaves the grave and returns to life as does the chick that comes out of the broken egg. In folk speech the verb *to break* has become synonymous with the end or the death of any personified object or phenomenon. Even bad luck dies or "breaks" when someone accidentally drops and breaks a clay pot. Since any privileged shelter of the soul either has no exit (the egg), or has a single one (the clay pot), the only solution for setting it free is the violent destruction of its shelter: knocking and breaking the egg at Easter, breaking the clay pot when the dead person is taken out of the house. The resemblance between the pot and the egg on one hand- as shelters which need to be broken for freeing the soul- and the human being on the other hand is well rendered in the expressions: "Man is like an egg", meaning that man is fragile and exposed to death at any moment; "his/her pot was broken", meaning that the person died.[80]

April 24

Dance on the Graves ("Jocul pe Morminte")

The funeral dance, usually practiced by girls in some cemeteries in Bihor on the second Easter Day, on Toma's Sunday or at Pentecost, is known under different names: The *Dance on the Graves, Moara, Milioara, Mioara* or *Felega's Dance*. The ceremony starts in the cemetery, for which reason it is also called The Dance on the Graves, it continues by a tour around the church and then, encouraging other people to join too, it goes round the streets of the village, over the fields towards the nearby villages. During the dance, the roles of companions from the world beyond, bearing names of flowers (Lioara, Viorica, Milioara), are played by their worldly counterparts.

"Lioara" (Game of the Graves), Udea de Jos, Bihor County (AIEF Photo Germina Comanici, Nr. 68 155)

The dance is made up of several ceremonial sequences: the girls form two uneven groups (one of them has an extra girl); they stand on both sides of a grave; one by one, the girls from the larger group exchange places with the ones from the smaller group in a certain order, which is contained in a text that the participants utter or sing in a dialogue form (the girls from the smaller group are asked to choose somebody from the larger group) whose purpose is undoubtedly to reestablish the balance between this world and the beyond; the girls make up pairs (one

---

[80] Ghinoiu, 2001, p. 178.

companion from *the side* and one from *the other side*); they form up a bridge, actually a tunnel, by the pairs of girls raising their arms and each girl holding either end of a bough, a handkerchief or a scarf; people who accompany the girls pass under the bridge (through the tunnel) from one world into the other. The text, which is uttered or sung on a melody typical of the children folklore, has lines made of five and six syllables that are characteristic of ritual poetry.[81]

In Colinele Tutovei area, The Dance on the Graves has been transferred from the cemetery to the death watch. The participants at the death watch divide into two groups: the girls are inside the dead's house and the boys are outside on the porch. In some villages, the girls take flowers' names and the boys call them from the outside by those names. Often, when there is only one girl left inside the house, she calls those who are outside. In the old variant, the last time it was the dead person whom they called (Odaia Bursucului, Vaslui County).

> *- More and more with us*
> *less and less with you,*
> *Give us, dear sisters!*
> *- Which one do you like?*
> *You are welcome to choose!*
> *Give us, dear sisters!*

Under various forms, the Dance on the Graves ("Lioara") and the death watch song ("Merioare") have passed into children's folklore.[82]

April 25
Marcus, the Bulls' Master

Young Bulls
(Photo Corina Mihaiescu, 1997)

Marcus, the bulls' master, celebrated on the 25th of April in the Folk Almanac, is the patron of big cattle, mainly of the bulls. On that day the bulls, the most important animals used for work in the old Romanian village,

---

[81] Traian Mârza, 1969, p. 36.

[82] Ciubotariu, 1986, p. 318.

were left to graze freely wherever and how much they liked, they were neither tied, nor yoked to the plough.

In the Romanian tradition, the bull is a fateful animal announcing to its master the arrival of Death, by refusing to draw the plough. The same message is transmitted by the dreams in which cattle appear particularly black bulls or cows tied with a rope or left free in the herd. Bulls were usually yoked to draw the funeral carts. Bulls are often invoked in funeral songs and laments (Izverna, Mehedinti County):

Dear bulls, dear bulls,
Who are you carrying?
Who are you walking?
Who are you taking away?

A reason for which "Zorile" goddesses of the dead person's destiny, are asked to wait is to have enough time to prepare the funeral cart and the bulls that are supposed to draw it (Runcu, Gorj County):

You, Zorile, Zorile,
Don't you hurry,
Don't you rush at us,
Until the white wanderer,
Has prepared,
A carrying cart,
Two drawing bulls,
For he is a traveler,
From one world to another,
From the country with yearning,
To the country with no yearning,
From the country with pity,
To the country with no pity..."

April 26

Death Tools: the Sickle and the Scythe

In the folk imagination, Death is the fierce woman, carrying a scythe on her shoulder, or having a sickle in his hand, which she uses to "mow" people's lives, like cutting wheat ears. From initially being symbols of vegetable death, the scythe and the sickle gradually became tools for human death.

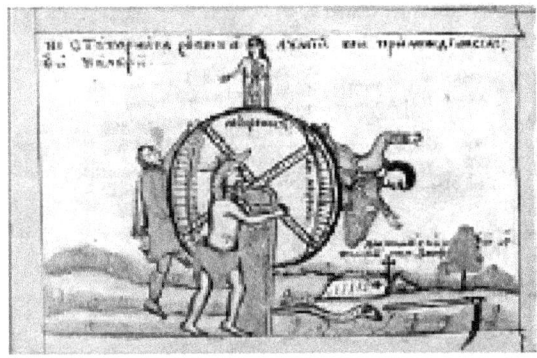

The Wheel of Life by Miniaturist Picu Patrut, 1844 (Patrut, 1985)

In prehistoric times, wheat growing was compared to man's shortened life formula: birth, marriage and death. The vegetable life cycle of the wheat begins with sowing the seed (a burial rite), it continues with sprouting (birth), then comes having ears, then bearing fruit (the death of the plant). According to the magic conception, the spirit of the wheat dwells in the body of the mother plant until it gets ears, when it withdraws into the impenetrable shelter of the grain. When it gets old, the plant becomes yellow and dry. It was sacrificed in the Neolithic Age by a beast with stone teeth in its mouth, and with metal teeth in the Bronze and Iron Ages. After the invention of the scythe in the Middle Ages, this new tool is carried by Death on its shoulder. As the Romanians call the edge of the scythe for *mouth* and the dents of the sickle for *teeth*, the verb *to mow* is actually a synonym for the verb *to die*.[83]

April 27
Tools for the Death of the Wheat: The Grinding Mill

The Death tools, which crush the spirit of the wheat "in the bud", are the grinding mill and the mill. In order to become bread or knot-shaped bread, that is sacred food often bearing saints' names (Christmas, Archangels, Saints, Little Saints, etc.) the spirit of the wheat must be set free, by violently crushing the wheat grain, thus breaking it into tiny particles in the ancient mill in the old times and later on in the grinding mill and in the mill. From breaking the wheat grain with his teeth to grinding it in the mill, man has gone through an impressive technological and spiritual process. First, he invented the ancient wooden bowl in which he used to crush the wheat grains, a prehistoric installation which,

---

[83] Ghinoiu, 2001, p. 173

similar to sowing with a stick or with a stake, is a technical transposition of the innate to and fro reflex of the sexual instinct.

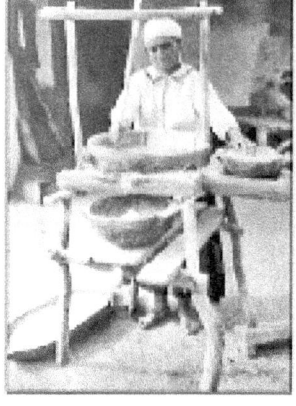

Grinding Mill
(AIEF Photo by C. Popescu)

Both the mill and the mill lake had an ill-fated significance. It was in those places where "moroi", "strigoi" and other phantoms would appear, and they were also the places where it was most effective to perform witchcraft and charms, or to steal objects for that purpose. The mill, considered the stone altar on which the spirit of the wheat was sacrificed, used to be stopped from working, in some villages, when the New Moon appeared (was born) in the sky, and also on the day called "Blagovestenie", when the Baby Christ was conceived in Holy Mary's Womb. The fateful significance of the mill is also reflected in a saying, often heard at funerals: "Everyone's turn will come too, as it does at the mill."

In the past, "someone's turn at the mill" meant keeping a record of the people who were expecting their turn at the mill. Brâncusi intuitively rendered the prehistoric altar function of the mill stones, by shaping such stones into a table, to create the memorial monument in Târgu Jiu.[84]

April 28
Breaking the Pot

Used continuously for 8,000 years from Neolithic times to the present-day, the clay pot is the best-known ritualistic symbol of man. It is "born" through molding of clay and then returned to its initial state through a violent death by ritually breaking it.

Gaining life by being burnt in the oven, the clay pot becomes an important ritual agent, manipulated by initiated people such as the witch, the midwife, the god mother, or the head of the male group of "Calusul" (horse) dancers. Thrown into a well or into a river during the hot summer days, the clay pot becomes a messenger sent by people to the divinity which releases the rain. By breaking it when a baby is given its first bath, the midwife makes the magic transfer of health and of the

---

[84] Ghinoiu, 1991, p. 10-13.

pleasant sound from the burnt clay to the new-born baby. At other times, breaking a clean unused clay pot by the godmother can repair the mistake of the girl who was not a virgin when she got married. When a clay pot is hung up on the outer wall of a house, facing the road, it signals to potential match-makers that there is a girl ready to be given away in marriage, whereas when the pot is reversed it means refusal to receive any match-makers. The reason may that a girl is too young and has not yet been allowed to attend the ring dance in the village, or her dowry is not yet prepared.

Neolithic Pot

The clay pot might also shelter spirits hostile to man. That is why, during the childbirth period, or in the days and in the nights when a dead person is kept in the house, or while performing spells and charms meant to cast away the evil spirits, the clay pots must be turned upside down in order to prevent the evil spirits to hide in them.

In most Romanian villages, after a dead person is carried out of the house, there is the custom of breaking a pot on the death place, or on the threshold or at the grave. The Romanian saying: "His pot was broken" (meaning that somebody died) reflects the fact that the custom is very old.

April 29
Bequest on the Deathbed

For comforting their soul and for making it easier to pass away old people who are on their deathbed usually call for those people whom they have judged wrongly in their life-time, or whom they have upset or treated badly, to ask for their forgiveness and also to take leave of them. Those who don't ask for forgiveness are believed to take to great pains for a long time before dying. The custom of asking for forgiveness on the deathbed, of solving old conflicts, of hugging and shedding tears is quite a dramatic scene.

The most precious heritage that man can leave after his death is ensuring continuity to his own descent, through his children, grandchildren and great grandchildren. Before passing away, or even on the deathbed, people usually left a verbal will to their children, which later on became the written bequest document.

The unwritten will left on the deathbed was a legal act. In some historical documents appears the phrase: *the share of the soul*, which means that a person bequeathed his possessions to a church or to another person in exchange for being buried and for being remembered according to all the religious customs.

Unlike the Medieval Western society in which the first born would inherit the house and the household, as a compensation for the fact that he was assigned the military tasks of the family, in the Romanian village it was the last born who enjoyed that right, for he was considered the descendent who had the chance to maintain the ancestors' cult for a longer time. The custom of a person's leaving on the deathbed his/her possessions, giving advice and entrusting secrets to his/her children is still practiced today.

April 30

Easter of the Clement Ones

The first Sunday after Easter, dedicated to Apostle Thomas in the Orthodox Almanac and to the souls of the dead in the Folk Almanac, is called *Easter of the Dead* or *Easter of the Clement Ones*. Thomas, one of the 12 apostles chosen by Jesus, who doubted about Christ's Resurrection, but believed it after touching His wounds, is celebrated in autumn, on October 6th, and not in spring, after Easter. The believers, after attending the service, lay rich offerings on their relatives' graves in the cemetery including pots, red painted eggs, lighted candles, and then eat together in the church garden. In the Beius area and in other parts of Transylvania, the funeral feast lasts until sunset, to the sound of the church bells.

Offerings on a Tomb, Butea, Iasi, County (Ciubotaru, 2002)

The *Clement Ones* are mysterious mythical representations of primordial humans, ancient ancestors synonymous with the Rocmanii (Rohmanii or Rugmanii). The Clement Ones live on the border between *our world* and *the beyond*, and on the banks of the River "Saturday" (The Death River) at the point where it flows into the Whirlpool of the Earth. They are celebrated at Easter of the Clement, usually the Monday following Thomas's Sunday. Their name has a literary origin and has entered the Romanian folklore through a very popular medieval novel called "Alexandria". People's beliefs concerning these creatures date back to much older times, definitely pre-Christian ones. As direct descendents of Adam and Eve, they took part in the creation of the world; they also support the Earth. As for their physical appearance, they look like naked short humans, their bodies are covered with hair.

Their men meet with their women once a year namely at "Easter of the Clement Ones" in order to conceive children. The boys are raised by their mothers until they can walk and feed themselves, after which they live with men separated from women. They are pious, kind-hearted, clement, wise, incapable of doing any harm, and they lead an austere life of strict fasting periods. Being simple people, they cannot count the days. They keep track of the holidays, particularly of Easter which they celebrate eight days later, or even more, when they see floating on the River "Saturday" the shells of the red eggs which have been deliberately thrown in a flowing water by housewives on Friday or Saturday of the Trials Week. When they see the eggshells in their remote country, they celebrate *there*. While *here*, we celebrate Easter of the Clement Ones or Easter of the Dead at the same time.[85]

On this day people lay offerings on the graves, lament their dead, distribute alms, do libations and lay out rich meals in the cemetery, in the churchyard or out in the field. (Moldavia, Dobrogea, Maramures, Bistrita-Nasaud)

---

[85] Marian, 1901, p. 175.

MAY

"FLORAR"

THE BLOSSOM MONTH

1	"Armindeni"
2	The Wormwood
3	The Lament
4	The Lament in Verse
5	"Zorile" song of the Departure
6	Song of the Fir-Tree
7	The Posthumous Wedding
8	The Alms
9	Making Clay lids for Bread Baking on a Hearth
10	The Funeral Boat
11	The Roller
12	The Wake
13	"Perinita"- Funeral Dance at Wake
14	The Dead Man's Cane
15	The Funeral Pole
16	The Dog of the Earth
17	Pentecost Couch
18	The Publicans / Paying Customs
19	The Coffin
20	The Tomb
21	Constantine of the Chicks
22	The Cemetery
23	Annexes of the Dead Man's Household in the Cemetery
24	History Written in the Sky
25	The Posthumous Land
26	The Posthumous Family
27	The Great Sacrifice in The Romanian Book of the Dead
28	Cult of the Fathers and Forefathers
29	Death Messengers
30	Sick Child Symbolically for Sale
31	Picking up a Godfather from the Road

May

is the third month in the Roman almanac which began on March 1, and is the fifth month in the Julian and Gregorian almanacs that both start on January 1.

The folk names given to this month indicate that it is a time of blooming ("Florar", "Florariu") and of exuberant vegetation growth ("Frunzar"). The weather being warm enough and the rainfalls quite abundant, with no hail, there are prospects of a rich year. "May is heaven!" is a folk saying which fully characterizes this month. In fields, orchards, gardens and vineyards, activity is in full swing, while the sheep herds, cattle herds and bee gardens are economically at their most efficient productivity. The folk holidays, few of which have fixed dates and many with mobile dates, involve customs and practices specific to the spring season.

May 1
"Armindeni"

Attaching a Pole with Boughs to a Gate, Dabaca, Hunedoara
(R. Isfanoni, by Doina Isfanoni, 1999)

Dedicated to the God of vegetation, protector of cattle, horses, sown fields, vineyards and orchards, the day is called *Armindeni*. He is celebrated on May 1 in Transylvania, Banat, Bucovina and in Moldavia, and on April 23 in Walachia and Oltenia. In Tara Lapusului the celebration is at Pentecost. To protect both people and animals against evil spirits, green boughs are hung on gate and house posts and entrances to cattle shelters. It is a custom, too, to stick a tall stake with green boughs on top, or even a whole tree whose trunk has been cleaned of branches almost to the top and decorated with flower wreaths and wheat ears. These are placed in people's courtyards, in the center of the village, at the sheepfolds or in tilled land.

In Moldavia, at outdoors feast people ate roast lamb and drank red wine mixed with wormwood to improve the quality of their blood and to protect themselves from diseases, mainly from plague.

> *Green wormwood leaf,*
> *Here we are, celebrating* Armindeni
> *The guests at table eat and drink,*
> *And have no fear of the plague!*

Armindeni marked the beginning of the summer season and the last almanac day of sowing the corn. The practice of hanging green boughs or of sticking the May Tree into the ground was later merged with the Christian tradition inspired from the biblical episode of the killing of infants by Herod. According to that legend, after having killed infants for a whole day hoping that one would be the infant Jesus, Herod hung a green bough to mark the last house he had searched and where he would resume the slaughter the next morning. In order to deceive Herod and save Jesus, people hung green boughs at every house during the night.

May 2
The Wormwood

Wormwood is a plant of the *Compositae* group taken as cure for malaria, stomach aches, swellings, and eye diseases and when mixed with wine to make the blood thinner. It is also used for dying wool, for making soap and for casting away evil spirits such as "Ielele." As a healing plant, it was gathered by local enchantresses who performed an established ritual, often naked and with hair undone, on All Saints' Day, "Armindeni," Pentecost and "Marina." Sometimes the enchantress was accompanied by another woman who played the part of the personified wormwood.

> *- Good evening, Great Wormwood,*
> *Your Highness!*
> *- I am glad to be welcomed,*
> *Take a seat!*
> *- I have not come here to sit with you,*
> *But to take out*
> *Forty-four of your devils . . .*

Wormwood is displayed at Pentecost, when people attach it to their hats, on their bosom, keep it in their pockets, decorate windows and icons, or put it on the table or on the floor to cast away the evil spirits. Even today, "Calusul" dancers tie-up wormwood leaves around the top of their flag as magic protection against evil spirits, especially the "Iele." At certain moments during the dance, they chew wormwood leaves. The wormwood gathered on May Day was kept throughout the year to be used in folk medicine practices.

Women purified their homes, their courtyards and the places where they ended with a ritual of carrying water forty days after a funeral and by sweeping those places with brooms made of wormwood leaves which had been gathered on "Marina" Day (July 17). The wormwood broom was also used in magic practices aimed at *making* a person who had left home *return*, or to *take out* and *cast away* an illness from a person's body, as in the charm:

> *Come out, you, foul monster,*
> *Out of George's body*
> *Where you have hidden,*
> *For I, the enchantress,*
> *Have made you drunk with the wine*
> *And plum brandy,*

Have swept you with the broom,
With the black wormwood broom,
And have thrown you in the garbage...[86]

May 3
The Lament

The spontaneous expression of grief, together with cries, calls, groans and desperate gestures caused by the death of a beloved person is called a *mourning song* (Transylvania), a *wailing song* (Moldavia) or a *lament* (Walachia).

Mourning at a Tomb, Dolj
(AIEF by C. Popescu, Nr.2304)

Lamenting is also expressed for animals and even plants with pain, tears, song, and cries. Over time, lamenting evolved into verse with lyrical and rhyming structures and a coherent and logical arrangement, meant to impress the audience and to express the grief of the mourners. In the plain regions of the country, if mothers, daughters or wives do not lament over their dead children, parents or husbands, they are considered indecent and disrespectful of the dead.

Until recently, one of the social aims for having children was the parents' wish to have descendents who would lament at their funeral. The role of

---

[86] Nitu, 1999, p. 173.

the lament is to comfort the sorrow of the one who leaves this world and to create a psychic balance for those who remain in this world. Lamenting is carried out, too, in the belief that the dead person's soul can see and can hear everything that goes on around the body. Another quality of lamenting is that it cathartic. It starts with an impetuous outbreak of sorrow and it ends with certain calm.

May 4
The Lament in Verse

The *lament in verse* is a link between the spontaneous lamenting and the funeral mourning songs such as "Zorile" (Song of the Departure), The Fir Tree Song, and The Death-Watch Song. Their main function is the initiation of the dead person's soul before parting from this World and going into the Beyond. Like ceremonial and ritual burial songs, the lament in verse contains many artistic elements. It is actually a monologue in which the woman who laments addresses the dead man's soul, in the second or the third person, as if expecting an answer that might never come. It is only women who lament. In some special cases, men can also lament, in secret.

Women lament in a pre-established order: first, the close relatives, then the remote relatives and finally the neighbors, the friends or any other woman who wants to send a message to her own dead relatives, through the dead one who is now leaving this world.

The musical composition is adapted to the occasion: a simple phrase, with one or two melodic ranges and with a mourning intonation, mainly at the end. Although the individual improvisation plays its own role, the lament in verse maintains some constant folk motifs within various regions and villages. The text of the song often contains issues such as the relation to the dead person: "My dear, my dear mother..." or "My dear, dear cousin..." offering a greeting:

> *Good day to you, John,*
> *Why don't you say a word?*
> *Why don't you answer, my beloved one?...*
> (Botosani, Suceava County)

Or, asking forgiveness from the dead person:

> *...And I beg you to forgive me,*
> *If I have ever hurt you..."*

In other cases, revolting against death:

> *Death, be cursed,*
> *For you never do what is right.*
> *You don't come*
> *Where you are called,*
> *You arrive*
> *Where you are not welcome.*
> (Hârtoape, Iasi County)

The verse might remind the dead one of his vain toil in this world:

> *Is this what you get for your hard work?*
> *Three deal boards!*
> *Is this what you get for your hard work?*
> *Two meters of land!...* (
> Ciprian Porumbescu, Suceava County)

It can describe a deceiving and merciless death arriving ves on horseback:

> *Death, may you be cursed!*
> *For wherever you go, you never do any justice,*
> *You have mounted on horseback,*
> *And you've ridden real fast,*
> *And you've tied your horse to our fence...*
> (Horodniceni, Suceava County)

It can point to way to a world beyond:

> *Dear mother, where are you going?*
> *And which road are you choosing?*
> *Don't take the road with thorns on it*
> *Take the road with flowers on it,*
> *For you'll meet our relatives ...*
> (Motca, Iasi County)[87]

May 5

"Zorile" Song of the Departure

Zorile are deities of destiny that are invoked in *The Romanian Book of the Dead* and asked to allow the soul some time to properly prepare its

---

[87] Ciubotaru, 1999, p. 283-305.

departure from this world into the next. The "Zorile" songs contain ancient lyrics of great emotional beauty and are interpreted in unison or by a group of antiphonic women at various moments during the funeral ceremony. The melody's impact comes from its archaic sound and the evocative power of its words.

Song of the Daybreak, Isverna, Gorj County
(AIEF, Nr. 541)

In the folk belief, "Zorile" are sister fairies, usually three of them, who by simply arriving before Sunrise decide upon the soul's passing from existence to post-existence. Old women sing these songs usually facing east while holding a stalk of sweet basil in their hand. Detached from the mourning family, they beg "Zorile" (in some variants heard in Gorj County) to take a longer time before they appear, or ask them (in some variants from Mehedinti County and from Banat) why they were in such a hurry to appear on the day of the dead man's departure.[88]

When begged to delay their arrival, varied reasons are invoked. For instance that there is not enough time for the dead person to prepare the funeral feast, to create the wax cake of which the dead man's cane is made, to make a piece of fabric that would be laid over waters as a substitute for the bridge, to find the ox-drawn carriage, to write letters inviting the relatives to come to the funeral feast and to say good-bye to the husband, wife, child or parent who has passed away. (Gorj, Mehedinti, Caras-Severin, Timis, Bihor, Hunedoara, Alba, Sibiu)

May 6
the Fir-Tree Song

Song of the Fir Tree, Runcu, Gorj County
(AIEF, Nr. 541)

---

[88] Ghinoiu, 2004, p. 155-161.

The *Fir-Tree Song* consists of a dialogue between a women choir and the prospective wife or husband of an unmarried youngster, who is substituted by a decorated fir-tree. Unlike variants south of the Carpathians, in which the fir-tree is lured into becoming the foundation, the floor, the clapboard or the rafter of a house, the Transylvania ones contain the promise that the fir-tree will be planted next to a well or that it will become *a dead man's companion*, which means the dead youngster's wife, and that it will be watered by the dead man's relatives in order to remain green for ever. The funeral function of the fir-tree, as posthumous husband or wife, is clearly expressed in the *"Buhas"* song from Bistrita Nasaud County (in that region, buhas is a young fir-tree):

We guess it will not be
The priest with his banners
To come and get you,
But it will be the wedding riders,
With their horses,
The wedding riders,
With their flag,
Not the priest with the church singer,
And we shall see the flag on the table,
Not the fir-tree on the house,
And we shall see the adorned flag,
Not the young fir-tree raised,
For you were worth living,
Not rotting in the ground.

In the Gorj region, one version is an artistic masterpiece containing ancient symbols. First published by Constantin Brailoiu, it begins with women asking the fir-tree a rhetorical question when it is brought from the mountain down to the village by some young men:

Dear fir-tree,
Dear fir-tree,
Who ordered you
To come down
From that rocky place,
To this wet ground?

There follows a long monologue in which the fir-tree tells how it was cut (sacrificed) and brought down from the mountain, then lured by some young men sent by the White Wanderer. The tree repeatedly expresses its regret for coming to life and for growing:

From the Wanderer
That I served
As shelter in winter,
As shade in summer.
From the village
Two strong lads
Called on me,
Their hair undone,
Their heads bent,
Dew drops on their faces,
Fog on their arms,
Hatchets tied to their belts,
Axes in their hands,
With knot-bread of wheat
And food for a month.
Had I known that,
I wouldn't have risen.
Had I known that,
I wouldn't have grown..[89].

May 7
The Posthumous Wedding

At the death of unmarried young people, a ceremony is followed commonly called the dead man's wedding or *posthumous wedding*. The wedding framework, which emulates a funeral one, addresses the problem of an unfulfilled life, namely a young person's death occurring before marriage and procreation. Fiddlers come to the young person's funeral to play songs that the deceased used to enjoy. The fir-tree is also present as a familiar symbol but as in mourning. In Moldavia, the funeral carriage is accompanied by one or more fir-trees, decorated with ribbons, towels and colored paper. The oxen drawing the cart wear knot-shaped bread around their horns. Also a small fir-tree called "buhas" is placed on top of the cart shaft and white headscarves or towels are tied to the yoke bolts symbolizing mourning.

Near the coffin stand an unmarried young couple, representing the godparents of the posthumous wedding, with candles in their hands.[90] Musicians playing their flutes and trumpets follow the procession. A highly emotional moment comes when the deceased bride or groom is dressed for the wedding.

---

[89] Brailoiu, 1981, p. 109.

[90] Ciubotaru, 1986, p. XXXI-XXXII.

*Oxen with the Hearse
(I. Godea, 2007)*

Sometimes, even the priest participates in the mock wedding, exchanging wedding rings for the fiancés (the dead young man with a girl or the dead girl with a young man) and absolving them from sins before marriage. A dead person's wedding and the exchanging of wedding rings was considered to have bad consequences for the partner who was still alive (not being able to marry, being visited by the dead partner in form of a "strigoi"- ghost-, or being forced to follow the buried partner into the grave), and therefore the episode of the posthumous wedding was eliminated, or the bride or groom still alive is replaced by a tree, a willow tree or a fir-tree.

May 8
The Alms

*Alms on the Ground at a Funeral
(AIEF by R. Maier, 1971)*

The alms given away by a person before death or by close relatives after death are offerings or sacrifices that the person will benefit from in the world beyond. They are presented during days preceding the funeral, at the funeral, after six weeks - at the departure of the soul - and yearly after the funeral, at certain almanac dates, over a seven-year period. Seven years after a person's death he is considered to enter the group of *fathers and forefathers*, therefore his name is no longer specially mentioned when alms are distributed.

During the Nineteenth Century, ethnographers found evidence of animal sacrifices at funerals, practiced much as in pre-historic times, in Moldavia, Bucovina and Banat. The night before the funeral, in the presence of a priest, people chose a black ram, oriented its body on the east-west direction, stuck candles on its horns and, after reading a prayer, sacrificed it by blood-letting in a specially dug pit called *ara*. Then, the head and the skin of the animal were taken by the priest, and the meat cooked and eaten by the participants. Reminding one of that ritaul is the expression *to give one's skin to the priest*, meaning to die.

The fact that the sacrifice took place in the dead person's courtyard, not in the cemetery, and also the farming name of the pit where it was performed - which was *ara* or *aratu* meaning to plow or till – are evidence of a connection that pre-historic man made between sowing seeds and burying the dead.

May 9
Making Clay Lids for Bread Baking on a Hearth

An important holiday for women in Oltenia, when they combined work with partying, used to be the Tuesday of the third week after Easter. The day had a special name, *Ropotinul testelor*, and was dedicated to making clay lids (*teste*) used for baking bread and maize flat-cakes over a whole year. Women from certain parts of a village, or those who were related, gathered together to make the lids by properly kneading the clay, mixing it with water and chaff on that day. The clay was shaped into lids for baking bread that resembled bells or bulging armors.

After drying the lids in the sun, the women smoothed them out by covering them with fine clay, so they not crack at high temperatures, then decorated them with green boughs and with wild flowers, and finally laid them on burdock leaves. After finishing work, the women had a party with food and drink, and sprinkled (honored) the lids with wine.

Baking Bread on a Hearth / Pre-Historic Oven
(R. Isfanonu, 2004, Photo by A. Mendrea, 1981)

The technique of processing the clay by hand, exclusively by women, on a particular day of the year, as well as the customs and the beliefs related to shaping and using the bread lid, are reminiscent of the pottery and farming practiced in Neolithic times, when the right to process and shape clay figurines belonged exclusively to women (Oltenia, Walachia, Dobrogea).

May 10
The Funeral Boat

The *funeral boat* is a means of transport from *this world* to *the world beyond*. Unlike a dead person's body which leaves this world three days after being buried, his soul is sent away after forty days on water, in a funeral ceremony called "releasing the water", or "freeing the spring." The custom is organized six weeks after a person's death and, in some regions, once a year for all the dead.

In some villages from the northern part of Gorj region, *the forgiven women* who cannot have children would come to the bank of a river or of a brook, having with them half of a dry pumpkin, two candles, red-hot coals, a stick, an apple-tree bough, a small coin, a piece of cloth (headscarf), a clay pot and a knot shaped piece of bread or a loaf of bread. The piece of cloth was laid on the bank of the river; water was poured over the cloth - as many pots or pails of water as will be carried to neighbors in the following days - the number of pails was marked by carving a sign on the stick; candles were lit; the little coin, the hot coals, the bread and flowers were all placed in the pumpkin, an improvised boat called "cotovaie"), and launched on the water; the apple-tree bough and the stick were thrown in the water; and the knot-bread, the clay pot and the piece of cloth were given away as alms to passers by or to children who watched the ceremony.

Each object has a symbolic significance. The apple-tree bough is the substitute for the dead man; the improvised boat is the funeral boat; the red-hot coals represent the funeral stake of the incineration ritual of the Geto-Dacians before being Christened; the little coin is to pay the boatman and for the customs duties; the clay pot is the preferred shelter for the soul; the knot bread and the piece of cloth are alms for the dead.[91] The boat floats until drawn to the shore, or until the water current capsizes it.

In the general archetypal conception, the boat is related to symbols for intimate dwellings: the cave, the house, the grave, the maternal womb. Through its shape which suggests a moon in its first and second phase, the boat acquires ceremonial significance.

---

[91] Ghinoiu, 2001, p. 13.

May 11
The Roller ("Sulul")

The roller or *sulul* is a god of vegetation, substituted by a log of wood (like the one of the weaving loom). Dressed up as a young man, he fertilizes the wheat fields on the first Thursday after Easter. Groups of girls from the same street or part of a village would take a wooden roller from the weaving loom to make a doll with head, mouth, eyes and arms, and dress up with nice clothes and with a flower at the ear. During Shrovetide on Wednesday afternoon, the roller was taken to the wheat field while the girls sang a sad song resembling the funeral laments or the *Calioanul* song. In the text of the song, the Roller is both young and old:

Roll, the Fertilizer God of the Cornfields, Sultana, Calarasi County
(AIEF Photo by N. Radulescu)

Old Roller,
Still unripe,
No one sees you off!
Young Roller,
Still unripe,
No one sees you off! [92]

Once in the field, the Roller was laid on the ground and fertilized the wheat that was still green. After dancing around it, the girls took it home. The next morning they carried the Roller to the fields again and to the woods before returning to the village where a meal - *alms* - was prepared by their mothers. At the end of the ritual the girls undressed the Roller. The custom was practiced in the villages from Mostistei Valley, Calarasi County, until the second half of the Twentieth Century. The Romanians from Transnistria called that holiday *Sulica*, coming from the Romanian word for roller *sul* and its feminine equivalent *sula* which de-

---

[92] Radulescu, 1969.

scribe the awl tool used by furriers and by shoemakers. In colloquial language it is a phallic symbol.[93]

May 12
The Wake

Funeral Feast on a Funeral 'Brick', Tomis - First Century A.D. (Preda, 2000)

The funeral *wake* takes place at night at the dead person's house plays much like a New Year's Party. In Romania, there are two types of wake. One, relatively recent, consists is watching the dead to ensure that no living creature (bird or animal) passes over or under the dead person so as to turn him into a "strigoi" (ghost). The second involves plays and enjoyment reminiscent of funeral feasts from ancient times. Practiced until the middle of the Twentieth Century in several parts of Transylvania (Western Carpathians, Luncani Platform, and Padurenii Hunedoarei) and of Moldavia (Vrancea). The plays take place in the room where the dead person is placed or in the room next to him with music, or in the courtyard, around the funeral stake. Unlike the wake games from Transylvania, dominated by fertility rites, those from Moldavia contained customs which brought fourth the fathers and the forefathers, through the use of death masks and by lighting fires reminiscent of the Geto-Dacian's cremation rite before being Christened.

The repertoire of wake plays is unlimited. Most of the time the plays ended with a kiss, given in front of the dead man, or on the porch. There were wedding scenes, masked performances representing pregnant women, and others, as if, when a man died, someone was staging the birth of another man, like in a well known song:

> *Men in the world,*
> *Are just passing by,*
> *When one is born,*
> *Another can die.*

---

[93] Ghinoiu, 2001, p. 185.

May 13
"Perinita"- Funeral Dance at The wake

"Perinita" is a ritual kissing game performed at a man's funeral but then transferred in modern times to the "funeral" of the year, namely when celebrating the New Year. On New Year's night, people drink and eat, often act impulsively, play games with masked players, and join in the kissing dance. All of these are obvious reminders of the ancient orgies.

New Year's party is a big party equaled in proportion only by the plays performed at wakes in some ethnographical areas until the middle of the 20th century. These kinds of wakes are organized "as a great time of enjoyment in the dead person's house. People laugh so loudly that the house shakes. The dead man's relatives also laugh, so do his children and everybody else; nobody minds the dead one, for...God forgive me, every man must die."[94]

May 14
The Dead Man's Cane

A century ago in many villages from the Sebes Valley, the cane used to be a substitute for the one who bore it. Propped up against the gate or against the door, the cane symbolically guarded the house when it had been left unlocked with padlocks or keys by the owner. The relationship between a man and the cane or stick was of a spiritual nature, like one between sworn brothers.

Shepherd and staff are inseparable except during the meals. Unlike the *sworn brothers* who are united until death when their ties are undone through rituals performed over the graves, the stick or the cane is a companion into the afterlife. In the Apuseni Mountain region, a stick cracked on one edge with a coin in it is laid in the grave next to the dead man. He can use it for walking or for defending himself against enemies and the coin for paying the customs on his long journey to the beyond.[95]

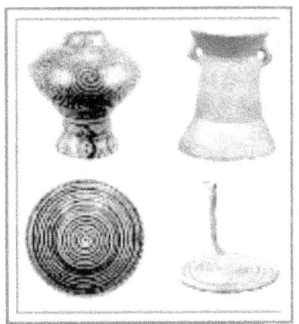

Spiral Motif: Pre-Cucuteni and Cucuteni Creamics; and Coiled Wax Scepter the Length of the Dead Person, Gheraiesti, Neamt County (Ciobotaru, 2003 and Contemporary Ceramics)

[94] Cornea I, 1940, p. 295.

[95] Frâncu Teofil, Candrea George, 1888, p. 173.

In Comana-de-Jos village in Brasov County, "not until long ago, people used to place a fir-tree stick in the hand of the dead person or in the coffin, next to him."[96] According to certain beliefs, the traveler needed the stick to defend himself against the dead ones' dogs, or *the dogs of the earth*, that would bark at him the first night after the funeral as they would do to any stranger. Such beliefs were the origin of the custom of making *a cane* for the dead, actually a long candle equal to the size of the dead man's body, coiled in a spiral shape, which is lit at several moments of the funeral ceremonial.

May 15
The Funeral Pole

The funeral pole is a tall tree trunk raised on the funeral day. It serves as a substitute for the deceased that remains among the living.

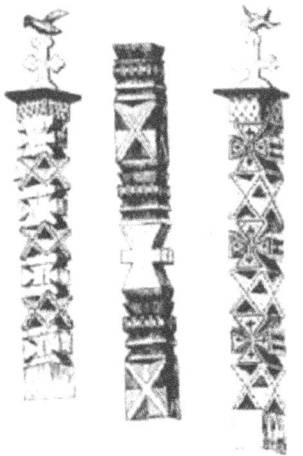

Funeral Pillar and Soul Birds,
Loman, Hunedoara County
(Pavelescu, 2004)

In Ancient Syria the divinities were represented in the same way, the male one by a stone column and the female one by a tree trunk. There are still villages in Southern Transylvania where a wooden pole instead of a cross is placed at the deathbed of a man or of a woman. In many places in Oltenia, the permanent wooden or stone cross is placed next to the funeral pole, six weeks after the funeral. In some places in Walachia, the stone cross which is placed next to the temporary wooden cross six months after the funeral is called a pole.

The wooden poles and crosses represent human figures with a head, eyes and mouth. The identity of the dead one, sex, age and often the social and material status, is reflected in the size of the pole, the ornaments painted or carved on it, and through other funeral symbols fir-tree, flag, spear placed alongside. On the poles and on the crosses there are rhombuses and triangles, solar rosette and moon motifs as well as anthropomorphic ones. In the cemeteries from Oltenia and Southern

---

[96] Ghinoiu, 2004, p.199.

Transylvania one can see artistic representations of soul birds, carved either entirely or partially on the crosses and on the funeral poles.

May 16
The Dog of the Earth

In folk beliefs, the *Dog of the Earth* is the guard of the 'other world'; it barks at the souls of the unknown dead during the first night after their arrival. A white dog with a long body and short legs, it is known as a contributor to the Creation of the World together with the hedgehog. It is blind with a shrill and frightening bark. At night, it comes out of the Earth and barks at tombs in cemeteries, or at roadside crosses, predicting death and various misfortunes. The poet Mihai Eminescu mentions it in his poem *"The Strigoi"*:

> *In the name of the Saint,*
> *Be quiet and listen*
> *To The Dog of the Earth*
> *Barking, under the stone cross!* [97]

As soon as a dead man has been buried, the Dog of the Earth checks the tomb and, if it finds something wrong with the burial ritual, it bites the dead person's nose or ears. It punishes those having no coin tied to a finger, or no coin between their teeth to pay passage fees. Family members frequently light a fire on the grave on the first night after the burial so that the dog will let the dead person rest in peace (Rucar-Bran mountain pass).

Dogs are also mentioned by the ancient Hindu in Rig-Veda X, 10: "On the path leading to the end, rush past the two striped dogs, with four eyes, belonging to Samara bitch; then go to your generous ancestors who are feasting together with "Yama."[98]

May 17
Pentecost Church

"Calusul" is a divinity which protects horses and the warm season of the year. It is celebrated in the Folk Almanac on the fourth Wednesday after Easter, under the name of Pentecost Couch or "Todor-

---

[97] Evseev, 1997, p. 75.

[98] Simenschy, 1978, p. 112.

usale." It is believed that on that day strong young men, called "Sântoader's Horses" meet beautiful young girls, called "Iele" or "Rusalii".

May 18
The Publicans / Paying Passage Fees

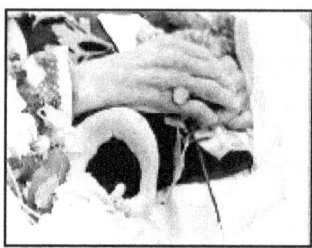

Coin for Paying Customs Fees in the Beyond, Varfuri, Dambovita County
(AIEF Photo by I. Dragoescu, Nr. 74974)

The *Publicans* are benevolent mythical representations that require the soul to *pay passage fees* in order to find the right road to Heaven. When a dead person is dressed up and laid in a coffin oriented towards the departure direction from east towards west, he is also given a coin to pay the passage fees. To make sure that he will not lose it, it is often put in his mouth, between his fingers, tied with a string through a hole in it to his little finger, dipped into wax and stuck to his palm, or placed into the crack of a stick put next to the body. Most often, the money for is put in the dead man's pockets, or tied in his handkerchief, or just placed in the coffin, or it is thrown over the dead man at stops made along the way to the cemetery or to the grave. There are two worries about the money taken by the *traveler*. First, he should not leave without it, and second, he should not lose it during his difficult and troublesome journey.

In some funeral songs from *The Romanian Book of the Dead,* the deceased is advised to stop at *a small fair* and buy some gifts for the Publicans, with the money tied to his finger:

> *...you should go to the fair*
> *And buy*
> *Three black woolen caps,*
> *And be most careful,*
> *For on your way,*
> *You shall meet*
> *Three young princes.*
> *Give them the caps*
> *To take you to Heaven,*
> *Where your house will be,*
> *Up the hill of joy.*[99]

---

[99] Kahane, Georgescu, 1988, p. 593.

Publicans may also appear as three old men:

...Just go straight on,
And be most careful,
For in your way
You shall meet,
Three old men;
They will take you by the hand
To the customs.
Then put your hand
In your bosom,
Take out three black headscarves
And pay customs
With these gifts.

They might be three virgin maids, or as a prince's child, or three wives:

Just go straight on,
And be most careful,
For in your way
You shall meet,
Three nice wives;
They will take you by the hand
To the customs.
Then put your hand
In your bosom
Take out three crape scarves,
And pay the duties
With these gifts.
(Pestisani, Gorj County)

The last and the most important customs point is at the entrance to Heaven, where the Mother Goddess appears. She keeps records of the dead people's souls and takes them:

To the middle of Heaven
For that's where
The real life is.

May 19
The Coffin

The posthumous shelter made of wood has a wide range of local names coffin, throne, chest, box, shell, trough, shelter, wooden house, or boat. It is built like an old traditional one-room house, with four walls and a four-sided roof. The carpenter of the village builds two types of houses, tall ones for the living and low ones for the dead. In Moldavia and some other parts of the country, the coffin has one or two small windows (square, rectangular or triangular) in the lateral sides of the coffin (where the head lies); sometimes they are glass windows. More rarely, the dead man's windows are placed on the "roof" (the lid) of the coffin, at the side where his eyes are. In the Neamt area the coffin has only one window which indicates the sex of the dead person, according to where it is placed: on the left side for men and on the right side for women.[100] The walls of the posthumous house are covered in white cloth in the same way as the house is painted with white lime.

Symbolic Meal in the 'Wooden House of the Dead,' Vrancea (AIEF, Nr. 219)

The coffin is a room for sleeping and a room for storing food, two basic functions of the ordinary house. Various objects are carefully placed inside. For sleeping a pillow, a bed sheet, blanket or a counterpane underneath the dead man are provided. For sustenance knot-shaped bread put on or around the dead man's hand, nuts, apples. Also offered are a candle, a wax cane and for lighting a fire flint steel, tinder, and even a lighter. There can also be soap, comb, mirror, razor, handkerchief, towel, as well as a bag for food, money in the pocket, a stick or a cane, personal glasses, shepherd's pipe, a doll in the case of mothers who leave behind small children, a crutch for an invalid, cigarettes and matches for a smoker, and objects related to the dead person's religion such as small icons, crosses and cross seals for placement on the dead man's chest.[101]

---

[100] Ciubotariu, H.I., 1988, p. XV.

[101] Ghinoiu, 2004, p. 211.

May 20
The Tomb

Tombs are a sacred place in which the peace of the ones at rest should not be disturbed. The tomb serves as a shelter of the dead man's soul built in the ground, like an earth hut. It is of the dead man's size, covered with earth, having a cover with four drainage sides and oriented in the east-west direction. In the funeral songs *"Ground of Dust, Ground of Dust"*, the dead man's soul is advised to ask the grave-diggers to make his tomb with windows and doors:

> *Ask the diggers*
> *To make you some windows:*
> *About three*
> *Through them to see.*
> (Zarnesti, Brasov County)

Tomb and Funeral Pillar,
Buciumi, Salaj County
(AIEF, Nr. 42 026)

The funeral rite of burial and the building of a posthumous house in the ground are significant elements for the cult of goddess, Terra Mater or Gaea. Through burial, the deceased is sent to the divinity's residence deep in the Earth. Like any other shelter, the tomb can be inhabited or un-inhabited as with cenotaphs. If someone dies far from his village or his country, a handful of earth is brought, which means that the man is buried in his homeland. If there is no body, a tree-trunk dressed with the dead man's clothes is sometimes buried instead.

Tombs can be either *clean* or *soiled* depending on the way in which the person dies. He can be called-by-death, commonly known as *natural death*, or gone-to-the-dead in an *unusual manner* by hanging or any type of suicide. The former are placed inside the cemetery, together with their fathers and forefathers, while the latter are placed outside it usually in a space between two villages. In a more recent practice, outcasts are buried in the cemetery but at a far end.

If tombs are found to have "strigoi" (ghosts), they are destroyed in the same manner as deserted or haunted houses in a village.

May 21

Constantine of the Chicks

On May 21, two saints, Constantine and Helen, are celebrated. In the Folk Almanac, there is a holiday dedicated to forest birds also called Constantine Starling or *Constantine of the Chicks*. In southern Romania, Constantine of the Chicks is considered the last day when corn, oat or millet could be sown.[102]

It is said that the voices of forest birds are freed on the January 11, Day of Vlasie, and that they mate and build their nests on February 24, Day of Dragobete. By May 11, Saint Constantine and Helen's Day, they are ready to teach their chicks to fly. In order to prevent any damage to cornfields or vineyards by these birds, especially by the starlings, many winegrowers do not work on those days dedicated to the birds.

May 22

The Cemetery

Depending on the region, the place of shelter and repose for the dead goes by different names: cemetery, graveyard, the garden of the dead, burial ground, or God's Acre.

In older villages and cemeteries, the one who inherits land on which the household is built in the boundaries of the village, usually the youngest son, also inherits the burial place in the precincts of the cemetery. In exchange for an additional inheritance received after the parents' death, also known as *the part of the soul*, the youngest son has the obligation to bury them and to carry out all the rituals required by the tradition.

In scattered Carpathian Mountain villages from the Carpathians (Luncani Platform, Tara Hategului or Apuseni), one can find family cemeteries placed in the courtyard or in the garden. In some localities, cemeteries are ethnically and religiously homogeneous.

Path in the Village of the Passed Away,
Dabuleni, Dolj County
(AIEF, Anca Giurchescu)

---

[102] Ghinoiu, 1997, p. 51.

Of special interest are cenotaphs, symbolical tomb that contain no mortal remains. Recent ones, located next to churches or in cemeteries, are dedicated to heroes who died in the two World Wars (Teleorman); some can be found at the gates of the dead people's household (Walachia); or at the cemetery gates for the ones who testified in courts of law (Gorj and Vâlcea Counties); others at the place where a violent death happened by drowning, struck by lightning or killed by wild animals. Unbaptised children, unidentified dead and thieves are buried separately at the end of the cemetery.

The identity of the dead in cemeteries by name, age, gender, social and economic status is easily recognized by the size, the ornaments and the notation painted or carved on the crosses or on the funeral poles raised at the head of the dead person. In southern Transylvanian and southern Oltenia cemeteries, one or two wooden soul birds are put on the top of the crosses or funeral poles. In the southern Carpathians, the wings of the soul bird are fret-worked in two wooden boards connected at an angle to emulate flight towards Heaven.

May 23
Annexes of the Dead Man's Household in the Cemetery

At a maiden's or young man's tomb, next to the cross or to the pole, stands the posthumous husband or wife represented by an adorned fir tree or apple-tree twig. Often an apple-tree is planted at the head of the deceased. In some cases a spear made of a fir tree stripped of branches from top to bottom is placed at the head of the tomb. On Saturday of the Dead, Palm Sunday, Great Thursday, tombs are cleaned and covered with flowers.

Wooden Alter in a Cemetery, Muscel
(AIEF, Photo by I. Vladutiu)

Beside the cross a small wooden table may be stuck in the ground, or an altar where the alms are laid. Occasionally a small shelter is built in which the candle or votive light is put, a broken pot used for incensing and a chair for resting.

May 24

History Written in the Sky

Significant events from Romanian's history are transferred from Earth by *writing* them into the sky. They can then be read by descendents following particular patterns of stars. It was believed that the Dacians who had been taken prisoners were sent to Rome via the Milky Way, also commonly known as the Slaves' Way, Trajan's Way or the Sheep's Way; lower class people traveled via The Greater Bear, while aristocrats traveled via The Lesser Bear. According to some legends recorded in the south of the country, prisoners taken by the Turks returned to their homes guided by the Milky Way.

In ancient times it was said that humans were better beings and that the sky was closer to the earth. Because their ill deeds over time ill, the sky which is the dwelling of the good ones, got further away from the world of the evil ones. Wanting to restore the initial harmony, people set out on their journey, guided by the stars: The Milky Way, The Greater Bear, The Lesser Bear and other stars which in Romanian bear names like: The Scythe, The Sickle, The Plough, The Clucking Hen with Chicks (The Pleiadaes), The Cowman (Bootes), The Shepherd (Venus). But the legend says that in order to stop humans, the Devil brought other stars in their way, such as: The Dragon, The Snake, The Hag and The Bear.

During the flight away from the Devil's forces, The Shepherd's milk pails were overturned and the spilled milk formed the Milky Way. Eventually after defeating the Devil, people created the same environment in the sky like the one on earth, while the army of stars which had been involved in the struggle against the Evil one remained for ever up in the sky, in form of constellations.[103]

May 25

The Posthumous Land

In *The Romanian Book of the Dead*, the other world is also called The Land Above, or The Land free of sorrow, in contrast to our world that is referred to as The Land Below or The Land full of Sorrow.

> *And down there,*
> *Is a big house,*
> *Its doors facing the valley,*

---

[103] Teodorescu, 1982, p. 55.

Its windows facing the sun.
There it is, our neighborhood,
Young and old,
And small children,
Groups of girls,
Groups of wives
And some small boys,
Could be some of mine.
Tell them all,
Tell each of them,
That we wait for them,
On great days
On Great Thursday,
With new clay pots,
With clean clothes
Washed in our tears,
Dried in the sun.
(Topesti, Gorj County)

The posthumous land is an Eden-like place where the souls of the dead meet their relatives and their friends who left this world before them. In all the variants of the song to "Zori" divinities, none of the tormenting elements from the Christian Hell are found: no Devil, no pitch barrels, no bottomless fire pit. Instead, it is a fantastic land, full of flowers, especially red peonies. In the funeral songs, there are names of places, like: *Hill of Joy, Field of Joy, Our Neighborhood*. Other descriptive words are used, *wide ring dance, flight of doves* suggesting a general peaceful state of spiritual unity and of group communion. The main drawback of the Posthumous Land is an ethical one. It is a world lacking in pity or compassion, as those feelings are left behind in this world.

During the funeral rights, the relatives from this world announce to the ones from the other world of the arrival of the dead souls by the ringing of church bells, blowing of horns, or through the beat of the wooden plate. So, when the souls reach that land, they will be welcomed with lots of good food and burning torches.

Go straight on,
As a tall house will appear,
And who is inside?
It's your dear father
Waiting for you,
With food on the table,
With filled glasses,

With burning torches...[104]
(Godinesti, Gorj County)

In terms of cardinal points, the living look to and love the east, whereas the dead look to the west. As required by the ritual, the dead man is washed, dressed up and then oriented with his legs forward on the direction that he will follow, namely: east to west. In order not to miss the right way, marked by the Sun descending towards West, the Dead are always buried in the afternoon. The same direction was also followed by the souls after death in ancient Egypt, in India of ancient Veda and in ancient Greece. The descendent way of the Neolithic man towards the maternal womb of the Goddess "Glie" (Earth) became, with Indo-Europeans and with Christians, an ascending way towards the Kingdom of the sky, into the seventh or the ninth Heaven, which is the home of God, Our Father. In relation to the Land Below, that is the Earth, the realm of the dead is the Land Above.

As he leaves today
His own house...
From the Land Below
He passes into the Land Above.[105]
(*"Zorile" from the house,* Ursatesti, Gorj County)

There the souls are grouped like in the Land Below by their belonging to families, to villages and to parts of villages. The only ones who are unhappy in that land are unmarried youngsters, "the monks," which on earth is an offensive name for bachelors, and those who end their lives before building a family.

May 26

The Posthumous Family

In many of the Romanian cemeteries, the fir tree, together with the pole (the cross) at the head of the deceased, form a posthumous couple marrying on the day of the funeral.

In the plain regions, the fir tree is replaced by a fruit-tree, usually an apple-tree o r a plum-tree. The role of the posthumous bride or groom played by the fir tree, is emphasized, when youngsters are buried and by the funeral verses sung in various ritual and ceremonial moments before

---

[104] Kahane, Georgescu-Stanculeanu, 1988, p. 582.

[105] Kahane, Georgescu-Stanculeanu, 1988, p. 546.

the tree is cut in the forest by some young men, when it is brought down to the village, while it is adorned by young girls, on the way to the cemetery, or when it is stuck at the head of the unmarried dead person. The burial fir tree was cut in the woods and brought in the village by seven young lads who had departed early in the morning, playing lament songs on the flute.

Post-Mortem Family in the Garden, Ursici, Hunedoara County (AIEF, Photo by E. Tircomnicu & L. David)

In Runcu village (Gorj County), the young men, wearing headscarves, would set off in silence. Once in the woods, they would choose a young fir tree, they would kneel in front of it, cut it by striking it a number of times equal to the number of lads in the group and bring the tree down to the village bearing it on their shoulders, with the top forward. At the dead person's house, the fir tree would be decorated with a wedding flag, the wedding ring, a flowery handkerchief, ribbons, flowers and bells.

The fir tree which is ornamented at a funeral, undoubtedly shows its ritual and ceremonial function symbolizing the posthumous husband or wife of the deceased. Ritual and emotional songs are interpreted for the posthumous partners, the dead man or woman and the fir tree, that leave this world together.

May 27
The Great Sacrifice in The Romanian Book of the Dead

As appears in many funeral songs from Oltenia, a cow, the heifer from the herd, must be offered as a blood sacrifice in preparation for the funeral meal. Pigs, sheep or poultry are not acceptable.

By invoking the "Zori," Goddesses of Destiny at Death, similar to the Fate Sisters at birth, the dead man is provided enough time to sacrifice a cow.

Oh, Zori
Oh, Zori,
Don't you hurry
To take away
The wanderer
John by name,
For he will pass
From the Land full of sorrow
To the land free of sorrow,
From the land full of pity
To the land free of pity.
Don't you rush
To take him away
Until you make ready
Nine little stoves for bread,
Nine barrels of wine
And nine of brandy,
Nine little stoves
For maize cakes
And bring from his house,
A fat, full-uddered cow,
With twisted horns
To be cut on the table
...
And they will cut
Nine little heifers
...
And a fat cow
Chosen from the herd
...
May a fat cow
Be his meal.

There is a record from 1936, in Poiana Alexii, Vaslui County, in which appear similarities between Indian and Romanian customs of sacrificing a cow at a funeral: "When the dead man is taken out through the entrance gate, a cow or a calf must be given as alms before the procession can proceed".[106]

---

[106] Muslea, 1972, p. 35.

May 28
The Fathers and Forefathers Cult

The Fathers and Forefathers Cult has its roots back in pre-historic beliefs that the deceased becomes a protecting god and therefore should be loved, respected and feared.

In India, in the ancient Veda period, sacrifices were brought to the dead ones at New Moon and Full Moon. In the classical Greek times, funeral meals and offerings were given three, nine, thirteen days and also one year after someone died. While in ancient Rome, the dead man would be invited to dinner, after the funeral, asked for his blessing, and finally separated by saying the words: "Salve, sancta parens!".

In a similar fashion Romanians preserve a widespread cult of the dead, fathers and forefathers. There are specific days in the Folk Almanac, when the dead ones are awaited with laid tables and open fires: Macinici, Great Thursday, and others.

In some villages from Moldavia and Bucovina, a festive meal with wine and different symbolical objects is laid for the deceased on Christmas Eve. The next morning, after consecrating the meal, the food and the drink from which the fathers and the forefathers ate, are shared with relatives and neighbors.

In some regions, at the Easter of the Clement Ones, at Pentecost or at other celebrations during the year, the living move for one day into the cemetery where they celebrate and eat together with the dead people's souls. The fathers and forefathers continue to be invoked in hard moments of people's lives such as natural and social disasters. They are called for help in solving earthly problems: healing diseases, marrying the girls, having prosperous crops and herds, punishing enemies.

The cult of the ancestors, kept alive in all aspects of the Romanian spiritual culture, is described by two pre-Roman words: "forefathers' precincts".

May 29
Death Messengers

The messengers of the Death God "Yama" from the Indian Pantheon, are the little owl and the dog, the same as in the Romanian Pantheon.

In India, he takes the human souls, while in Romania, he takes the lives of plants and animals. In ancient Indian belief, the souls of the dead would meet their parents after the funeral, in the underworld Land of the God Yama and later, in the sky. Yama is not the only common god for both the Indian and the Romanian tradition. The Indian God of Rain,

Rudra, is invoked by groups of children who carry a strange phytomorphic mask, *Paparuda* during arid summer days. Furthermore, the Indian God Shiva would be enchanted with the Shiva carol at the winter solstice, on Christmas or on New Year's Day.[107] In southern Romania, the expression "to be struck by *Iama*" (birds, animals, cornfields) means to die or to dry.

May 30
Sick Child Symbolically for Sale

It was believed that a sick child's life could be saved, among other methods, by selling him symbolically to a mother whose children were all living.

"And I sold the child to my sister when he was brought from church. I was in the house. The midwife and my sister were outside. The midwife handed me the baby through the window, and I gave him to my sister through the same window: 'I sell you this child, John by his name! – I'll buy him,' she said. And she gave me some money which I put behind the chimney. After that, the child called my sister 'Mother', and I was called 'Soi'. The same thing happened to a woman from Almaj. All her children died, so she got herself a godfather from the road. A wandering gypsy passed by, and that's what they did. They took him to the barber, and he got a shave. They made him godfather, and so the child is still alive. No child has ever died after taking a godfather from the road!"

On this occasion, the name of the symbolical dead child was changed with another one, usually representing a wild animal – Bear or Wolf – which will scare off death and illness.

In other cases, the sick child was introduced three times through the top end of a shirt, and then pulled out through its bottom end symbolizing death and rebirth. In the therapeutic burial case, the sick child was introduced into a hole dug in the ground and pulled out healthy through a small tunnel, another hole.

No matter what method was chosen, the principle was the same: the symbolic death of the sick child. The soul enters through one end and then is released through another end in the form of a healthy child.

---

[107] Ghinoiu, 2001, p. 88, 143-144, 175.

May 31
Picking up a Godfather from the Road

In cases of high infant death rates, the Christian name was often changed through different practices. The best known one, *picking up a godfather from the road,* was identified in many regions

In Tara Almajului: "If the woman has many boys and they all die, and if she gives birth to another one who lives, then she swaddles him and a woman takes the baby outside, lays it down in the middle of the road and leaves him there. And anybody who picks the baby up from the ground (a man, a woman or a gypsy wanderer), is asked to come inside the mother's house and to dip him into water (baptism), thus becoming a godfather."

Or in the villages from Danube's Clisura: "I had two girls who died and later on I gave birth to a boy. So, being afraid that he would also die, I changed his godfather. Early in the morning, the midwife took the baby to the centre of the village and she stood there till one woman passed by, returning from the mill. And one of my relatives appeared too, knowing my plans, of course. But the midwife wouldn't pick him up, because he was aware of it. So she went after the woman coming from the mill and asked her to be the godmother of my baby 'Oh, Lord, I am so happy! God Almighty, how happy I am to be the godmother of this child!' So she got dressed up and they all went to church to baptize him".

The ritual of a godfather from the road calls for a few compulsory steps: taking the child out of the house early in the morning, leaving the baby in the middle of the road, asking the first person passing by to baptize him, bringing the child from church home through the door, if he had been taken outside through the window, and through the window if he had been taken out through the door.

JUNE

"CIRESAR"

SWEET CHERRY'S MONTH

1	Ascension and Saturday Before Whitsuntide Ascension
2	Horses' Easter
3	The Boiled Wheat Cake
4	Cousins and Sisters
5	The Girl of the Woods
6	Plants for Healing Drunkenness
7	Flowers of Love
8	The Oath
9	The "Calus" Divinity and the Church
10	Small Saints in the Folk Almanac
11	Summer Forefathers or "Wheat Vartolomeu"
12	"Iele" or Spirits of the Pentecost
13	"Calus" Mute
14	War Between "Calus" and Pentecost Spirits
15	Calus Dancers- Disease Healers
16	Sworn Brothers and Sisters
17	The Horse and the Wolf: Almanac Clocks
18	The Divine Herd of "Calus" God
19	The Effigy of "Calus" God
20	Breaking the "Calus". The Silence Rite
21	Beliefs Related to the Origin of the "Calus" Dancers
22	Midsummer's Day Torch
23	The Almanac for Gathering Medicine Plants
24	The Midsummer Goddess - "Drăgaica" or "Sânziana"
25	When the Cuckoo is Struck Dumb
26	Midsummer Wreath
27	The Glowworm
28	The Origin of the Girls' Fair
29	Summer Saint Peter
30	Saint Peter's Curse

Midsummer Dance, Zimnice, Teleorman County
(AIEF by C. Popescu, Nr. 12515)

June

is the fourth month in the Roman Almanac before Caesar and the sixth month in the Julian and Gregorian Almanac, dedicated to the goddess Juno, Jupiter's wife and the protector of the married women.

Because cherries ripen in this period, being the first fruit of the year, the month June is called Sweet Cherry's Month or Little Cherry. It is also the time of the summer solstice, with the longest day of the year and with the most powerful sun, when vegetation reaches maturity. Even so, no matter how promising the crops are, any storm or pouring rain followed by hail can destroy the wheat fields, fruit orchards or vineyards.

In the struggle between good and evil forces, people, unaware of who the winner will be, exalt Christian saints dressed in pagan clothes (Timoftei, Vartolomeu, Onofrei, Elisei, Saint Peter), but they also celebrate the pre-Christian divinities, dressed in Christian clothes (Dragaica, Sânziene). Other holidays are added to these, in a year with a mobile moon-set date for Easter, on April 23rd, such as Good Sunday, Pentecost, Beak Thursday, The Green Sunday, Saturday Before Whitsuntide or Saint Peter.

June 1

Ascension and Saturday Before Whitsuntide Ascension

Ispas, the mythical character who witnessed Christ's Ascension and the ascension of the dead one's soul ascension to Heaven, is celebrated on the sixth Thursday after Easter. On their way to Heaven, the dead ones' souls could get lost and return to the earth in shape of a "Moroi" or a "Strigoi" (Ghost) and in so doing bring fright to animals and especially to milk cows. For this reason, during the day and the night of the Ascension, precautionary measures against the "Strigoi" and against their evil actions were taken. This involved gathering leaves and twigs of nut and hazel-nut trees, sycamore maples or lovage herbs, "pummeling" cattle and people with lovage, blowing the horn (bucium) to scare away the evil spirits, making a lovage waist band for girls and women to wear, calming dead people's spirits by giving them rich alms, and performing spells or charms.

Ascension Day was considered a deadline for various agricultural activities. This was the last day for planting and corn-sowing, the oxen and the heifers were taken to ir mountain meadows, and the lambs were marked through cuts in their ears. A Christian Orthodox greeting is used on this particular day: "Christ has risen! – Christ has truly risen!" Because Christ was thought to have been a joyful man, the believers are also in a good mood on His day. He was celebrated like a true Saint and, in many cases, like the patron of a household (Walachia, Moldavia, Oltenia). Bloody sacrifices were made (the lamb), the tips of the horned cattle's tails were cut, popular country fairs were held (The Blaj Girl's Fair).

This holiday is known all over Romania with people bearing the name of Ispas were celebrating on this day. Also in some local variants, alms are given for dead people's souls on Ascension Eve called Saturday Before Whitsuntide Ascension. It is said that the food taken as alms by women, usually green cheese, unleavened bread, green onion and brandy, eases the dead soul's hunger as it rises to the sky on Ascension Day.

In the Dobrogea region, women would walk on village roads bearing pots full of cooked food so that, before rising to Heaven, the dead souls floating in the air could enjoy the aroma. (Banat, Walachia, Dobrogea, Bucovina)

In southern and eastern Romania, summer fairs were held every year, after Ascension, one week before Pentecost, where clay-pots, pans and cups and wooden spoons were sold. In Blaj, on the day of the fair, eligible girls come with their most valuable jewelry and objects in hope of meeting young men for marriage.

June 2
Horses' Easter

*Thracian Knight Hunting
(Scorpan, 1967)*

Horses' Easter, or Mare's Thursday, is a cabalistic holiday, celebrated in the same day with Ascension - on the sixth Thursday after Easter - when people thought that for only one hour of the entire year, horses would graze till they satiated.

On this day, when spring vegetation first flowers, horses were free to graze whenever they wanted, while the oxen and the heifers would journey to mountain meadows. In older times, Horses' Easter used to be a day of deadlines, when transactions among people were either signed or ended. Unlike Saint George on April 23 or Saint Peter on October 26, which are holidays with a fixed date in the Folk Almanac, Ascension is celebrated on a day that can vary with some length from year to year.

Because of these variations in timing, the "deadline function" of this holiday gradually faded and eventually acquired a pejorative meaning. Today, the expression *at the Horses' Easter* means "never returning the thing that was borrowed" or "never keeping a promise".

Some legends connected to Jesus' birth and also some carols which are trace back to the origin of this holiday, say that the Virgin Mary was disturbed by the clattering, neighing and foraging crunching of horses during Christ's birth. For this reason she put a curse on horses not to ruminate and to be permanently hungry.

June 3
The Boiled Wheat Cake

The most common sacred food made of wheat is the boiled wheat cake. This cake, representing the sacrifice of the crushed wheat's spirit in the felting mill, is boiled in water, sweetened with honey and decorated with nuts and candy. The boiled wheat cake is a sacred meal with great symbolical significance, and is now prepared only by Christian Orthodox believers for important holidays of the year, especially those which commemorate fathers and foregathers, or at funerals.

June 4
Cousins and Sisters

Those girls who, during the childhood, have sworn oaths to one another at certain spring and summer holidays ("Sântoader", "Mosii de Vara" meaning Saturday Before Whitsuntide, "Matcalau") call themselves *cousins or sisters*. Similarly, men call each other sworn brothers, brothers or cousins. In the same way, the girls who take part in the sacred processions of certain rituals, such as: "Paparude", "Caloian", "Dragaica", "Lazarelul", are known as sisters and they also address each other with the word "Sister". While they are alive, they meet every year on that particular holiday when they become sworn sisters, feast and offer each other gifts.

In Oltenia, on the burial of one of the sisters, certain separation rituals were performed before the tomb was covered with earth. In Bihor, the sisters who stayed alive symbolically met the dead ones in a ceremonial called "Lioara" or "The Dance on the grave," during one of the holidays dedicated to the dead. In southern Transylvania and in central Walachia, the sworn brothers and sisters call each other *cousins*

Such ceremonies, which was meant to ease one's longing after the dead sisters, have gradually disappeared. But they are still preserved in a well-known children's rhyme, in which the *"longing Mary"* refers generically to the dead women and the *"longing sisters"* to the ones who were still alive.

June 5
The Girl of the Woods

The *Girl of the Woods*, daughter to The Hag of the Woods, is a mythical representation of wood-based civilization. She lives in the middle of the woods, where she is brought by winds and storms, and she takes the shape of a young lad's girlfriend or of a fairy. She travels only by night and can also take the shape of an old woman, or of a creature half girl, half fish, or of an animal, usually a mare. She lures young men which she then kidnaps later to give birth to their children and she eventually leaves them wandering in the woods.

Unlike The Hag of the Woods that is tormented because people kill her children (the trees of the forest), the Girl of the Woods is happy and even sings and dances. Her anthropomorphic representation is that of a tall girl, with long hair down to her feet wearing wooden boots. She wanders either naked covered with her hair or dressed in bark and tree-moss. Seen from the front, she looks like a woman, but from behind, she looks like a hollowed tree trunk. In some regions, The Girl of the Woods is the same as Hag of the Woods.

Any young man can get rid of her love with the help of certain witches who create a human figurine of straw that is dressed up with the man's clothes and then taken to a crossroads. Tricked, the Girl of the Woods hugs (makes love with) the straw-man and in this manner leaves the young man alone. She avoids luring men who wear a waist-band, a belt or a lime-tree waist-band; the one who manages to tap her waist can take all her power and find out all her secrets. Her enemy is the Night Man or Dusk Man that can catch her, tear her apart and burn her.

June 6
Plants for Healing Drunkenness

In old times, people could not prevent the extinction of some plant and animal species by declaring them legally protected species. Instead, the power of faith was stronger and more effective than the rule of law.

One example is be the Superb Pink *(Dianthus Superbus L.)*, a beautiful flower from the *Caryopillaeceae* family, which grows in the high meadows and orchards. Women from Vrancea County, experts in folk pharmacopoeia and cosmetics, used to consider this plant as bringing hatred to one. They believed that people would hate you only by picking it up or by bearing it with one.

Dozens of other plants could be picked up and used in cooking, in folk medicine and cosmetics, in cloth-painting, in building the roof of the houses or as vegetal fibers for manufacturing clothes. The columbine *(Aquilegia Vulgaris L.)* from the *Rununculaceae* family, with blue or colorful flowers, is a wild plant or can be grown by man in gardens, for personal use, in cloth-painting (blue), and in folk medicine against drunkenness. The columbine flower, mixed with another plant, "Strigoaia", was boiled in brandy yeast and consumed against drunkenness.

The snowball tree *(Viburnum Opulus L.)* from the *Caprifoliaceae* family grows in the woods and in wet bushes and has round, red, sourish and refreshing fruit. These fruit are used for coloring cloths in red and in the folk medicine for curing some diseases. The legend says that this tree grew out of Father Noah's blood when he cut his finger while building the arch. The name of the plant appears often in folk verse, including shouts:

All girls, come to the snowball tree,
'Cause you are not made for dancing,
You are silent like grass
And old like my mother![108]

---

[108] Butura, 1979, p. 61.

June 7
Flowers of Love

People cumulated impressive knowledge of plants that grow in the wild. They could be used for various purposes such as food, folk medicine and cosmetics, cloth-painting or magical practices. One special category were the so-called *Flowers of Love* which include
- *Stork's Bill* is a melliferous plant *(Delphinum Consolida L.)* with blue flowers, beak-shaped, which was invoked in the charms made for women who could not give birth to children. The plant is also known as the *child-making-weed*, or the *lifting weed*. The stork's bill tea has aphrodisiac qualities, if it is drunk at night, before going to sleep. (Oltenia)
- *Love Flower* also locally called *love (Sedum Fabaria L.)*, from the *Crasulaceae* family, is the personification of a plant which is protector of the family and the household against enemies. It has spear shaped leaves, purple-pink flowers and it grows near the creeks in the high regions. The plant was transplanted from the place where it naturally grows, to a clean spot in the garden of the village. In order to find out if a young couple will marry or not, two love flowers would be planted, one for the girl and one for the young man. By the way in which they grew, that is, with the stalks close to each other or far from each other, the plants could foretell if the marriage would take place or not.
- *Bullocks* is a general name for some plant species from the *Primulaceae, Orchidaceae and Orobanchaceae* families, used in empirical medicine and in the charms for fertilizing cattle and sterile women. Some plants could stimulate the sexual functions through their shape or through their active substance. These plants were given to cattle, mixed with the forage, and women used it when bathing. (Oltenia)

June 8
The Calus Divinity and the Church

By dancing the Calus and according to the *similia similibus* principle, individuals tried to absorb the virility, power and elegance which raised the horse from animal to god in pre-historic times. Of the Calus it is said:

"Christ sent the Holy Spirit on earth, and the Devil made the *Calus*."[109] (Bârca, Dolj County)

---

[109] AIEF, mss. 1972.

"The days when the Calus is danced, are devilish days. Nobody works on that day. They say that the one who works will be kidnapped by the Devil living inside the Calus or inside the Iele goddesses; the Calus Dancers, chewing wormwood and garlic, hopped over the *kidnapped one.*" (Perieti, Olt County)

"The Calus Dancers swear the oath by the lake. If they ever let out anything of their vow, they get sick and die." (Bârca, Dolj County)

"The Calus Dancers from Sirineasa, Vâlcea County, would worship "three goddesses left by God on Earth to make people look ugly."[110]

Viewers who watch the Calus ceremony from outside may get the impression that members of the group are seized by some devilish spirits, that they have separated from church and from God and that they have signed a secret pact with another divinity.

The Calus Dancers identify with the cabalistic divinity which they worship through everything they do. Their Christian names (Ion, Vasile, Nicolae) are changed with horse names; they wear spurs and bell harnesses tied to their boots, bells tied to their waist-band over their chest that look like harness, while dancing; they mimic horse tramping, galloping and they execute acrobatic moves of mounting on horseback or of horse shoeing. In some groups, one of the dancers even initiates a horse neighing.

June 9
The Oath

Ritual of Tying the Gag in 1976, Osica de Sus, Olt County
(AIEF by Anta Giurchescu, Nr. 76.908)

When joining the group, each Folk Dancers take an *oath* to Calus in front of the *Mute*, a mask representing the cabalistic God, and the "Calus" Flag, proceeded at Pentecost Strode, at Pentecost Saturday or at Good Sunday holidays. These made up a ritual known as Tying the Flag or The Vow.

---

[110] Fochi, 1976, p. 43.

The ceremony was secretly held being kept away from the eyes of curious ones. The oath guaranteed the unity and solidarity of the Dance Group in the days when the Calus Dance was performed to confirm total loyalty to the Calus, obedience to the chief and denial of human pleasures.

The Calusari (Folk Dancers) would all shout their vows in reply to the chief's words: "I swear, on the souls of my forefathers, on my horses and cattle, that I will respect the Calus and its laws until the Flag is undone!"; "I swear that I will praise the Calus in faith, honor, obedience and fear of God!" They also swore that they "would not get drunk, nor quarrel" (Cetate, Dolj County), that they "would be like brothers and share their money" (Dobrun, Olt County), that they "would be clean and refrain from sexual relationships during the time they dance the Calus (Rusanesti, Olt County) and that they "would heal people" (Susani, Vâlcea County). The only dancer, who would not take an oath, was the Mute who "would cover his mouth so that the Pentecost spirit would not take him away." (Tetoiu, Vâlcea County) The oath sworn by the Calus Dancers to their Chief, or by the Calus Group to the Calus divinity was evidenced everywhere this custom was practiced.

Today, the oath is still sworn by the Calus Dancers from Oltenia and South-Western Walachia, but it has changed in having lost its deeper sacred nature.

June 10

Small Saints in the Folk Almanac

The four Christian saints celebrated in June 10 (Saint Timofte), on the 11th (Saint Vartolomeu), on the 12th (Saint Onofrie) and on the 14th (Sait Elisei) are called the *Small Saints* in the Folk Almanac. They are believed to take care of maturing and ripening of the wheat in the fields. Because time recorded by the old style almanac lagged behind exact astronomic time, year after year, the tasks attributed to the old time saints of fertilizing the crops and making them ripe no longer corresponded to the development stage of the cereal plants. This led to these saints becoming less and less relevant in terms of evaluating and planning specific events. Though not forgotten by people, these saints were made responsible for some negative weather phenomena which are frequent experienced in June: hail, strong winds, storms and heavy rains.[111]

There was evidence of these saints and their diminished importance in the Folk Almanac in Moldavia, Walachia, Oltenia, Banat and Southern Transylvania.

---

[111] Ghinoiu, 1997, p.182.

June 11
Summer Forefathers or "Wheat Vartolomeu"

The holiday celebrated on Saturday before Pentecost, dedicated to the dead, the fathers and the forefathers, is called *Summer Forefathers* in Moldavia, Dobrogea, Walachia, Oltenia and Eastern Banat.

The regional names given to this holiday emphasize the importance of that day (Great Forefathers) and its place in the Folk Almanac (Great Sunday Forefathers, Pentecost Forefathers). It was believed that the souls of the dead, after leaving their graves at Great Thursday and walking freely among the living ones, would return in an upset mood to their underground shelters on the day of Summer Forefathers.

Bed and Clothes Given as Alms at Six Weeks after the Burial, Cotofenii din Jos, Dolj County
(AIEF by Ofelia Vaduva, 1975, Nr. 72 034)

To comfort them people would distribute alms consisting of clay or wooden pots (bought at the fairs) which they filled with wine, water, milk, cooked food, bread, flowers and lighted candles. When giving alms, people followed a strict ritual. Certain phrases were uttered and pots containing food and drink were distributed before any member of the family tasted from them. On that holiday, so many pots were distributed and received, that people didn't need to buy new ones for their own use.

Other practices dedicated to the dead were also carried out on that day. Those included cleaning and watering tomb plots and lamenting the dead. People were convinced the peaceful manner in which their dead could return to their underground world depended on how well they were comforted and on the abundance of accompanying offerings.

The summer solstice day in the old style almanac, when it was believed that the wheat roots dried out and the grains were ripe, was called "Wheat Vartolomeu" in the Folk Almanac.[112] The name of that mythical representation was borrowed from Saint Vartolomeu in the Orthodox Almanac. In the old style almanac, the day when that saint was celebrated corresponded to the day of the summer solstice. As a result, Vartolomeu's day used to be an important landmark in counting time over the year. Daytime and the daily sunshine periods grew shorter as of that date; in

---

[112] Ghinoiu, 1997, p. 211.

the forest, the leaves of the elm, the poplar and the lime trees twisted themselves and in the night, the Pleiades constellation appeared in the sky.

In its personified version, Wheat Vartolomeu had the features of a terrible god who would punish all those who did not observe his day by sending hail, strong winds and storms on earth. When the almanac was corrected and when celebrations of holidays were transferred from the old style into the new style almanac, the agrarian significance of Wheat Vartolomeu diminished. (Banat, Oltenia, Walachia, Southern Transylvania)

June 12
"Iele" or Spirits of the Pentecost

Table for Requiems in the Churchyard, Salt Valley, Vrancea County (Cherciu, 2003)

Iele are feminine mythical representations which appear at night before the rooster sings and between Easter and Pentecost. They have a wide range of regional names: The Holy Ones, Field Girls, The Beautiful Ones, Miraculous Ones, Pentecost Spirits, Falcon Girls, Bear Girls, The Fairies. Iele are rebel spirits of the dead which refuse to return to their underworld homes, after leaving tombs on Great Thursday and celebrating Easter with the living ones.

Unlike the "strigoi"- dead people who appear and make trouble to the living ones during winter - Iele are present only in the summer. They have an anthropomorphic appearance as maidens dressed in white. ele wander accompanied by fiddlers (flute and bagpipe singers), they ring the bells, beat the drums and blow the trumpets, they dance (ring dance and other folk dances), they lay tables on green grass, drink, have fun and sing all together:

> *Hadn't God created on Earth*
> *Lovage, valerian and water hyssop,*
> *The world would have been all for us!*

Similar to the "Philippes", the "Sântoader" spirits, the "Circovi" and the "Calus" Dancers, Iele travel only in groups that come into sight in odd numbers (3-5-7-9) and rarely in even numbers (2-4-12). Their homes are in virgin forests where no man has ever set foot, in the skies, on the plains and on large water bodies. They can be seen by night, floating and fluttering in the air, by the wells, in the trees or under the overhanging eaves of the houses. I

The grass turns into red and dries on the place where Iele perform the ring dance. If someone happened to see or to hear them, that person would neither move nor speak. Iele usually punish human malefactors, the ones who do not respect their days, who sleep under the trees or in open air by night, or who go out to the well to bring water, by lifting them up in whirlpools, by making them look ugly and by mutilating them.

Various forms of rheumatism and neuro-psychical diseases bear the name: "seized by Iele", "hit by Iele", "grabbed by Iele", "left falcon fluttering", "crippled by them." People can heal from these diseases only through Iele charms, *prayers at monasteries*, by becoming a member of the "Calus" Group, or by being hopped over by Folk Dancers.

In the regions where Iele are known as Bear Girls, they predestined children at birth and foretell people's death. People protect themselves against Iele by wearing garlic and wormwood tied to their waistbands at their greatest almanac feasts of Pentecost, Midsummer's Day, and the first day of Saint Peter fasting.[113]

June 13
"Calus" Mute

Mask of the "Calus" - 1976, Negoesti, Dolj County (AIEF by Anca Giurchescu)

The silent mask from the "Calus" dancers who play the role of Calus, the protecting god of horses and of the warm season of the year, is called *Calus Mute*, God, or Calus Father. Mute, a strange and mysterious creature, is dressed in patched clothes, wears a wooden phallus tied to his waist band and holds primitive weapons, bow with arrows, club, axe, broadsword or a whip. He also wears a mask made of goat-skin, a goat-beard, a kid-hair cap or smears his face with soot. He carries with him in his bag the Calus Beak, a wooden totem of the divinity, and various remedies for diseases.

---

[113] Ghinoiu, 1988, p. 267-274.

The man who plays Mute's role is one who stands out through his exceptional inborn qualities as a dancer, an athlete, an acrobat or an exceptional artist. He polarizes the attention and interest of the audience by the way he dresses and especially by dancing on his hands, on the ground or on roof ridges, by climbing to the top of the high and branchless trees and or executing acrobatics on the roofs of the buildings, which even an experienced circus artist be reluctant to do.

The Mute is both feared and respected for the divine spirit that lies within him. During the dance, he enjoys himself, dances, has fun. A fee-spirit, he does whatever he wants and does not answer to the chief's commands. He hugs and kisses married women and does all kinds of irreverent things with a wooden phallus. He is the prototype of long-gone gods. But there was one thing which he is not allowed to do, namely to speak during the days when the Calus dance is performed. Breaking this interdiction is harshly punished, even with death.[114]

June 14

War Between "Calus" and Pentecost Spirits

The "Calus Dance" is a great show in which Calus and his group, the Folk Dancers, mimic through their dance, gestures, ritual acts or cries, their well known victory in their struggle against Iele or the Pentecost Spirits.

They recount, through dancing, the terrible battle of an crowd armed with bludgeons against the Iele that are invisible enemies or seen only by the fighters. During the dance, the calm atmosphere before the battle rendered by horse-stepping called *The Stroll*, gradually changes into a tormenting gallop. In some groups of Dolj County, there are victims among the Dancers, a ritual custom suggestively called "Knocked down by the Calus." They frighten the enemies by knocking sticks, by brandishing their weapons, by tapping the ground with their feet, by ringing their bells.

This preparation for battle, together with the Chief's commands and the dance shouts make up a real war journal in the Densusianu Questioning:

Come on to Calus
Up! Up!
(Grânciova, Dolj County)

---

[114] Ghinoiu, 2003, p. 23-26.

Up on the saddle!
Up on the saddle!
(Pârvu Rosu, Costesti, Arges County)

Starting the attack:

Let's hop on it
On it again!
(Slavesti, Vâlcea County)

Following and punishing the enemy:

Look, it's here!
Hop on it!
(Mischii, Dolj County)

Once again
Go on, go on!
(Orlesti, Vâlcea County)

Warning the dancers of danger:

Careful, careful
Hop on it!
(Bârca, Dolj County)

Encouraging the cabalistic crowd:

Come on! Come on!
Go ahead, again!
(Neajlovu, Giurgiu County)

These shouts and commands are of ancient origin with unusual and obsolete words like "jalda" and "obze" (Urdarii de Sus, Cârligei, Gorj County, Bragadiru, Teleorman County) and others.[115]

---

[115] Ghinoiu, 2003, p. 59-60.

June 15

Calus Dancers- Disease Healers

The Calus Group hastens the marriage of girls at Pentecost, as well as fertilizes sterile women by sending them to the Calus Ring Dance and by touching them with the wooden phallus held by the Mute.

The role that made the dancers famous was actually curing people *Seized by Pentecost*. The ritual of healing these neuro-psychical diseases had two steps. At fist consulting the sick person to find out if he or she suffered from *"seized by Calus* disease and then treating the patient. Usually, a relative of the sick one would go in the Pentecost days to the Calus Group's chief, asking him to *"release him-her from the Pentecost illness."* The chief would come to the patient, followed by musicians playing dance songs. If the sick person reeled or moved a hand or a leg when he heard the Calus songs, it was evidence of being *seized by Pentecost* or *by Calus* and thus he could be cured.

The Calus dancers never try to heal epilepsy, neurological diseases or paralysis. But they can heal the so-called *disease of the girls who never danced*, a girls' mental depression caused by severe parental treatment in fear of their daughters losing their virginity before marriage. The treatment is done at home, where the sick person lies on a blanket in the courtyard, or in a forest glade where she is taken by horse-carriage. This treatment is based on what nowadays we refer to as *"psychotherapy," "chino therapy"* (tapping the sick man's feet with a club) or *"melotherapy."*[116]

June 16

Sworn Brothers and Sisters

Commemorating Dance at Six Weeks after the Burial of a Young Bachelor, Dalbovita, Mehedinti County (AIEF by I. Ghinoiu, Nr. 70 320)

An oath lasting until death is taken by children and adolescents (9-14-year-olds) is based on

---

[116] Ghinoiu, 2003, p. 67-69.

friendship, sex and common beliefs and usually carried out in the days of "Sântoader," "Summer Forefathers" or "Matcalau". The custom takes place in a field, the cemetery, in the house or its courtyard, where the participants are either pairs of children (two girls and two boys), or larger groups of ten to twelve boys and girls mixed together.

As part of the ritual, the children utter the oath, then exchange knot-shaped bread or clay pots accompanied by lighted candles followed by hugging each other as brothers and sisters do. They eat the ritual knot shaped bread and boiled wheat cake and finally have fun together. After this ceremony, the children call each other *sisters, brothers* or *cousins* for the rest of their lives and treat one another as real brothers or sisters. They discuss intimate and serious problems and keep each other's secrets. Never will they marry their brother's sister or, respectively, to their sister's brother and help and protect one another even with their lives. When one of them dies, the surviving sister orbrother who remained dresses in mourning clothes and, in some regions, a separation ritual is carried out at the tomb on the day of the funeral.

June 17
The Horse and the Wolf: Almanac Clocks

In prehistoric times, the horse was considered, everywhere it lived, a glorious animal perceived as a God. Indians, Greeks, Romans, Celts, Dacians worshipped the horse in different ways. In Romania, the Calus traditions kept the cabalistic cult alive. The horse has a privileged place in the Romanian Pantheon, due to its intelligence, its beauty and its body elegance.

The cult of the horse and wolf are connected to a pastoral almanac structured in two seasons: *winter* ruled by the wolf and *summer* governed by the horse. The Moon and the Sun, the stars that measure people's time, are magical links between these two Indo-European zoomorphic divinities - the wolf and the horse. The wolf is associated with the Moon which it enchants with dog's howling in the night, and the horse is associated with the Sun which it helps climbing in the sky from dawn to midday, every day.

Lacking any instrument of measuring time, the prehistoric man used the astronomical and biological clocks manifest in nature. One of these clocks was giving birth to foals in the vernal equinox period which is an astronomical phenomenon celebrated by many ancient nations as New Year. Except the donkey, the horses' close relative whose pregnancy period is 360 days, no other biological clock on the Romanian territory could mirror the length of a tropic year for prehistoric man through the rhythm of the reproduction cycle. The mare has usually two reproduction periods both being close to the equinox periods: the summer one and the winter one. In practice, the beginnings of the two basic seasons in the cattlemen's almanac are marked by the two periods when the mares mate and bring forth the spring season of March and April and the autumn one.

June 18
The Divine Herd of "Calus" God

After Christ's rise into Heaven on Ascension Day, the Earth and our world are left for a most critical period without God's protection for ten days, until Pentecost when The Holy Spirit descends to earth. Those who take advantage of this situation are the "Rusallii" (Pentecost), rebellious dead souls that refuse to leave for the other world and cause serious trouble for people on earth. People try to please them by giving them alms on Pentecost Saturday or in the Pentecost morning, they call them "Fairies", "Lovely Girls."

Specific Dance of the Calusari: "The Stroll," Icoana, Olt County (AIEF by Anca Giurchescu, Nr. 43 430)

However, a tough magic practice involving threats by the fighting Calus Dancers. They make up a divine herd of the Calus God who is born on Pentecost Couch Day. They entertain him by dancing during the Pentecost week but finally kill him and then bury him on Beak's Thursday. The cabalistic troop is called *"Calusari"* or *"Calus"* in Walachia, Oltenia and Dobrogea, *"Caluceni"* in Banat and in Moldavia and *"Caluserul"* in Transylvania.

Free of the magic function of older times, today the Calus Dance is part of widely appreciated artistic repertoire of some ensembles both home and abroad.[117] The leader of the group selects his dancers according to strict criteria. The men have to be skilled dancers, healthy and fit. During summer events they have to dance to the point of exhaus-

---

[117] In 2005, the dance was recognized by UNESCO as a unique contribution to Romania'a "intangible heritage."

tion, moving from house to house in their village and even in the neighboring ones.

"I agreed to take a man in the group, said one leader, only "if he was able to stay in the air as long as possible" or "when he dances, you should not see his legs." Harry Brauner, a well-known folklorist, who accompanied the Calus dance group from Padureni (Arges County) to London in 1935, described how the leader strengthened the dancers' muscles while traveling by train. "The dancers had to lie, each of them, on the seats, while the leader and his assistant were hitting their leg muscles with a club."[118]

June 19
The Effigy of "Calus" God

The cabalistic effigy, made of a ceremonial Binding and worn by Mute or by the Leader during the "Calus" dance, is called *Beak, Hare* or *Calus*. It is a peculiar totem made of a twisted piece of wood or carved in wood by the Mute or by the Leader. It can be in the shape of water fowl's neck and beak, or of a horse's neck and head, a wolf's head or of a dog's mouth. The totem is wrapped in healing plants and in hare skin fastened with a long thread whose measure is equal to the size of the Calus Dancers. It is fastened on top of a stick, or carried in a bag by the Mute.

During the dance, certain groups place the Beak in front of the musicians or next to the Calus flag to 'watch' the performance dedicated to it. Most of the times it is hidden from the sight of the profane or, in some cases, part of the head can be seen sticking out of the bag thereby increasing the mystery surrounding it. Every time it is seen, the Beak is considered a devilish thing more feared and respected than the Christian Cross. People believe they can become sick or mad merely by touching it. On Beak's Tuesday it is buried in a secret place where it was made. The funeral ceremony, called *Breaking (death of) the Calus, Breaking the Flag* or *Memory Eternal,* consists of special ritual actions.

June 20
Breaking the "Calus" - The Silence Rite

The last sequence of the Breaking the Calus Dancers' ceremony, in which the Calus god dies violently on the Beak's Tuesday (the second Tuesday after Pentecost), is called variyably from region to region: *Breaking or Burial of the Calus, Memory Eternal,* or *Breaking the Flag.*

---

[118] Ghinoiu, 2003, p. 28-32.

*Symbolic Death of the "Calusar" - 1976,
Optasi, Olt County (AIEF by Anca Giurchescu)*

The funeral ceremony is usually held in the same place where Calus was symbolically born on a hillock, on a hill or in an isolated clearing in the woods. The funereal remains of the God, substituted by the flag, the Beak and Mute's mask or sword, are subjected to unusual rituals. The objects are either thrown away or abandoned, laid on water, cremated or buried. The period between Calus birthday (Pentecost Couch) and the day it is buried (Beak's Tuesday) is a ritual time equal in length to a lunar month, that is a thirteenth part of a solar year. The birth of Calus takes place before sunrise, whereas its death, Breaking the Calus, always occurs in the evening, after sunset. After a year, on the Pentecost Couch Day, the Beak is unburied and if the hare skin decayed it is replaced with a new one. (Oltenia and Banat) (Ghinoiu, 2003, p. 44)

In some cases, before Breaking or death of the Calus, the dancers free themselves from their oath by taking another oath: "We swear to God, that we have obeyed the Calus, by its law!" In its older forms, the funereal Calus ceremony ended with a *rite of oblivion:* the members of the group ran from the site of the ceremony and hid in the forest or in the wheat fields and then, while returning home or to the place of the oath, they told each other that they had been to a fair to trade some things. After participating in the death ceremonial of Calus God during which they chew garlic, the dancers never mention a word about what they had seen or done then.

It is that rite which lies at the origin of a Romanian saying that refers to keeping a secret: "No garlic have you eaten, so no smell of it from your mouth."[119]

---

[119] Ghinoiu, 2003, p. 69-72.

June 21
Beliefs Related to the Origin of the Calus Dancers

Throughout the Middle Ages the Calus was a defining characteristic of Romanian identity for those living to the north and to the south of the Danube. To the North of the compact area where the Calus custom was practiced, some traces of it were found with the Carpato-Russians from Galitia and, moving towards Western Europe, more rare and more faded elements have been identified.

Surprisingly, towards western Europea, a similar variant of the Carpato-Danubian Calus model can be found. "In England, the *Hobbyhorse* Calus also appears in some dancers' society - who wore bells tied to their feet and were called *Morris Dancers*. They would go around dancing at Easter, on May Day, on Ascension, at Pentecost and during feasts. In Shakespeare's time, they performed in theatres after the play ended in order to animate any depressing mood created by the tragedies."[120]

June 22
Midsummer's Day Torch

Diana from Efes - The Carpathian Goddess
(Popa-Lisseanu, 1928)

In some ethnically distinct regions, the Midsummer's Day Torch is the burning of a torch on the night of June 23 to 24 to symbolize the invincibility of the sun at the summer solstice. The torch is made of a dried piece of fir-tree wood which is cracked at one end and then filled with resin and spruce fir-tree slivers which are tied with spun yarn. In the evening, on Midsummer Day's Eve, young men gather on a hill outside the precincts of the village, they make a circle, light their torches, then line up and start drawing circles in the air with their burning torches, rotating them from east to west while shouting "Watch

---

[120] Romulus Vuia, 1975, p. 113.

the torch!"

By passing the torch between their legs, they look as if hopping over the fire or riding a horse of fire. When the torches are about extinguish, the young men descend to the village, surround the gardens with them and then stick them in the middle of the fields and orchards. The fire-circles made by spinning the torches in the same direction as the sun's apparent movement in the longest day of the year, express people's joy for the victory of light over darkness, of heat over cold, of fertility over sterility and also their determination to help the star of life keep the height that it reached in the sky at summer solstice.

The smoke and the strong smell of burnt resin, loud shouting, as well as the lighting of torches and sticking them in gardens and orchards, constitute the core of a spectacular night ceremony flooded with divine fertilizing rituals. (Maramures, Bistrita-Nasaud)

June 23

The Almanac for Gathering Medicine Plants

Collecting Medicinal Roots, Apuseni Mountains (I. Godea, 2007)

The *Almanac for gathering medicine plants* is the distribution over the year of favorable day for harvesting specific flowers, leaves, seeds, fruit, roots, bulbs and rhizomes of the healing plants.

Unlike the deadlines for harvesting the edible plants which can vary according to the weather conditions, medicine plants are picked up following a almanac with fixed dates and moments of the day or of the night, rigorously established by tradition. The days when these plants can be gathered are grouped around the vernal equinox ("Sântoader's Horses" Week, Palm Sunday, Great Thursday, Sângiorz, Sângiorz of the Cattle), around the summer solstice (Todurudale, Ascension, Midsummer's Day, Summer Circovi, Ilie Palie, Foca) and around the winter equinox (Holy Mary's Birth, Holy Mary's Death, Cross Day).

The *Folk Almanac* indicates not only the day and the time of day but also the most favorable places for harvesting. They should be clean, that is from places where no animal, bird or man set foot before and where dogs cannot be heard barking. Those who gather the medicine plants have to be clean both physically and spiritually, they must recite magical words when picking them up, wear certain clothes, and reward the Earth where the plant grew with bread, salt or seeds.

The most important day of the year for gathering these plants is Midsummer's Day. Picking up the healing plants on the night of Midsummer, before sunrise wouldn't be done by any expert in folk medicine unless a real or imaginary reward was expected.[121]

June 24
The Midsummer Goddess "Dragaica" or "Sânziana"

In the Romanian Pantheon, *Sânziana* is an agrarian goddess, protector of the wheat crops and of married women. She is identified with Diana and Juno in the Roman Pantheon or with Hera and Arthemis in the Greek Pantheon.

As a goddess of fecundity and of maternity, the Midsummer Goddess is called *Dragaica* in Walachia, Dobrogea, southern and central Moldavia and *Sânziana* in Oltenia, Banat, Transylvania, Maramures and Bucovina. She is born on May 9, on the day of Mother Dochia's Death; she grows miraculously until Midsummer's Day on June 24, the day of the summer solstice when the plant bearing her name blooms.

On the day of the summer solstice, the Midsummer goddess sings and dances with her nuptial procession formed by maiden fairies and beautiful girls, she wanders over hills and woods and she floats in the air. In the "Dragaica" groups from southern Walachia, the girl who plays the role of the agrarian goddess is dressed like a bride, with a white dress and a wreath made of Sanzania (Our Lady's Bedstraw) flowers on her head, representing marriage. During the nuptial ceremony, Sânziana brings grains to wheat ears, smells to healing plants. She cures diseases and ailments, especially children's diseases; she protects the field against hail, storms and whirlpools; she foretells the predestined husband. When the day of her celebration is ignored, she provokes storms, whirlpools and hail and lifts away the fragrance and the healing power of the flowers.

After Midsummer's Day, the days become shorter and the nights grow longer, the wheat root dries while it ripens, the Pleiades constellation appears in the sky, the flowers lose their smell and their healing power, the cuckoo stops singing and the glow worms appear in the woods.

In the western Apuseni Mountains, on Gaina (Hen) Mountain, the feasts of praising the agrarian goddess have become special occasions for youngsters to meet and get to know each other as marriage prospects

---

[121] Ghinoiu, 1988, p. 269-270.

and to attend. To this day, it remains to this day a famed and popular fair.[122]

June 25
When the Cuckoo is Struck Dumb

The cuckoo song, both a way of measuring time and a melancholic source of inspiration for the sorrow and grief verse, is first heard at Annunciation or Cuckoo's Day on March 25. Because it stops suddenly three months later at Midsummer's Day or summer's solstice, the day is also called *The Cuckoo is Struck Dumb* in the Folk Almanac on June 24.

According to the legend, on that day, the cuckoo chokes on a barley grain and turns into a hawk for six months. People observed that the short spring period during which this migratory bird singing starts and ends when two important astronomical phenomena, indispensable for calculating any almanac, take place, the vernal equinox and the summer solstice. Because the cuckoo can foretell people's luck, health, marriage or death, the cuckoo is loved by Romanians.

June 26
Midsummer Wreath

The wreath made of Sânziana flowers (Our Lady's Bedstraw) and of wheat-ears in the morning of Midsummer's Day. Symbolizing the agrarian goddess, it is hung by a window, by the gate-poles, around crosses on the road side and in the cemetery. This divine effigy has miraculous powers worn on the head by a maiden at the ceremonial is called "Dragaica Dance."

This *midsummer wreath* protects people, animals and crops against the natural calamities. Thrown on the roof of a house or a barn, it indicates through special signs whether the person who made or threw the wreath will live or die, whether a young girl will marry during the year and what her future husband will look like (young or old, handsome or ugly, healthy or sick) or whether she will have prosperity or loss in her home.

---

[122] Ghinoiu, 1988, p. 267.

*Bride's Knot-Saped Bread and
the Scepter of the Groom,
Farcasesti, Iasi County (Ciubotaru, 2002)*

The Midsummer wreath which adorns the goddesses' head during her nuptial dance has the same significance with the wheat knot-shaped bread laid on the bride's head by the godmother in a ceremony before going to church, and with the royal-like crowns laid by the priest on the bride's and groom's heads. In all cases, a fertility transfer is made from the sacred knot-shaped bread or wreath to the bride and groom.

The custom of making the Midsummer wreath and all the traditions related to it is evidenced among Romanians throughout the country.

June 27

The Glowworm

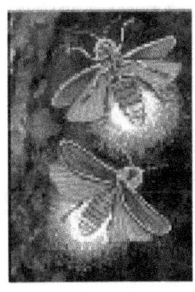

The *glowworm*, also known as *little torch, God's fire, spark*, an insect from the Coleoptherae family whose female produces a phosphorescent light, was meant by God or by Saint Peter to lighten the way of the people who get lost in the woods by night.

Another legend says that when God descended on Earth, He was followed by angels from the Sky. They enjoyed the sights of this world and one angel fell in love with a shepherd's daughter. Returning to the skies, God changed the angels into stars so they could watch the world's beauty from above, and he threw the enamored angel to Earth transformed into a glowworm.

The glowworm is a mysterious creature with two qualities. One is positive: "The blind man who gathers nine glow worms will regain his sight" or "If you put glowworms in a child's bathing water, he will become bright." Another is negative: "The glow worm is the Devil's Eye" or "The one who has glow worms around his house is thought to be the Devil's friend."[123]

---

[123] Evseev, 1997, p. 227.

June 28
The Origin of the Girls' Fair

Alphorn Women at the Women's Market on Gaina Mountain
(AIEF, Nr. 1214)

The still widely popular *Girl's Fair*, held on the Gaina (Hen) Mountain in the Western Apuseni Mountains, traces back to Juno, the goddess protecting married women. The name of the mountain and of the fair held on it around summer solstice - The Hen - refers to the bird symbolizing the Neolithic Mother Goddess of fertility. Starting with "Sânziana" or "Drăgaica" holiday on June 24, the day of the summer solstice in the Folk almanac, the old people in the village used to follow the movement in the sky of the constellation called "Clucking hen with chicks," the folk name of Pleiades. This group of stars belonging to the Taurus Constellation, helped determine the right time for sowing the autumn wheat. The hen, a fantastic bird with golden wings and eggs, marks the sacred place where the fair bearing its name takes place. The holidays around the summer solstice which gather people from Carpathian areas to worship the Goddess of fertility have acquired new functions including trading of products, entertainment and an occasion for young people to meet in view of finding a marriage partner.

June 29
Summer Saint Peter

Summer Saint Peter, a divinity indicating the middle of the agrarian summer and the harvesting time, took June 29 and its name (Saint Peter) from the Orthodox Almanac. In the Romanian Pantheon, Summer Saint peter is separated from his brother, Winter Saint Peter, patron of the wolves. The two saints' days are celebrated at about half a year time difference from each other. In the folk tradition, Saint Peter appears both as an earthly character and as a divine one. Since ancient times, it has been believed that Summer Saint Peter walked about Earth, alone or accompanied by God, and that God often consulted him when taking decisions.

In Romanian folk tales, Saint Peter is an ordinary man. He wears peasant clothes; he farms, raises cattle, and mostly fishes. Unusually for a Saint, he is involved in humorous incidents. His horses or his oxen are stolen from him right when he needs them for harvesting; he enjoys himself with song and dance at the village pub and is beaten when he gets drunk; he has a girlfriend who likes to fish. And though he becomes the Devil's servant, he is God's spy on Earth. Being hard working, faithful and a good advisor, Saint Peter is brought to Heaven by God and charged with the gates and keys to Heaven. While in heaven, he also oversees the food stores and distributes food to wild animals; moreover, he heats the hail so that it melts into smaller pieces, thus making it less harmful when it falls. On certain almanac holidays - Christmas, New Year, Epiphany, Forty Four Martyr's Day, "Sângiorz", Midsummer's Day, he can be seen on Earth at midnight, when the sky opens for a moment, sitting at the holy table on God's right side.

In certain regions, Saint Peter's holiday is announced by terrestrial or cosmic signs, or when glowworms appear, the cuckoo stops singing or the Hen (Pleiades) Constellation appears in the sky.

June 30
Saint Peter's Curse

Old people from the gold-mining Rosia Montana mountain region recount that long ago, when Saint Peter was strolling on Earth, he arrived once at Rosia Montana. Like any traveler he went to the pub. The locals being very hospitable offered him brandy but Saint Peter refused them. Offended that an old man dared to refuse them, they started a fight. Why can't you drink with us? Who do you think you are? Someone important, or what? We asked you to have a drink, out of great generosity!

They beat him black and blue. When he finally managed to escape from the gold washers, Saint Peter cursed them harshly.

I curse you, people from Rosia Montana, to go searching for gold in the mine with your empty bags and no matter how much gold you find, you shall not be able to keep it. Whatever you may earn, you shall lose at the pub.

They say that saints are very good at cursing and that their curses come true. And from then on, people from Rosia Montana kept drinking and offering strangers to drink. Only the old people know about the curse, for bags have always been empty. The young people just laugh and don't believe the old men's story.[124]

---

[124] Soit, 1974, p. 23.

JULY

"CUPTOR"

OVEN MONTH

1	"Ana-Foca" and "Cosmadin"
2	The Blackwort (and Empirical Orthopedics)
3	Chicory
4	Lovage and Valerian
5	Folk Treatments for Curing Diseases
6	Charm Techniques
7	The Rain Maker (Paparuda)
8	The "Pricup"
9	The Sun Eclipse
10	Shearing the Lambs
11	Fairs Held in the Mountains
12	"Caloian"
13	"Pantelii" - Solomon Hail People
14	The Dough, Archetype of Genesis
15	"Ciurica" and Limping "Chiric"
16	Summer Circovi (Midsummer)
17	Pastoral Nedeia Feasts
18	A Miner's Folk Tale
19	Macrina - Santilie Forefathers
20	Santilie
21	The Church Patron
22	The Dittany - Flower of Fire
23	"Oparlia" and "Foca"
24	From the Ring Dance to the Disco
25	Rites of Integrating Each Sex Into Its Own Community
26	"SAntilie" Ring Dance
27	"Rudari" Gypsies Coupling
28	The Living Fire
29	Devil's Inventions
30	Guide Marks for Measuring Daytime
31	The Goat's Horn (Beliefs About Driving Hail Away)

July,

the seventh month of the almanac, is dedicated to Julius Caesar, the reformer of the ten-month-long Roman Almanac. In Romania, this is the hottest period when the wheat ripens and is harvested. This is why people called it Oven Month.

Sunday Dance (Photo by J. Berman National Geographic Magazine - April 1934)

The *Folk Almanac* has many holidays and customs dedicated to the harvest and to nature's more harmful powers such as hail storms, lighting triggered fires, or droughts. In order to prevent and minimize their effects, people ask for help from various mythical persona that are celebrated during this month: Cosmadin, Ana-Foca, Pricopul, Panteliile, Ciurica, Summer Circovi, Macrina, Santilie, Ilie-Palie, Foca, Oparlia, Saint Ann, Pantelimon, Pintilie the Traveler. During dry years, holidays of Rain Making such as Paparuda and Caloian are added.

July 1
"Ana-Foca" and "Cosmadin"

Ana-Foca, a holiday celebrated on July 1, bears the names of two celebrations, in the Christian Almanac, namely the Death of Saint Ann on July 25, and Saint Martyr Foca on July 23.

Ana-Foca is a mythical representation in Transylvania and Banat which brings a scorching heat that withers and devastates crops, especially vineyards.

Another mythical representation praised on July 1 in the Folk Almanac, is called "Cosmandin" which has its origins in the combination between two disease healers saints, Cosma and Damian. This holiday is considered to be a favorable ritual time for folk medicine practices and for charms against abdominal fever and epilepsy. Beliefs in these Saint-doctors, who cured people without asking for payment, are found in Moldavia, Bucovina, Banat and Transylvania.

July 2
The Blackwort and Empirical Orthopedics

Tatin's weed or the *blackwort (Symhytum Officinale L.)* is the personification of a healing plant used for curing wounds, burns, rheumatism, displaced bone joints (luxation) and fractures.

Blackwort (Parvu, 2000)

Gathering the plant followed an ancient ritual lasting two days. On Tuesday evening the plant is spotted and marked in the place where it grows and after three days, on Friday Morning, it is picked. A physically and spiritually clean woman, initiated in folk medicine, goes to the plant and makes fifteen bows in front of it. Then respectfully she says to it:

Lady Tatin's weed,
I won't pick you up rotten,
I'll pick you up ripe
To mend flesh with flesh,
Bone with bone
To make them look as before!

The woman explains for whom and why she picked it up from the ground. At home she boils and mixes it with barley wheat. With this blackwort mixture to which "luxation charm" is added, the enchantress treats the bone fracture like a surgeon. Mixed with garlic, wormwood, water hyssop and other plants, the blackwort also guarantees magic protection against "Iele" and "Strigoi" (ghosts).

Resigned that their power can be annihilated by some plants, "Iele" bemoans:

> *Hadn't God created on Earth*
> *Lovage, valerian and water hyssop,*
> *To all of us would have been the World!*[125]

July 3
Chicory

Chicory *(Cichorium Intybus L.)* of the Compositae family grows in hayfields and often in vacant lands or road-sides. The plant is used in folk medicine for obtaining vegetal coloring. It is invoked in charms for unmarried girls, to enamor the matchmakers. It is believed that the young girls who laid chicory together with the beloved one's shirt under the pillow, would see him in their dreams, while the girls who got smoked or washed with chicory flowers would get rid of hatred and also of witches' charms.

Harvesting Wheat, Runcu Mare, Hunedoara County
(R. Isfanoni, 2004, Photo by Doina Isfanoni, 1996)

In a beautiful Transylvanian legend, chicory is associated with the Goddess of the Flowers who would wash with dew drops before sunrise, so as to go unseen. But the Sun saw the Goddess one morning and fell in love with her and sent two stars to ask her in marriage. The earthly goddess refused him:

---

[125] (Butura, 1979, p. 117)

The sun, husband-sun,
Is always a traveler,
Over villages by day,
And over waters by night!

Angry, the Sun changed the goddess into a chicory flower her eyes following the Sun.

When I rise, she joys,
When I fall, she parches;
When I set down
She will be picked.

From that moment on, it is said that the chicory always followed the sun's position, until late autumn. The flowers close in the evening and open in the morning at sunrise.

July 4
Lovage and Valerian

At Pentecost, in southern Romania and at Ascension, in Transylvania, *lovage* is displayed to cast away the "Iele" and the evil brought by them. Lovage stalks and leaves are hung on windows and doors. They are tied around milk cows' horns and tails or mixed with porridge and given as food to animals. In some cases they are tied on women's waist bands, used for pummeling children or for embellishing the horses which young men ride by the village's crosses on Ascension. (Sibiel, Sibiu County)

A bundle of lovage and flowers hallowed at Ascension is also kept next to an icon and used at variously to overcome hard times during the year. This bundle is used for the same purpose in making the "Calus" flag at Pentecost and the "Dragaica Flag" on Midsummer's Day. In folk medicine, lovage is used for treating headaches, convulsive coughing, indigestions and twinges, and, mixed with valerian and wild garlic to heal some cattle diseases. It is used, too, in to treat neuro-psychical and heart diseases

Valerian (Valeriana Officinalis L.) is a plant with miraculous powers which together with garlic, wormwood, water hyssop and other plants, assured protection against "Iele", "strigoi" (ghosts) and dragons. The plant was invoked as a divinity to bring love to young girls and luck to married women.

To be protected against dragons, the maidens from Apuseni Mountains bathed in valerian, lovage and black grass water, before going to dances, to feasts or to places at the edge of the village.

July 5
Folk Treatments for Curing Diseases

Veterinary at the Sheepfold, Draghina Mountain, Arges County (AIEF by Ion Ghinoiu, 1975, Nr. 75 511)

Psychotherapy, phytotherapy, chino-therapy, melotherapy and balneotherapy are modern names of ancient healing techniques involving curing plants, massage, or mineral waters. Many of these empirical healing techniques are also part of *the charm* practices, which are nowadays unfairly and mistakenly taken for witchcraft and deceptions by paranormal healers. The charm is based on *word-therapy* which is combined from case to case, with phyto-, psycho-, chino- and melo-therapy.

In the charm verses, diseases to be cured are personifications of evil sent through witchcraft by *uninitiated people,* through curses by *enemies* or through punishments by *God, the Virgin Mary and Saint Friday.* The charms embody precious knowledge and observation related to the appearance, the manifestation and the empiric healing of the diseases. Women invoking the charms have strong personalities, capable of provoking and hindering some psychic processes. They have knowledge of human anatomy, healing plants and, of course, healing or ameliorating techniques.

The so-called *stung clay-dolls,* discovered by archaeologists in their excavations and by ethnographers in their field work, constitute a strong evidence that *acupuncture* was used in the Carpato-Danubian-Pontic region. Moreover, at least some of the enchantresses, especially the ones who used the "drawing technique" (massage), also used or practiced bioenergetics in treating diseases. The length of the charm verse varied from a few words to dozens of lines. Like any folk poem, the charms were orally handed-down. Because the verse and the charm techniques were kept secret, they had to be *stolen* like any other skill or transmitted secretly sometimes soon before dying.

July 6
Charm Techniques

A cure's effectiveness depends on the enchantress' knowledge, experience and skill in combining and dosing for each illness as well as her *charm techniques*. There are charms against anaemia, drunkenness, jaundice, Saint Anthony's Fire, epilepsy, ugliness, the evil eye, evil thoughts, bitterness, neck-ache, heart beat.

Except the *evil eye* charm, which is done at any time of the day or of the night, especially for children who could not be left to suffer, the perfect time for incantation and for the treatment to be efficient differs depending on the disease. The charms can be performed at New Moon or at Old Moon, in the morning or at sunrise, on an empty or a full stomach. However, treatments are so varied that a complete inventory is impossible. Combinations of healing plants, different aliments and drinks, substances and mineral waters are used.

The mysterious atmosphere, favorable for suggestive psychotherapy, is created by choosing an optimal time for the charms, by the old pentatonic melodic verse, by the temped rhythm and the grave tonality with pianissimo voice, or by the dramatic dialogue with the evil spirit and the disease itself. The charms are usually sung as though battling an enemy in war thus personifying the illness. During this "war", the sick person is rubbed or "drawn." A poultice is applied and the person massaged, treated with fresh or dried herbs or with mixtures of tea, inhalations, ointment, washes, mineral or organic substances. It might follow several stages starting by identifying the disease, determining the name of the one who sent the illness, threatening and cursing him through words, gestures and energetic actions, "pulling out" and scaring away the disease so that it would never come in contact with the sick one by sending it "in the heel of Hell," "in the wolf's head," "in the Black Sea," "over ninety-nine borders," "where the sun never rises," or into "in the stag's horns."

July 7
The Rain Maker (Paparuda)

Paparuda, the goddess invoked by a feminine group with the purpose of releasing rain in the hot summer days, is related to the Indian God, Rudra, master over weather phenomena.

In Romania, Paparuda has various names: "Papaluga," "Paparuga," "Barbaruta," "Dodoluta," "Matahula," or "Pepernie." Initially, the custom was held on a fixed date around the vernal equinox. Later under Christian influence, the holiday was shifted to the third Thursday after Easter; nowadays it is an occasional custom, practiced in the summer in times of drought.

Young Boys as Rainmakers in Dobrita, Gorj County
(AIEF, Nr. 37 846)

In folk beliefs, Paparuda is envisioned as a "tall and slim saint," "a goddess who controls the rain," who "breaks or blows away the clouds," or "a woman who deals with rain."[126] In the Paparuda carol, the ceremonial and the ritual role of the rain goddess is played by a little girl or an unmarried girl, by a boy or a lad or by a pregnant woman. The person, dressed in a specific costume, made out of dwarf elder and common burdock leaves and rarely of other plants, dances around a well or on the shore of a stream, river, or lake. Occasionally the head is decorated with flowers or flower wreaths. In some cases, the chosen person holds a wooden cross.

Admired for her divine procession, Paparuda dances, enjoys herself, and is welcomed with respect in village homes. The ceremony includes three ritual and magical sequences:

- *Birth of the goddess:* A Paparuda group or procession is gathered of pure persons, usually little girls or unmarried young women; an individual who will play the role of the sacred character, Paparuda, is chosen; a mask or the vegetal costume is made out of dwarf elder and common burdock leaves or other plants and put over the naked body; the goddess person is then decorated with flowers or flower wreaths.
- *The goddesses' enjoyment:* The procession walks through the village to pay visits to people's homes and to water wells; the dance by Paparuda is performed to a simple melody sung by the participants who also clap in rhythm. Paparuda and her companions are drenched with water and sometimes with milk or whey before receiving gifts of food, money, and wooden pots. The Paparuda verse invokes the rain through poetical phrases and on occasion invokes practical outcome such as rich crops, good health. Also mentioned are gifts received from the host.
- *Death of the goddess and the funeral rite:* The vegetal mask is taken off, usually at the same place where it was put on and floated on the water; those "dead" ones transported to another world on running water are mourned with Paparuda songs and ritual

---

[126] Fochi, 1976, p. 224.

bathing of the members who formed the group. Gifts are shared and sometimes a funeral feast.

This custom is evidenced in different evolution stages throughout Romania. In some regions during the Twentieth Century it was taken over as money-making entertainment.[127]

July 8
The "Pricup"

The *Pricup* is a mythical figure in the Folk almanac represented by Saint Martyr Procopie in the Christian almanac. His role was to hasten the ripening of cereals which had been sowed in spring (Moldavia) and to protect the crops, particularly the hemp, from hail and whirlpools (Walachia, Oltenia, Transylvania, and Bucovina). If his day is forgotten and not observed, the Pricup can bring scorching heat and drought to the cereals before they ripen.

Pricup is an example of a mixture between pre-Christian and Christian beliefs. According to the Orthodox catechisms for July, Procopie was a real person who lived during Emperor Diocletian's reign and fought against idol-believers. Church stories recount that Pricup was taken to the idols' chief and pulled down all the idols' statues through the power of his faith. Over time Saint Procopie from the Christian Almanac became Pricup in the Folk Almanac, a meteorological mythical representation, an idol who parches and devastates the crops before they ripen.

July 9
The Sun Eclipse

According to ancient Romanian beliefs, eclipses are provoked by werewolves. These are depicted as monsters who ravenously bit the Sun's holy body. When it was devoured, rivers of blood poured from the Sun's body, an apocalyptic scene. Fortunately, the Sun recovered quickly, recomposed from the pieces which fell from the werewolves' mouths.

Werewolves which eat or darken the Moon and the Sun are said to be the third or seventh born children of an unmarried woman and that they live among the clouds or above the clouds. In winter, when werewolves can turn human, they descend over the fields and torment anyone they meet in their way.

---

[127] Ciuceu 1988, p. 110-132.

Eclipses may be caused in other ways. The Sun can be eaten by the Hag of the Woods, it can be brought down from the sky by certain spellbinders, or it can deliberately cover its bright face in order not to see all the bad deeds and sins that people are capable of on Earth.

This dazzling astronomical phenomenon was also interpreted as the expression of God's punishment and as an ill omen sign. Seized by fear, people would make the sign of the cross, genuflect, burn incense and produce loud noises by beating the wooden bell board, ringing bells, hitting old iron objects or metal pails, shooting their guns, snapping their whips and shouting. All this was intended to scare and cast away the werewolves when they were biting the Moon and the Sun. When the eclipse was over, people would burst into joy as both the Sun in the sky and the humans on the Earth were saved from extinction.

July 10
Shearing the Lambs

Shepherds usually live in social groups, made up of ten to twenty people isolated for long periods from their village communities. They manage on their own when confronted by natural threats and cumulated impressive knowledge of meteorology, astronomy, ethno-botany and folk medicine. Shepherds lead a peaceful and lonely life, feeling more closely related to the surrounding nature than to the people living at the foot of the mountain. This changes suddenly at "Santilie" (Saint Elijah) on July 20) when sheep owners and the shepherd's wives climb up to the sheepfold to shear the spring-born lambs.

First Outing,
Bran, Brasov County
(Photo by. D. Dimancescu, 2005)

While lambs were sheared at the sheepfolds in the middle of the shepherd summer, mature sheep and rams were sheared in the village before being taken up to the sheepfolds (during the period between "Sangiorz" and "Armindeni"). This is not only a practical activity but also a long expected occasion for the shepherds to meet their wives and children.

Unlike the sheepfolds in Marginimea Sibiului and in Tara Oltului from the north of the Carpathians where, starting with the Nineteenth century, women came to play a leading role and to be in charge with the work at the sheepfold, in the southern Carpathian regions shepherds are neither allowed to descend to the village nor to be visited by any female before "Santilie." To maintain the prosperity of the herd, they have to stay clean, that is to stay away from women. It is said that "before Santilie holiday, no woman should set foot on any sheep track."

In some areas (Zabala in Covasna County), the young shepherds descend in the village at "Santilie" to accomplish the ritual of asking their beloved girlfriends to take part in the ring dance. On the day preceding that holiday, the young men give their girlfriends presents such as a distaff or a piece of green cheese beautifully shaped as a baby symbolizing their love and marriage intentions.

July 11
Fairs Held in the Mountains

For the last two centuries, under Austro-Hungarian rule, Romanians living in Transylvania were subject to abuse when engaged in traditional practices. Those attending the "Gaina (Hen) Mountain Fair" in the western Carpathians were accused of "selling their daughters like animals."

The inhabitants of the Western Carpathians called "motii", "topii" and "Crisenii"), who worked in the gold mines to enrich mine-owners who slanderered them, kept unchanged their millennial tradition of climbing up their sacred Mount Gaina once a year. That mountain where the fair is held lies at the border between two ancient ethnographic areas: Tara Motilor and Tara Crisurilor inhabited by the "motii" in Vidra de Sus and respectively by the crisenii in Bulzesti.

The celebration, dating to pre-history when people worshipped the goddess protector of the married women, was identified with Artemis, Juno and Diana by archaeologists, and with "Sanziana" and "Dragaica" by folklorists. In time the event acquired new functions. One was to barter. Pots brought by the crisenii were exchanged for wooden pots by the motii. Another was for entertainment and enjoyment. Such fairs, initially a ceremony for invoking the goddess protector of the married women and of the marriage, were also organized in other places such as Halmagiu County (Kiss Fair or Wives' Fair), Teius, Blaj, Recea (Girls' Fairs). To these one could add the famed "Dragaica" Fairs held in southeastern Romania.

Astrological evidence may explain the prehistoric timing of the Girls' Fair on Mount Gaina. The date corresponds to the time when the Hen Constellation (Pleiades) appears in the sky. All the holidays at the summer solstice, including the one held on Mount Gaina, belong to the cultural and historical patrimony of the ancient European civilization dominated by the Mother Goddess. This spiritual goddess brings fertility to cultivated fields, to married women, makes the birds breed and gives fragrance and healing power to the flowers.

July 12
"Caloian"

The doll made in the summer in times of drought, out of clay, straw and twigs and dressed with rags is one of the effigies of the great Neolithic goddess. When she was invoked to bring the rain, she was called Rain, Rain's Midwife, Mother Caloiana, Wandering Mother, Holy Mary, The Fairy or Scaloiana. And when she is begged to stop the rain she became Drought, Mother Draught, Father Sun, Holy Sun, Sântilie. "Caloian" or "Scaloian" are some messengers frequently sent to the worshipped divinity to beg her to release or to "bind" rainfalls:

*We send you, Caloian
High up to the sky.
Go and ask: To open the gates,
To free the rain,
So it falls like rivers,
Dear Caloian,
May rain pour,
Like our tears,
Day and night,
May water fill the ditches,
And make vegetables
And all herbs grow...*

Mourning of the "Caliona," Gropeni, Braila County
(AIEF 972, Nr. 56254)

The ritual scenario of Caloian usually starts on a Tuesday when the doll is made of clay and of other materials and then buried. Two days later, on a Thursday, the funeral ritual continues by digging out the doll which, varying from region to region, is buried again, chopped into pieces, abandoned on the ground or on water by laying it on a wooden board to float, sinking in water or throwing it into a well. And lastly there is the funeral meal when Caloian is sent as a messenger to the divinity that can release or stop the rain. These actions are invoked through ritual sung texts.

The funeral ceremony, reconstructed from ethnographic studies and from from folk texts, consists of several ritual sequences:
- *Forming the group* of young and unmarried girls;
- *Caloian's birth* by making it of clay in most cases; *messenger's terrible death* by a young boy or a young girl;

- *Caloian's burial* in a secret place in a manner similar to the burial of unmarried young people with a priest, a psalm reader, a funeral flag or pole, and laments with lots of tears; then *disinterment* (resurrection) after three days;

- *Caloian is sunk into water,* thrown into a well, or laid on a wooden board to flow on a running water;

- *Funeral feast* with food and drink, which sometimes ends with Caloian's ring dance.

When the messengers consist of pairs, for instance a Caloian and a Caloiana, or Mother Rain and Father Sun, they are sent to the divinity through a funeral ritual by burial or sinking in water. They carry different messages: *the Female* for bringing rain and *the Male* for stopping rain on the earth. The custom is practiced, in its various stages of evolution, throughout Romania. The ceremony once had a fixed date, usually in the third week after Easter, but in recent times it became a sporadic practice, held in spring or in summer, whenever there were long periods of either drought or of rain.

July 13
"Pantelii" - Solomon Hail People

In the Folk Almanac and in the Romanian Pantheon, *Pantelii* on July 13 amd 27 are Saint Ilie's sisters, fearful meteorological figures who set on fire and mercilessly burn the crops during the Oven Month. It is thought that their destructive power could be diminished by various work interdictions after Santilie on July 20.

"Solomonarii" are people who know how to disperse clouds filled with hail wherever they want to. They are faithful believers possessing supernatural powers.

"They have a school where they learn all these."

"They have a book to read from."

"They study in the town or the fortress of Babar."

"Solomon Hail People are God's men and only one out of seven ordinary men can become a Solomonar. They can bring hail to punish the ones who don't respect the holidays or who disobeyed God. The hail is produced in a Dragon's tail; hail falls where the Dragon casts its tail. That is why, no matter how warm summer can be, the Dragon remains cold; the water from the wells without any snakes or frogs in it cannot be cold in the summer. The Solomon Hail Man travels with the Dragon towards east and there, in those countries, he sells bits of the Dragon, which people put by their windows to keep the house cool in their hot climate." (Bucovina, Apuseni Mountains)

July 14
Dough, Archetype of Genesis

Dough, sacred material out of which women make normal and knot-shaped bread, like clay is an archetype of genesis. The growth cycle of wheat, starting with sowed seeds and ending with the harvest, is analogous to man's birth, marriage and death. According to folk belief, the spirit of the wheat lives inside the mother-plant's body until it produces seeds, dries and dies.

The spirit of the wheat which passes on from the dead plant to the seed becomes immortal through its new life-cycles. In the transformation process of the wheat into bread, the old crushing pot, the grinding mill and the mill are treated as sacrifice altars. This why there are spiritual and technical similarities between the making clay-pots and of making bread.

The process liberates the wheat's soul from the seed and the clay's spirit from the earth through cutting, crushing, beating and grinding; adding water to obtain both the dough and the clay; kneading and letting the mixture rise; shaping the faces, forms of pots and knot-shaped bread which bear the names of mythical representations: Archangels, Little Santas, The 44 Martyrs, Little Fir Trees. Because they are brought alive by baking them in the oven, they can be substituted for the divinity and the human being in different magical practices and customs.

In biblical stories, God made the human face out of clay, just like the Neolithic man had made the divinities' bodies out of clay and dough. God animated His creation (the man) by blowing life over it, while the Neolithic woman animated her clay-divinity figurines and pots as well as the dough divinity as bread, knot-shaped bread by baking them in an oven.

July 15
"Ciurica" and Limping "Chiric"

Gods of nature Identified with Dionysus (lft) and Arcanda (rt) from the Getycal Funeral Thesaurus of Agighiol, 4th Cent B.C.
(Photo by George Dumitru)

Ciurica is a fearful mythical representation who gave women the right to punish their husbands in her celebration day on July 15. On this day, people avoided any kind of hitting, fights or misunderstandings in the family so that such misbehavior would not occur over the year.

The memory of this scary patron is kept in some idioms which are used as a threat for misbehaving children: "Calm down, or else Ciurica will come" or "be a good child! Otherwise, you'll be taken by Ciurica." (Walachia, Oltenia)

The fire-bringing holiday from the Folk Almanac Limping *Chiric*, took over the name and celebration date of Saint Martyr Chiric from the Orthodox Almanac on July 15. The Orthodox Catechism of July tells the story of *Chiric* who was born in the time of Diocletian Emperor. He was beaten to death by nonbelievers when he was only three years old. In Folk Almanac lore, Chiric remained lame after he was beaten. But knowing that the divinities with handicaps are very powerful - Limping Philip, Limping Sântoader, Limping Little Fates which cut the thread of life while foretelling the fate of a child at birth, Limping Chiric and others, he would be feared and respected through different work interdictions. (Southern Nistor Valley)

July 16
Summer Circovi (Midsummer)

Summer Circovi is a three-day holiday in the middle of July, on 15-17 or 16-18, dedicated to those evil forces that bring neuro-psychical diseases ("seized by Circovi" or "beaten by Circovi"), hail on the crops, fires in the households, wolves and other wild animals into the cattle herd. During these days, severe work interdictions are established with gathering wormwood and motherwort stalks for making brooms as the only permitted activity.

Summer Circovi are placed in the middle of the pastoral summer (Sangiorz-Samedru), in the same way as their brothers, Winter Circovi on January 16-18, are placed in the middle of the pastoral winter (Samedru-Sangiorz).

July 17
Pastoral Nedeia Feasts

The *Pastoral Nedeia Feasts*, held in Carpathian Mountain areas, are related to the celebration of a pre-Christian holiday dedicated to the god of fire and sun.

After the Carpato-Danubian people were Chritsianized, they made this holiday similar with Saint Ilie on July 20 commonly referred to as "Sântilie." Although the ancient name of the god was lost, people continued to observe its cult on mountains heights to be closer to the sky and the sun.

Nedeia or Sântilie is first identified in documents dated to the year 1373.[128] These mountain feasts certainly included complex ceremonies dedicated to the sun and the fire and later assimilated the exchange of products. In some cases, these celebrations descended to the villages at the foot of the mountain, but the old places where they originally held are easy to identify after their Carpathian toponomy: Nedeia Feasts, Sântilia, Little Nedeia Feasts.

Irrespective of what they were called, Sântilia or Nedeia Feasts, they functioned as fairs where shepherds products were sold, where all necessary products for the sheepfold were brought, but also where youngsters' parties were held.

The historical significance of the pastoral "Nedeia Feasts" is connected to their old origin and their role in establishing economic, matrimonial and cultural connections between Romanians from the southern Walachian and northern Transylvanian sides of the Carpathians. The Nedeia Feasts had no borders. Some feasts were even called "fairs in two counties" or, in Vrancea Mountains "fairs in three counties" which gathered people from Moldavia, Transylvania and Walachia.[129]

July 18
A Miner's Folk Tale

There is a miner folk tale that a "long time ago, this place was inhabited by fairies. But they died, one by one, and so did people's faith. The ones still alive hide in dark places where no man has set foot. They dance on the mountain peaks without stopping till dawn when their fear of people scatters them. One night, a fairy fell in a mine pit while spinning in her dance. Her sisters, thinking she had died, mourned her and then forgot about her. But the fairy had not died. She was found by a miner who told her:

"I'd like to take you home. But you are too beautiful to stay in my poor hut. What am I to do with you?"

In answer he devised an idea. He would smear her with soot so that nobody would recognize her when taken her outside the mine. The Fairy accepted. After getting out of the mine, the miner asked her:

"Now where do I take you?"

"Wait until day becomes night and take me to my sisters."

---

[128] Cornea, 1937, p. 73.

[129] Cornea, 1937, p. 48.

When they reached the heights of the mountains, the miner left her alone to wait for her sisters. But the fairies not recognizing her killed her with stones and rocks. Only afterwards realizing that she was their sister, the fairies were deeply grieved. They mourned over her death day and night and they finally decided to bury her. They took her to the Jiu River to wash her coal off. Ever since, they have kept on washing her and crying over her."[130]

July 19
Macrina - Santilie Forefathers

Macrina, who appears in the Folk Almanac as the protecting goddess of dead children's souls, took over the name and celebration date of Saint Martyrs Macrina from the Orthodox Almanac on July 19. On this day, mothers distribute green wormwood brooms, chicken, boiled maize and flowers as alms. From wormwood stalks they make large wreaths through which their children passed in order to protect them from diseases. The houses and the courtyards were swept with the wormwood brooms kept in the house attic. (Oltenia, Walachia)

Santilie Forefathers is a tradition held mainly for the offerings of fruit, cracknels, cooked food accompanied by lighted candle given in memory of the dead. This done on the day or the eve of Santilie. It is believed that on that day, the souls of the dead, especially those of children, would return to their homes to receive good food from the living ones. The family commemorating dead children invites little girls and boys to their home, and, in their garden, they shake apples off a tree from which nobody had eaten in that year, and giave children apples to eat. They clean tombs in the cemetery and along with other rituals give away pots filled with food or water.

July 20
Santilie

Santilie, God of Sun and Fire
(Popa-Lisseanu, 1928)

Santilie, the god of Fire and of the sun in the Romanian Pantheon is

---

[130] Soit, 1974, p. 58.

identified with Helios from the Greek mythology and with Gebeleisis from the Geto-Dacian mythology. Under the influence of Christianity, Sântilie took over the name and celebration date from Saint Ilie on this day. At Santilie, in the middle of the pastoral summer, the well known Nedeia and Santilia Fairs were organized. Santilie, a solar and meteorological divinity, provokes fires in hot summers, thunder and lightning during the storm; he can stop or releases rain decides where and when to drop hail.

As a profane character, Santilie appears in the Folk customs as a soldier, a hunter, a farmer, a cattle-man or as a cattle-tradesman. Being lured and deceived by the Devil, Santilie murders one or more members of his family (father, mother, son, daughter or sister). He expiates sins in different ways. God forgives him, places him among the Saints and raises him to Heaven in a carriage with fire-wheels, drawn by two or four white winged horses.

In the sky, the Saint rushes through the clouds, he thunders, roars, rattles, rumbles, and peals); he sends lightening and beats devils with the fire-whip. Scared, the devils hide in trees, under overhanging eaves, in church spires and even inside some animals - especially cats and dogs. Willing to catch all of them, Santilie strikes with lightning even trees, people, cattle and churches where the devils hide.

The symbols which define Santilie as an authentic solar god are the carriage with fire-wheels and winged horses. There are also his whip and fire arrows, thunder and lightning with which to light up a cloudy sky.

The divinities which bring scorching heat and fire in the Oven Month, many of them being Sântilie's sisters (Parliile, Panteliile), his brothers (Ilie Palie, Pantelimon) or simple coachmen at his heavenly carriage (Foca), are subordinated to him.

July 21
The Church Patron

The *Church Patron* takes over and maintains the name of a Saint or of a Christian mystery when the construction of a worship building, a church or a monastery is finished. The activities of the people living in an area are thought to be protected by that saint. In many cases, the church patron name also becomes the name of the settlement where a fair is held. After holding the ceremony dedicated to the cult of the saint in church and after commemorating the dead in the graveyard, the saint patron is honored with food and drink and with joy in the households. Families, or an entire village community, celebrates in the churchyard or around the church, in parts of their land usually in mountain areas. Over time, Church Patrons have preserved the spiritual and material cohesion of people in both villages and larger regions.

Church Patron's Days were favorable occasions for lots of people to meet and to get to know each other especially in view of marriage, to have fun and enjoy themselves, to apologize for all the harm they have done to each other during the year, to make agreements and to exchange the needed products. These festive occasions had different names: prayer, church patron, fair, nedeie-fair.

July 22
The Dittany - Flower of Fire

The *dittany*, a plant of the Rutaceae family with white flowers and a penetrating smell, grows wild in arid places, near forests and bushes. Enchantresses invoke it to scare away the "Iele" and to prevent harm they bring to people.

The dittany is also called the flower of fire because the oil released in the hot summer days "takes fire" by forming a bright halo around the bloom. People suffering from weakness and dizziness bathe in water with dittany. The plant is also used for curing epilepsy in the form of a brandy and yeast mixture.

To determine whether the sick person will get well or not a magic practice is carried out. A person is taken on an important summer holiday to a field, in a place where dittany grew, and required to sleep there for a night. In Banat on the night of Todurusale, when it was believed that "Iele" break the top of the dittany plant, leaving it without smell and healing powers, people "seized by Iele" (crippled) and the ones suffering from epilepsy, sleep in places where the miraculous plant grows. In Oltenia, the sick ones are transported in carriages to the place where dittany grows on the eve of holidays like Saint George, Midsummer's Day or Ascension. They are laid on the ground in the order of their arrival, and various offerings of bread, salt, a pot with vegetables and one filled with water are put beside the dittany root to help them be cured. The next morning, a sick person's condition is foretold from the signs left by dittany plants placed in a pot of water.

The ritual meal custom takes place at a table filled with knot shaped bread, brandy, clay-pots and frankincense, where the enchantress invokes the dittany to change the Fate's decisions taken at the sick man's birth.[131]

---

[131] Nitu, 1999, p. 91-93.

July 23
"Oparlia" and "Foca"

Oparlia is the mythical representation in the Romanian Pantheon which can provoke fires and burn marks on people's bodies if her day wasn't respected and observed on July 23. In Moldavia and Dobrogea, Oparlia was called "Foca." She punishes people for the same reason with fires, scorching sun heat and hail.

The goddess took over the names of the Saints: Foca Saint Martyr, Foca the Gardener and another Foca who lived during the time of Emperor Traian. In the time of the Emperor Diocletian, know in history as a great Christian prosecutor, Saint Foca was also respected as a patron of sailors.

The names itself of "Foca" implies fires simply through its meaning since in Romanian "foc" means "fire." (Moldavia, Dobrogea)

July 24
From the Ring Dance to the Disco

The Boreal Crown (Top) Artifact from Frumusica, Bodesti, Neamt County, First Half of IVth Millennium B.C., and Ring Dance (Bttm) from Mehedinti (end of IInd Millennium A.D.

Sunday feasts take place on days not designated as fasting days or other special holidays. They are attended by the entire community organized by age, sex and social status. This is a time for the *ring dance* in Moldavia, Walachia, Dobrogea and *dance* in Transylvania, Maramures, Crisana and Banat.

The main activity is the ring dance, an imposing dance in which participants with straight backs hold hands forming a circle, a symbol of perfection. The dance is a slow one, creating a peaceful mood in contrast to other Romanian traditional dances that are quicker (Sârba, Brâul) and even stormy (Ciuleandra, "Calus" Dance). Although the ring dance bears different names and has various local and regional variants, it is an unique dance in terms of choreography. A ritual of great complexity, it is performed on major calendar holidays including Easter, Christmas, Santilie, and Nedeie.

Led by young men of the village, an important function of the ring-dance is the asking young girls to take part. This recognizes the fact that the girls are prepared to be asked in marriage and that from that moment they belonged to a new social group. By the way in which the young men organize the ring dance - choosing and paying the fiddlers, selecting and arranging the place for the dance, ensuring that order, discipline and the local rules were observed - they gain or lose the appreciation of other age and gender groups of people in the community.

Evidence of the ring dance goes back more than 5,000 years ago in the Carpathian area. In Bodesti Village (Neamt County) Cucuteni area, a group of four anthropomorphic clay-figurines dancing a ring dance on a stand were discovered by archaeologists who called it Ring Dance from Frumusica.

The dance had a ritual function in customs belonging to the Almanac cycle (Perinita, Young Men's Dance, "Calus" Dance) and in those belonging to the family cycle (Wedding Ring Dance, Bride's Ring Dance, Ring Dance given as Alms, The Dead's Ring Dance), a festive function (Union Ring Dance) and an entertaining function (Party-Ring Dance, Sunday Ring Dance and Ring Dance at various holidays over the year). Unfortunately today the ring dance is replaced even in the villages by discos, which no longer play the traditional role and thus losing the meaning of old functions.

July 25
Rites of Integrating Each Sex Into Its Own Community

Growing up in a traditional society means creating strong personalities, male and female, with distinct sexual characteristics. Beyond the sexual and biological differences between men and women allowing for reproduction other differences are psychological, educational and social ones. People know intuitively the importance to the community of not raising boys in a feminine manner or girls in a masculine manner. Any effeminate traits in young men meant diminished changes for marriage. From birth boys and girls are differentiated by names, clothes, specific toys and games, also by sex confirmation ceremonies (cutting the forelock for boys and breaking the flat bread for girls). Girls usually engage in household activities, whereas boys are taught to use tools for fixing things in and outside the house. Homosexuality is never mentioned in the traditional village.

July 26
"Santilie" Ring Dance

Santilie ring dance is a prenuptial custom performed during the middle of the shepherd summer, when the shepherds descended from the mountains "to ask their beloved girlfriends to dance the ring dance." For a girl, being introduced to and participating in the ring dance in front of the entire village community, represents a compulsory step prior to possibly being asked into marriage. The girls not introduced to the dance can only watch and have to wait one more year. In farming villages, introducing girls to the ring dance usually takes place in spring on the Second Easter Day.

One day before the Santilie Ring Dance, shepherds offer gifts to their girlfriends, such as a distaff carved during their lonely time up in the mountain when they long for their girlfriends (Voinesti, Covasna County), or a piece of green cheese, beautifully shaped as a baby in a special mould (Moinesti, Covasna County), as well as other love tokens and symbols of their marriage intentions.

In older times, the dance included ritual symbolism related to fertility of the fields, to earning one's living by practicing various occupations, to resolving certain deals between the dead and the living ones. Among these, the most well preserved customs were those connected with the funeral rite, especially the game given away as alms in the areas outside the Carpathians, forty days after a funeral.

July 27
"Rudari" Gypsies Coupling

In Campulung Muscel, the last day of the "Santilie" Fair called Pantelimon or *Rudari Gypsies Coupling*, is dedicated to the occasion for the "Rudari" gypsies, living in the villages on northern and southern sides of the Middle Carpathians in Arges, Dâmbovita, Brasov and Sibiu counties, to meet and to get married. The "Rudari" arrived in the morning or in the evening of July 27; girls who are supposed to get married put on Romanian folk dress and young people meet and had fun together during the day of July 27. That night they hide in the woods to couple somewhere on the "Gruiului" Hill in Campulung. When morning comes the marriages are acknowledged by the larger Rudari community in the square of the old part of the town. There they dance the "braul" to the sound of flute music so that everyone can see who got married to whom. On the same occasion, divorces are settled. Married spouses who had had arguments during that year and decided to split go away in the company of other partners during Pantelimon night.

"Rudari" Girls (Gypsy) at the Coupling Fair
(AIEF, Photo by I. Ghinoiu, 1973, Nr. 22 281)

As late as the 1970's for the Rudari, official marriages registered at the authorities or the religious ones in church were less important than the traditional coupling custom on Pantelimon Day. The girls and their mothers, however, would have certainly preferred an official marriage which would have regulated the legal status of the couples' future children. Instead, they had to obey a severe, unwritten law and could only comfort themselves thinking: "That's the custom!"

Pantelimon or Pintilie the Traveler, Santilie's brother, a mythical representation whose day of celebration is July 27, is an important landmark in the almanac time register. It was believed that, from that day on, the planets in the sky started to travel on their orbits towards autumn and winter, that the migratory birds, mainly the storks, were gathering in flocks, preparing for the journey to the warm countries, and that the stag stopped bathing in the river, which was the sign of the water becoming cold. (Moldavia)

July 28
The Living Fire

Lighting the Living Fire,
Bucovina Mountains
(Tiberius Moraru, 1935)

When the sheep are driven up to the sheepfolds in the mountains, a fire is first set alight by rubbing two dried sticks. Called *The Living Fire*, it is kept lit till "Santilie" when the sheep descend from high grazing pastures.

It is thought that by keeping the fire lit, it could destroy all evil spirits. It could scare away witches around the sheepfold who were responsible for the many calamities cast upon people, cattle and crops such as diseases, hail, damage done to the cattle herds by wild animals and insects, obstacles against getting married.

Destined to purify the space through its light, its heat and its smoke, the living fire lit at the beginning of the pastoral season is different from other ritual fires at New Year, Easter Shrovetide, Forty-Four Martyrs, Great Thursday, Midsummer's Day, and other times. This difference is recognized in the prehistoric rubbing method of making it and its long period of continuous burning. There are many arguments, too, demonstrating that it is a ritual fire and not an ordinary one. It is lit only by men, usually by unmarried virgin youngsters, at fixed dates when the pastoral season starts, or when the sheep are taken to the sheep folds; the shepherds hop over the fire and sometimes pass the animals through its smoke while magical sayings are uttered.[132]

July 29
Devil's Inventions

According to folk beliefs, the Devil, an ingenious and crafty creature, invented lots of things, plants and animals on Earth by mistake or by playing, by his own will or at his Brother's (God) suggestion

Being God's brother, at the beginning he contributed to the making of the Earth and to the creation of the World. However, though powerful he is less intelligent than God. His creations remain unfinished and he doesn't know how to use them or sees them only for destructive purposes. He builds a house without windows or doors; he invents the sieve for carrying water with it: he tries hard to stick both of his feet in one boot. His creations are often taken over by God who knows what to do with them by creating a real house, a pot, a pair of boots. Competing with each other, the two gods create animals, plants and objects on Earth. The Devil creates the goat; God creates the sheep. The Devil creates the pub, God the Church. Devil invents tobacco and plum brandy while God invents frankincense and wine. All the important beings on earth have their origins attributed to the Devil. But all his faulty creations are positively modified or fixed by God.

---

[132] Muslea, 1972, p. 389-396.

As the Romanian philosopher Lucian Blaga once noted: "The world and all its living creatures are both cooperating and competing with each other. However, the collaboration of the two is indeed spoiled and undermined by the Devil's intuitions. Even so, God's magic powers, His intentions and actions are less vindictive and more oriented towards Good. The Devil ambitiously and enviously wishes to do something himself, but he only manages to mimic in a bad manner the good deeds made by God."

July 30
Guide Marks for Measuring Daytime

Daytime is indicated by two clocks - a cosmic one by the sun's position in the sky, and a biologic need for daily meals. The *Lance in the Sky* is a sub-unit for spatially estimating the daytime the equivalent of about half an hour. A summer day is 18 lances long: nine from sunrise till noon (at dawn – one lance, early midday – three lances, and so on) and nine from noon till sunset. The daily units for time are:

- *Dawn*, the morning moment for determining time, synonymous with daybreak and early in the morning. Dawn lasts from Sunrise to Early Midday when the Sun has risen as high as one lance up in the sky;
- *Sunrise* marks the beginning of the day and the appearance of the Sun at the horizon;
- *Early Midday*, synonymous with Little Noon, indicates the time between 8 and 9 hours during the summer. At Early Midday the Sun has risen as high as the lances in the sky, which represents one third of its ascent;
- *Great Noon*, synonymous with Under-Noon, marks approximately 11 o'clock;
- *Noon*, a moment when the sun reaches its highest point at 12 o'clock, is synonymous with Good Noon, Noon at the Cross, the Crossing in the Sky. According to the folk tradition, at noon the Sun ends its ascent rests for a moment, and after drinking a glass of wine and eating a piece of communion bread, it starts its descent. Like the Sun, the peasant who tills the land must also stop working and rest.
- *Afternoon*, synonymous with Small Dinner, represents 14 to 15 hours;
- *Vesper Bell* is determined by the Sun approaching the horizon, when the vesper bell sounds at the church and people stop working in the field.
- *Sunset* marks the time when the Sun goes down beyond the horizon and is synonymous with the sinking of the Sun.

July 31
The Goat's Horn
(Beliefs About Driving Hail Away)

The Capricorn on the Horoscope from the Sucevita Monastery (Prut, 1972)

The Goat's Horn is a meteorological personification of the Capricorn constellation. If thunder and lightning comes from the direction people normally see the Goat's Horn Constellation in the sky, then rain will certainly come. People make the sign of the cross and pray that the rain will be clean and without storms. (Walachia, Oltenia, Moldavia)

AUGUST

"GUSTAR"

TASTING MONTH

1	Bear's Mating Day
2	Saint Mary Fasting Time
3	Prehistoric Origin of Carrying Heavy Things on the Head
4	All Roads Lead to Rome
5	Transport by Rolling and Dragging
6	Transfiguration Forefathers
7	Gathering and Washing Laundry in the River
8.	The Yoke and the Knapsack
9	Wearing the Cap, the Knapsack and the Hood
10	The Village Furrow
11	The Shape and the Size of the Ancient Village
12	Memorizing the Documents of Oral History
13	Span Between the Celebrations
14	Virgin Mary in the Folk Almanac
15	Great Virgin Mary
16	Hag of the Woods
17	Mother of the Fields and Devil's Mother
18	Mother "Gaia" (Jackdaw)
19	Playing Mother Gaia
20	The Dwarf Elder, A Phytomorphic Divinity
21	The Man and the Pot
22	The Earth, Our Mother
23	"Valva", A Spirit of the Earth
24	Birth and Being Driven Out of the Intra-Uterine Heaven
25	Beliefs About the Sun
26	The Good Moment
27	Techniques for Hindering Childbirth
28	From the Fates' Table to the Table of Silence
29	The Midwife
30	The Fates – Goddesses of Destiny
31	The Baby's House

August

is the sixth month in the Roman Almanac and the eighth in the Julian and Gregorian almanacs. Since 8 B.C., it carries the name of the Emperor Augustus, when the 6th month of the year (sextilis) became the 8th month. In the Romanian language, August was regionally called: August, Augustru, Maselariu, Tasting Month (the ritual of grape tasting) or Harvest Month.

August has a smaller number of holidays - Day of the Bear, Macavei, Holy Mary's Death, Autumn Saint John - because it is a period of the year when harvesting, maintaining the crops, second mowing of hay arm work have to be carried out rapidly and on time.

August 1
Bear's Mating Day

This day is commonly called Macavei or *Bear's Mating Day*. On Romanian territory, the bears mate at the end of summer and beginning of autumn, a time when they cause a lot of damage to the sheep herds, the orchards and the bee gardens. In Tara Hategului area, people put offerings in the bear's way, usually a veal-chop and they would loudly say to it: "Here you are, Bear!"

Father Martin, an important god of the Carpathian Pantheon is also celebrated at Winter Martin's Day (1-3rd February) when the bear brings forth, on Bear's Day (2nd February) and on Bear's Saturday (one week before Palm Sunday Forefathers).

Bear (Photo by Christian Charisius)

In folk customs, the bear was considered much more useful than harmful. At a child's birth, it influences the Fates positively; babies smeared with bear grease grew healthy and fit (a practice still known to occur in recent times); the child who suffered from *scare-disease* could get cured if he was smoked with burnt bear fur. And men who are literally *walked over by the bear* in springtime are cured of back-aches in summer. At people's funerals during death watch nights and on New Year, fantastic spirits hidden under bear masks appear. Bear-teeth are often worn as talismans.

Over time immemorial, the bear has been perceived as an ordinary man, either a miller or a shepherd in his village. In some tales, the bear has human feelings and behavior. He loves a woman whom he kidnaps and takes to his home in the village; he is intelligent; he builds a shelter for the winter (den); he foretells warm or cold weather. But, there is one thing that he cannot do, namely to make fire.[133]

August 1 is dedicated also to Saint Martyr Macabei who was caught by the pagans and burned alive in an oven. On this day people sprinkle their gardens and orchards with consecrated water. They hallow some wheat ears with their hands, mixing the grains with all the seeds which were going to be sown in autumn. They remove honey from the hives to be used in folk medicine practices and gather healing plants. (Oltenia)

---

[133] Bârlea, 1976, p. 422-426.

August 2
Saint Mary Fasting Time

The Holy Virgin Mary's holiday preceded by one of the great fasting periods of the year, starts on August 1, at Bears' Mating Day, and ends on August 15, on Saint Mary's Death. At Transfiguration on August 6, the most important holiday of this fasting period, people are allowed to eat fish. The fruit and vegetable abundance, from the end of the summer to the beginning of autumn, make it easier to keep the fast of Saint Mary. It is also said that this fast period was taken out of the Easter Lent period. While four fasting periods which are followed over the year (Advent, Lent, St. Peter's Fast and St. Mary's Fast), people also for marrying girls, for healing certain diseases.

During these periods interdictions are more severe, the so-called "black (total) fastings." Black fasting, which meant total restraint from food, one day per week in seven weeks running, was kept for catching and punishing bad people or thieves. The person who keeps the black fasting, usually a "forgiven woman" referring to one after menopause, unmarried or widowed, isolates herself and spends some time in a state of physical and spiritual purity. (Northern Moldavia, Bucovina) Black fasting is sometimes kept on Wednesdays or Fridays for the family's health and prosperity. (Walachia, Oltenia)

August 3
Prehistoric Origin of Carrying Heavy Things on the Head

Transporting pots with food and with water on the head is an ancient practice, especially for women. This custom drew Ovid's attention who, in referrence to Geto-Dacian women's occupations, wrote: *"Femina pro lama cerialia murtera / Suppositoque graven vertice portat frangit aquam"* ("instead of weaving wool threads, the Dacian women were weaving mostly hemp and flax yarn, they were crushing the grains and they carried the pots with water on their heads").[134] After two millennia, Romanian women, particularly the ones from the south-western part of the country, use the same technique as their ancestors, in special situations. With their child or the water pot on their heads, walking straight and looking forwards, these women look like statues, their demeanor a reminder of that of their distant predecessors

---

[134] Ion Cornea, 1940, p. 155.

August 4
Therapeutic Burial

This is a magical practice of healing by symbolic death and rebirth of the sick person. In the case of a very young ill child, he or she is put into a hole dug into the ground and removed through a small tunnel connected to an adjacent hole. On such occasions, the name of the symbolically dead child is changed into a new one. The preferred new name is usually *Bear* or *Wolf* in order to scare away death or disease. As a result these names are frequently found in Romanian anthroponomy thereby confirming the widespread use of this practice.

August 5
Transport by Rolling and Dragging

Transporting weights by dragging is older than carrying them on the back or on the head. In order to do that, people did not need a path or a road. Certain activities like forestry could not be accomplished without using this means of transport. In the mountain areas, people still use a dragging device quickly improvised of tree branches, transporting hay in bumpy areas. In previous centuries and millennia, man took full advantage of dragging because the object that is dragged becomes itself a means of transport and, because when descending gravity provides an added advantage.

Photo by J. Berman (1930s)

Transporting hay during 1930s and 2005,
Bran, Brasoc County
Photo by D. Dimancescu (2005)

A technique similar to dragging is rolling or sliding. Rolling was used by ancient mountain people as an efficient way of fighting and protection technique against enemies. In the *Painted Chronicle From Vienna*, (Chronicon Pictum Vindobonese), a Latin manuscript from 1358 containing important details related to the founding of Walachia by *Basarab the First* and to his fight for independence, Romanian warriors appear fighting against the Hungarian army, by rolling rocks down steep mountain slopes. The resulting victory obtained against king Carol Robert of Anjou in the fall of 1330 established once and for all the independence of Walachia.[135]

Dragging is used on grazing fields in the summer time and on the mountain paths and on snow in the winter time when hay is transported from the hilltop hayfield to households in the village.

Dragging manure, Slavei (AIEF by R. Vuia, Nr. 16)

Hay Sled, Apuseni Mountains (AIEF by R. Vulcanescu, Nr. 6 662)

August 6
Transfiguration

The holiday in the Orthodox Almanac on August 6, *Transfiguration* (or "*Probejenia*"), marks the line between summer and autumn in the Folk Almanac.

In some regions, people believe that on transfiguration day storks and other migratory birds start their journey south. From that day on, the leaves of the trees in the wood start changing their colors, the grass stops growing, the waters cool and are "spoiled" by the stag; the snakes, lizards, salamanders, insects hide in preparation for hibernating. The custom says that people are no longer allowed to bathe in the rivers or to kill a snake which gets in their way.

But, on transfiguration day, people are allowed to eat fish and grapes as the holiday occurs during the *Virgin Mary Fasting* period. On this

---

[135] Maria Bocse, 1973, p. 378.

day, healing plants and fruit are gathered: hedge water hyssop, lovage, garlic, chamomile and bottle gourd flowers, peanuts and plums.

As with other borderline moments of the almanac, practices for commemorating the dead are also carried out. Alms of grapes, grapes must and honey combs offered on this day are called *Transfiguration Forefathers* during which star gazers make observations and astronomical anticipations. (Walachia, Oltenia, Moldavia, Bucovina) Grapes, consecrated in church, are called Tutova or "grapes flat cake" in some localities of Moldavia. Tasting the first grape was ritualized along with the expression: "New grapes in old mouth." (Moldavia and Bucovina) This ritual of tasting the grapes as well as other fruit on Transfiguration Forefathers' day explains why August received the name of Tasting Month. (Central Walachia, Western Oltenia)

August 7
Gathering and Washing Laundry in the River

Washing in the River, Campului, Hunedoara County
(AIEF by R. Vuia, 1957)

People can bathe in rivers or lakes only during a well established period marked in the Folk Almanac. It starts at Sangiorz on April 23 and closes at Transfiguration on August 6. During this 105-day period women can wash laundry and sheep wool. The reason, it is said, is the waters are "spoiled by the stag which relieves itself in the river," but after Transfiguration time the waters start cooling and the bear also stops bathing in certain places. (Moldavia, Walachia, Oltenia and Banat)

This does not pertain to unused water kept for ritual bathings practiced in a family's life-cycle: bathing a baby after birth and baptism, child-wife bathing, or dead man's bathing. This applies, also, and in the almanac cycle for the girls' and wives' bathing at Sântoader, bathing in the flowery meadows at Midsummer. At the same time, Romanians believe in the value of consecrated water; of foul water in deserted wells, of healing water locally called 'stinking water' due to its strong mineral contents, and of life-giving water. The life-giving water is said to be found at the end of the Earth, in places where no man has set foot and the one who succeeds in getting there and drinking from it, remains forever young.

August 8
The Yoke and the Knapsack

Prehistoric man discovered balance when using *the yoke* on which to hang loads at both ends of a stick. In Oltenia, the yoke is frequently used for carrying water pails. And still at the beginning of the Twentieth century peasants in the capital-city area of Bucharest transported milk and dairy products on the streets and to the markets of the town with the same yoke held on the shoulders.

The same system of balancing the loads is used in the case of *the knapsacks*, a kind of double sacks. The importance of the knapsack for traditional and contemporary way of transporting is so great that it is a compulsory component of the traditional dress in some regions of the country.

Similar to other items of clothing some knapsacks are worn on holidays/celebration, some at fairs and other in working days. The traditional knapsacks are made of woven wool and, rarely of hemp. The decoration consisting of alternating two black-white or white-grey stripes, is one of the first chromatic patterns used by man.

Another ingenious and practical peasant transport devices is *crosnia*, brushwood carried on people's backs, wooden crooks or sacks hung around the neck.

August 9
Wearing the Cap, the Knapsack and the Hood

By long-held tradition men have to wear a cap between Virgin Mary's Death on August 15 and Sangiorz on April 23, and a hat between Sangiorz and Virgin Mary's Death a custom that is respected everywhere in Romania. The ones who forgot to change the cap with the hat at Virgin Mary's Death are reminded to do so with the traditional expression: "Saint Mary is here, forget about the hat!"

Young Shepherd in the Valcan Mountains
(AIEF by R. Vuia, 1957)

The knapsack, a symbol of the traveler, is still worn by people in Maramures and used as ritual object in some funeral customs. Not many decades ago, a woman was rarely seen leaving her house without the woolen knapsack hung around her neck or over her shoulder. It is likely that modern purses have their origin in transporting things with a knapsack.

The "Motii" Romanians living in the western Carpathians sowed their small fields with wheat and corn seeds in their knapsacks, and shepherds never left the sheep fold without carrying their knapsack full of food.

Women had an additional reason to use the knapsack. When in the fields watching or gathering cattle, they needed to have their hands free to spin, to knit socks or other clothes, or to carry their children. In many cases, they were seen with their aprons tied to their waists, which created a comfortable and efficient means of carrying things called the apron tail.

Other pieces of the Romanian traditional dress gained new functions. The *hood-coats*, which shepherds used to cover their heads and their backs when it was raining, were also served for carrying food or bedding. The hood-coats which were long-haired on the outside, so that the water would fall easily off them when it was raining, were boiled in 'poisonous' water after being woven, to protect those who wore them from insects.

August 10

The Village Furrow

Drawing a furrow around the precincts of the village was a magic practice used to symbolically protect the village or larger settlement. Traditionally, the furrow separated villages and even the Romanian provinces Moldavia and Walachia, until their union in 1859.

An ancient Roman legend says that "the first thing that the glorious founder of Rome, Romulus, did was to draw a furrow around the Palatinum. The earth that was dug out symbolizing the wall of the fortress, the furrow was the ditch and in the place of the gate, a plough in upright position created a free passage towards the exterior." Romulus' twin brother, Remus, ridiculing the wall and the ditch hopped over them in one go, and this is the reason why his brother killed him cursing: "Anybody who dares pass over my wall will die!"[136] The custom of drawing a furrow as a border between villages, which could not be trespassed without serious consequences, has been kept till our days.

The furrow symbol persisted in the Carpato-Danubian area due to the two ground-hills built by the Romans, and called "Novac's Furrow" or "Trajan's Furrow" by the Romanians.

---

[136] Grimal, 1973, p. 16.

August 11
The Shape and the Size of the Ancient Village

Similar to the founding of the precincts of the village, propertied lands around it were chosen following established rituals. The main concern of the founders was choosing a productive territory large enough for satisfying their need for food and a surface which could be tilled by the villagers.

Historic documents from 1411 say: "... and the land of that deserted place shall be as large as a village needs for its living - year 1502;" "... and the land of this village shall be large enough for 20 houses to use for all their needs", "... enough land for a village to live on with sufficient food and with 40 houses."[137]

The size of the property was equal to the area which a man could walk round in a day and a night going on foot or riding. An interesting spiritual practice onbserved in Oltenia was beating of the wooden church board in the middle of the village and extending property limits up to the places where the divine sound of this prehistoric instrument could no longer be heard.

One can infer from this that, assuming a flat georgaphy, the ancient shape marking the limits among villages was generally round, in accordance with the concentric sound-wave propagation. This is reflected in the folk verse "the little round village/ I can go round it in no time!"

August 12
Memorizing the Documents of Oral History

Once land boundaries were determined, anyone who tried to trespass or to change the boundaries was harshly punished. The boundary had to preserve its unique value, namely marking the limits of the village area, distinct from everything else situated outside it. People thought that plague, death, "Iele" and "strigoi" (ghosts) haunted anything beyond. Village boundaries were considered to be totally unfit for sleeping or building houses, and that was where criminals, people who got drowned and those who had taken their lives were buried. But as the population grew, the boundaries became the most disputed and regulated ones from a legal point of view.

Among the old practices for determining and for recognizing boundaries, some of them also confirmed by historical documents, are oath taking practices, such as: "with furrow earth on the head ", "by hit-

---

[137] Ghinoiu, 2004, p. 99.

ting the head on the stones", or by "pulling the hair".

Crucifix at the Entrance of Ulm Village, Hunedoara County (R. Isfanoni, 2004)

In one special day of the year, the old people of the village would take a young 7-8 year old boy and walk with him on the boundary line passing from one sign to another. When they reached the key-point of the boundary, called "the joint", they would beat the child really hard so that he should remember everything he had seen and that he should bear testimony, when old, in case any misunderstanding among the neighbors ever arise.

In a society based on oral communication, in which people could not read or write, the custom of beating children, which nowadays is condemned, was thought to necessary and useful. Punishing children for a thing which they forgot to do at a given moment, was sometimes called "giving them a mother's drubbing." An old man from Merei, Buzau County recounts that this method was practiced by some landowners (boyars) who "would pick up a man and beat him on the boundary so that people should know how wide the limits of his land were."[138]

August 13

Between Two Virgin Mary's Days

The draughty period of the year, though favorable for sowing wheat, rye and barley, the time-span between the celebration of Death of Virgin Mary on August 15, and celebrating the Birth of Virgin Mary on September 8, is called *Between Two Virgin Mary's Days* in the Folk Almanac.

After repeated trial and error over the millennia, Romanians determined the most suitable periods for sowing cereal plants. This transmitted from generation to generation by the saying: "The wheat must be sowed in autumn in dusty soil, and in spring in the muddy soil." Under specific climatic conditions, the *autumn-wheat* had to be sown between the two Virgin Mary's Days, a period lacking rain, while the *spring-wheat* had to sown in March, when the snow is almost melted and the soil very humid.

---

[138] Ghinoiu, 1979, p. 204.

August 14
Virgin Mary in the Folk Almanac

In the time passage from summer to autumn, the Folk Almanac keeps the memory of the death and birth of ancient Mother Goddess, over which the Church established the celebration of the Death and the Birth of *Virgin Mary*.

By reversing the days which begin and end the Virgin's life - first she dies on August 15 and then she is born on September 8 - the Christian church actually absorbed the prehistoric model in which the old mythical representation dies first and bearing the adopted name of Great Virgin Mary and then is born which is became Little Virgin Mary.

Although the religious verse encourages people to rejoice at the birth of Holy Mary on September 8 by hailing "let the trumpets of faith sound!" or "Joachim is happy and Ann celebrates; may everybody dance, David rejoice...,"[139] Romanians are more inclined to celebrate Virgin Mary's Death on August 15.

Virgin Mary is identified in the Romanian Pantheon under various names: Great and Little Virgin Mary and Great Holly Mary and Little Holy Mary.

The importance of Great Virgin Mary's Day for the almanac is characterized by the two-weeks of fasting (1-14 August) prior to the celebration, by pilgrimages organized at the start of an important wedding season (16 August -14 November), by beginning the fall-fair period, and by commemorating feasts for the dead and by giving alms for people still alive. In addition this is a significant time in making certain changes such as the sheep descended from the mountain, as reminded by the saying: "At Great Virgin Mary/ the sheep go down the slopes!" This the period, too, when men change their hats with caps, bathing in the rivers spoiled by the stag and sleeping on the porch are no longer allowed, vineyard guards were hired and magical measures for protection of the vineyards were taken against birds and nut-gathering starts.

August 15
Great Virgin Mary

To the Romanians, *Great Virgin Mary* is the feminine divinity rivaled only by their love for Jesus Christ. She is often invoked by girls for hastening marriage, by pregnant women for having an easier childbirth by victims for catching the thieves and by enchantresses for healing diseases. She has characteristics of the ancient Birth-Giving Goddess, of the Great Neolithic Goddess, invoked by people in the hard moments of their lives.

---

[139] September Catechism, 1984, p. 98-116.

In some customs, Virgin Mary, identified with the Moon or the Earth begs God not to destroy the world, not to cast away the useful winds.

Virgin Mary of the Black Valley, Vrancea County (Cherciu, 2003)

Holy Mary blesses the oxen, the cows, the sheep and the pigs because they kept her warm and fed her when she gave birth to Jesus in the Christmas stable. And because they announced Christ's birth, She blesses swallows.

However, She curses horses because they disturbed Her with their stamping and crunching during Christ's birth and because they ate the hay in which she had hidden the baby; she also curses spiders because they are faster than She is in spinning as well as the carpenter because he builds a heavy cross for Jesus. She changes the mischievous young man who scared her, while She was carrying Jesus in her arms, forty days after his birth, into hart's tongue, a weed used for love charms.

In fairy tails, She helps the heroines to get out of trouble, but She also punishes them if they disobey Her commands, She heals serious diseases, she helps the girl whose stepmother made her blind recover her sight, She helps the sage maiden marry a prince.

August 16
Hag of the Woods

In the Folk Almanac, young mythical representations appear grouped between the vernal equinox and the summer solstice (Sanziene, Dragaice, Pentecost, Iele and others), while the mother goddesses are predominant between the summer solstice and the winter equinox. These mothers of the Romanian Pantheon display lots of analogies with basic features dating back to 8000 – 2500 B.C..

One of them, the *Hag of the Woods*, is the master of everything that is born, grows and lives in the woods. Together with other characters like Forest Father, the Man of the Woods and the Girl of the Woods, She belongs to the clay and wood civilization. She is a mother-of-the-mothers who lives in the forest, in old trees, in hollows, or in the plant called Hag of the Woods. But she is a sad mother: she moans, she groans, she mourns and she sighs because humans kill her children when they cut the trees in the forest. She knows all her trees as her children in the woods whom she feeds when they are little; she scolds them if they get crooked; she calls them by their names or by their nicknames and she curses them to be cut off by men or stricken by lighting if they disobey her. As a great goddess, she can be either good or evil. She punishes the thieves, she helps the poor and she shows the right way to children who get lost in the forest.

In time, though her qualities of a good mother gradually faded. Nowadays she is mostly known as a malefic representation, an old hag, a man eater, the patron of the spirits which populate the woods by night. An ugly and hideous creature with her long hair touching the ground, she laments through the woods to attract the travelers. She can appear as a mare, buffalo-cow or cow, or as a woman, dressed in bark of moss, with long undone hair or plaited falling down to her heels. She can be as tall as a house or a hay stack, as little as a hare, as beautiful as a fairy, or as hideous as a monster.

She punishes the women who spin on Tuesday, men who whistle or sing in the forest and wake her children, the lumberjacks who disregard the rules governing in the wood, people who gather apples, wild pears, peanuts in the woods on Transfiguration Day on August 6, by making them dumb or crippled.

She travels on foot or riding on a horse with nine hearts. She appears suddenly like a ghost, she brings winds, whirlpools, bad weather, she goes into people's houses slamming the doors and the windows. Her children are ugly and always grumbling, they can hardly speak even many years after they were born, a reason for which she tries to replace them with children from the village.

August 17
Mother of the Fields and Devil's Mother

*Mother of the Field*s is the goddess of everything that grows and ripens in the fields. Unlike the Hag of the Woods' grumbling children, Mother of the Fields' children are good and calm. She became the ideal of beauty and perfection attributed to the Neolithic Mother Goddess (Mother Earth, Terra Mater) after being usurped by the Indo-European Father God and the Christian God. All her positive features are expressed in and reflected by other names: The Virgin, Holy Mary, Great Mary. The mothers in the village with grumbling children thought it was unfair and tried to make things right with the help of charms:

Mother of Fields!
You have a child

And I have a child
Mine cries all the time
Yours never cries
From this day on
Yours shall cry
And mine shall be quiet!

In opposition to Mother of the Fields, the *Devil's Mother* is a mythical representation evoked by the Romanians in swearing, curses and arguments. She is believed to have given birth to demons, but to have created tobacco and encouraged the habit of smoking. She looks like a hag, as black and as ugly as the darkness of Hell, with horns and her head twisted like reels, with a long and crooked nose, with teeth like a boar's fangs, with claws like sickles, with a cattle-like tail, with a big pipe between her teeth, with flames coming out of her nostrils and stinking of tobacco. (Valcea)

August 18
Mother "Gaia" (Jackdaw)

"Gaia" (The jackdaw) is a day-bird of pray, mysterious and ferocious, and it belongs to the Falconiformes species, together with vultures, falcons, eagles and hawks. It has a stout body, four sharp claws, a curved and slightly flattened beak and feathers which change color with age. Sight is its most developed sense and it foretells rain during the droughty summers. It is one of the most beautiful and one of the strongest among the birds of prey. This invincible bird was also chosen as model by the artist Brancusi for his evocative bird sculptures.

In some of the "Zori" verse sung at funerals in some villages from Oltenia, Banat and south Transylvania, The Death Goddess appears in the form of a night or day bird of prey: a raven, a jackdaw, or a vulture. Several sources support and describe the existence of a bird-like Death Goddess ("Gaia" or "Gaea") in the Carpato-Danubian pantheon. One finds it in the funeral texts in the Romanian Book of the Dead, some folk expressions used to scare naughty children (*to meet Gaia* or *to meet the Devil, watch out for Gaia*).

August 19
Playing Mother Gaia

Children's games, rhymes and folklore, as well as the spoken language, are great preservers of prehistoric relics. One example is the game called *Playing Mother Gaia* (also called "Gaia" or "Gaia and the Clucking Hen" or "Chick Gaia"). "Each of two vigorous children choose to play the roles of Gaia or of the Clucking Hen. Then they make up two equal groups of children who stand in a row, holding each other by the waist, while Gaia sits on the ground and digs a hole with a stick. The Clucking Hen with her line of chicks comes up and starts a dialogue with Gaia: ' What are you doing here? – I'm digging a hole! – What for? – To make a fire. – What for? – To put the cast iron kettle on it (in some variants there is a frying-pan). – What do you need a kettle for? – To soak one of your chicks in boiled water!' Gaia stands up and gives the Hen the stick she has been digging with. The Hen and her chicks spit on it and throw it away as far as possible. While Gaia runs to get the stick, the Hen and her row of chicks move in circle around the hole and sing 'three times around the pit' and croak to tease Gaia. Then the two groups start struggling as Gaia and the Hen try to grab each other's chicks. During the struggle the children express their fear of being seized by the claws of death, by Mother Gaia. When they have finished capturing each other's chicks altogether, Gaia and the Hen wrestle and the winner is to play the Hen's role in the next game. This ancient childhood game was enjoyed until the middle of the 20th century.

August 20
The Dwarf Elder, A Phytomorphic Divinity

Dwarf Elder
(Parvu, 2000)

A phytomorphic divinity, the *dwarf elder* (*Sambucus ebulus* L.) of the Caprifoliaceae family, is invoked to release rain during the "Paparuda" ceremony, to heal snake bites and to drive away lightning during storm. Its green stalks are the sacerdotal attire worn in the Paparuda ceremonial by the person who plays the role of the goddess of rain. Its dry boughs, gathered by children or by clean or forgiven women, become funeral stokes lighted in courtyards or on graves in the cemetery, on Martyrs' Day, at Shrovetide and at Great Thursday.

Under the influence of the Christian religion the dwarf elder became a malefic plant, also called Devil's fruit. In the soil, where its roots grow, it became said that it hides the male devil and out in the air, among its boughs hides the female devil. According to some beliefs, the dwarf elder is a female divinity married to the common elder (sambucus nigra) which is a male divinity. When a man cuts off dwarf elder stalks and throws them in places where common elder grow, he is rewarded by receiving good advice from it.

When people gathered the dwarf elder, they invoked and respected it like a divinity: "Good morning, dwarf elder! I honor you with bread and salt and with nine genuflections and you should also reward me with health to my cattle: worms shall not stay in their wounds longer than priests, mayors and high officials stay in Heaven." Its fruit gathered in late autumn, are used to color textile and wine, while its leaves and stalks gathered on the Day of the Cross (14 September), are used to heal cattle wounds especially snake bites.[140]

August 21
The mand and the pot

In folk language clay pots are commonly compared with man's body and soul. The clay pot has mouth, lip, neck, belly, arm, glove, hand and foot; if it has been properly made (burnt), it has a nice sound; if pieces are broken of it, it has a hoarse sound; a virgin maid is compared to a brand new, unused pot; *sinful* girl is compared to a cracked pot and an old woman to an old broken pot.

The common element that makes a spiritual connection between man and pot is the earth, which in folk beliefs appears as a living organism endowed with intelligence. Like a man, the earth also needs to rest during the night. In the northern Bucovina it was a sin to dig the earth after sunset and particularly in the night because it had to rest. In the cosmic heterogamy, the Earth is the mother who brings forth and feeds the children and the sky is the man, the children's father.

In over 140 Romanian proverbs and sayings referring to clay pottery, the clay pot is present as a multipurpose term for comparison.

"It sounds like a pot," meaning that somebody is seriously ill or that someone is dying.

"He has now become pots and small pots," meaning that someone died a long time ago and became earth or clay which is now used for making clay pots.

---

[140] Butura, 1879, p. 31-41.

"She has eaten from the pot!" meaning that a girl has lost her virginity.

"Nobody knows what is boiling in a pot covered with a lid!" referring to false and hypocritical people.

"I may not be so keen-witted, but I won't fit in just any kind of pot!" meaning "I may not be very sharp, but I am not very stupid either."

"If you don't trample the earth, you'll not be able to make clay pots of it!" meaning that a child should not go unpunished when he makes a mistake.

"To be as empty as a pot!" meaning a heartless woman.

"The drunkard comes across pots of wine everywhere, even the Devil offers him some!" referring to people who often get drunk.

Other expressions (containing pots) define notions like: honesty, purity, poverty, wealth, greed, meanness or people's age.

August 22
The Earth, Our Mother

Blidaru, Dacian Fortress from the Surianu Mountains (Isfanoni, Photo by Eugen Pecaru, 2002)

The Neolithic personification of the Earth, Mother Earth, appears in the most unexpected and hidden corners of Romanian traditional culture. For their documentary value, some of the beliefs are presented which are relevant in this context.

"The Earth complains to God about the hard time man gives to it: 'Dear God, man scrapes me and cuts me, I can't bear it any more! – Be patient, says God, now man prospers on you expense, but then it will be your turn to take advantage of him!>'"

"The Earth is sacred: you must genuflect on it, you must worship it, for it feeds and supports all of us, we get food and water from it, it keep us warm, the Earth is our mother. 'Genuflect and kiss the Earth, I say to my children, and pray that it shall provide us, because from earth we come and to earth we shall return.'"

"The earth is half man and half woman, because God creates Eve from Adam's rib!"

"When cursing, one can say: May dust eat you up! May earth eat you up!"

"The Earth is a man at the surface and a woman in the inside. It is jealous of his woman and complains to her: 'People cut me, till me, but they don't trouble you at all, you're just fine. Not only are you idle, but you are also fed by people.'" The latter is a reference to the funeral ritual.[141] (Bucovina, Moldavia)

August 23
"Valva", A Spirit of the Earth

Valva is an earthly goddess that has a composite of features belonging to several female mythical representations. In some traditions she is assimilated with Varvara, patron of the miners, celebrated on December 4. As a spirit of the Earth, she is present in all things and in all places: in mines (Valva of the mines), in forests and in trees (Valva of the woods), in waters (Valva of the waters), and in the fields (Valva of the crops).

Mother Goddess with the Hands on the Womb found in Gheraeisti-Nedelea, Neamt County

---

[141] Voronca, 1903, p. 156-160

When she guards treasures, she is called Valva of the Treasures, and when she is patron over the days of the week, she is called Valva of the Days, synonymous with Saint Sunday and Saint Friday. She has anthropomorphic appearance as a beautiful woman with a distaff tied around her waist, or like an old man with a pipe in his mouth, also like an old woman, a dwarf or a child. In a zoomorphic state, she takes several forms as a cat, a hare, a ram, a lamb, a hen, a sparrow, a snake or a dragon. All these Valva representations announce their presence through sound and visual signs. This includes singing, speaking, hitting a rock in which there is gold with a hammer.

In western Carpathian areas, Valva protects people from thunder, hail and strong winds, She brings rain clouds and it also shows the miners where to find gold. She flies when she travels, like the Hag of the Earth and like other mythical representations, but She can also be seen walking on the earth or riding a horse. These earthly spirits can be good ones and bad ones: some help people, while others punish them; the former are dressed in white and the latter in black.[142]

August 24
Birth and Being Driven Out of the Intra-Uterine Heaven

The fetus that receives everything it needs during its intra-uterine life (food, oxygen, constant temperature, protection against noises, etc.), is driven out at birth into an unknown world, where it suddenly has to face all kinds of feelings and sensations of hunger, thirst, cold, lack of air, bothersome light. It seems strange then that a new-born is celebrated with noisy feasts. This contrasts with the Geto-Dacians who, according to Herodot's records, used to sit around the new-born baby crying: "... all the misfortunes it will have to suffer, once it has come to this world. Hereupon all human sufferings are mentioned" (Herodot, History, V, 4). His records are referred to in the words Pompeius, Mela, Valerius Maximus and other writers.

Human Destiny being thrown Away - Peasant Miniaturist Picu Patrut
(Patrut, 1985)

---

[142] Ionita, 1982, p. 26-29.

August 25
Beliefs about the Sun

In folk beliefs, the Sun, personification of the day star, wakes up in the morning, like a ordinary working man, and rests in the night. He has human qualities and features.

"In the morning, when the Sun wakes up, he is a seven-year-old child who travels the whole day and sees all the bad things that happen in the world, which makes him grow a long white beard reaching his waist by evening. His mother then bathes him in fresh milk and he becomes a child again."

"The sun is a human. There, in the sea, lives his wife. The Sun has wings of fire. His wings are so round that they get together and make it look round, but in the middle of it there is a man with a cross on his back."

"The Sun is a clean young man, who has not sinned. The Moon was very fond of him and kept courting him and loving him. Then the Sun said to her: 'Am I not sending enough burning heat to the world? If I were to get married and have children, what would become of the humans? The whole world would burn to ashes and all the people would disappear.'"[143]

The Sun is reborn at Christmas and respectively at New Year. At winter solstice he is small like the day, then he grows and becomes quite strong at vernal equinox when the day is equal with the night, and his power reaches the highest point at the summer solstice, when the day is the longest of the whole year. After the summer solstice the power of the sun and the length of the day decrease all the time until they reach a balance at autumn equinox, after which they are overrun by the forces of darkness and of the night.

The Sun's erotic inclination and his incestuous relationship with his sister, the Moon, are frequent motifs in the Romanian and in world folklore. Sometimes the Sun is a married man, his wife being the Moon, whom he meets in the nights when she gets *refreshed* and she does not appear in the sky; at other times, from their incestuous marriage the stars are born. Most often the astral incest is prevented by God's intervention.

---

[143] Niculita-Voronca, 1903, p. 27, 509, 588.

August 26
The Good Moment

The favorable moment at a child's birth, when it was believed that a star appeared in the sky that would guide the child's life until death, is commonly called *The Good moment*. The entire Universe takes part in man's birth and death (his coming to this world and his leaving it), through spectacular changes such s the appearance and the fall of stars. Romanian beliefs in the cosmic greatness of existence (life) is expressed in some lines of the "Miorita" ballad: "And when I die / A star will fall. "

A child's baptism in Runcu Village, Gorj County (AIEF by F. Lorint, Nr. 36 943)

It is also found in the belief of farmers from Baragan plain who, whenever they see a bright comet in the sky, say that another man has just died. The Romanians think that their children's future is influenced not only by the Fates' predictions, but also by the circumstances in which the birth took place: day time or night time, and the position which the day of birth occupied within the week, the season, the year and the lunar time. Evidence from modern-day research in medicine and astrobiology suggests connections between biological processes including the intrauterine ones and terrestrial and cosmic rhythms.

The days of the week and of the year that were considered favorable for giving birth are Sundays and the great holidays. As for the best time of the day, that is some time between midnight and dawn after the first rooster's crow.

August 27
Techniques for Hindering Childbirth

Names commonly used by people to designate a pregnant woman are related to the gift received from God referred as a "woman in the state of gift", to the weight carried during pregnancy or a "heavy woman, or with burden", to the change in form or "thick woman." However, for the same condition, a young girl who gave birth to a child outside marriage would be attributed offensive names such as "big with child," "with bones in the belly", or "pot-bellied."

Women in the traditional village had enough knowledge of ways of *hindering childbirth*. The most efficient contraceptives were those made of plants.

"There is a weed to be used against having children. It's not good to fill up the world with children! It happens that neither the man nor the woman can bear fruit."

"It was a bitter weed, but I ate it with bread. I used to take it when I remembered to. I was glad when a woman showed me that weed, but now I regret it, because I am old and I am alone."

A method for delaying a new pregnancy was prolonging the nursing of the baby. There are old people who remember asking mothers to nurse not by crying, as is usually done, but with words, which was a method likely to delay a consecutive pregnancy up to three years. However, the most common method was continence on religious grounds. Sexual interdictions were imposed during fasting days on Wednesdays and Fridays during the 52 weeks of the year, in the four fasting periods of Easter, Christmas, Saint Mary and Saint Peter, in the days between Christmas and Epiphany, in the first week after Easter, in the Day of the Cross as well as in other days of the folk almanac such as the beginning of ploughing, of harvesting. Together these made up over two thirds of the almanac year. Not only the work and food interdictions, but also the sexual ones were reminded to those who did not comply, in the lines of the dance chants:

Forget about love, my dear girl,
And look for the swaddling band,
Forget about your ugly man,
And look for the swaddling clothes,
For, in one or two months
You'll need a new cradle
A new cradle made of green wood,
As the baby starts to show![144]

August 28

From the Fates' Table to the Table of Silence

The person who is the intermediary between the Fates and the child whose fate is to be predestined three days after birth, and only rarely 5, 7 or 9 days after birth, is the child's midwife. She is the one who gives the two ritual baths to the child and to the confined mother, who cleans the house and prepares the Fates' Table.

---

[144] Trebici, Ghinoiu, 1986, p. 209-210.

The traditional farmers' table is round and low, it is placed in the middle of the room and its role is that of the altar, which is filled with offerings that necessarily include know-shaped bread, salt and a cup or glass with wine or with water for the Fates. On the table are also laid some objects of a symbolic value, which are meant to suggest to the Fates some ideas they can use in their predetermination: a plough share in the farmers' villages, a flute in the shepherds' villages, a notebook and a pen to help the child be good at school, and other objects.

Left: Laying the Fates' Table, Dablaca, Hunedoara County (Isfanoni, 2004)
Right: Gherla Icon Representing the Angel, the Midwife, and the Fates' Table at the Virgin's Birth (Irimie, Focsa, 1968)

All the things displayed on the table are aimed to satisfy the Fates and hopefully to make them predestine good health, luck and fecundity to the child. Some of the gifts on the Fates' Table often announce the second major step in one's life, namely marriage. The place where the predestination ritual is performed differs from region to region. It can be outside, at the window, in the child's room, at the head of the bed or around the table filled with offerings. The Fates sing or call out their predestination, whatever that might be. But what they have predestined can be found out indirectly, by interpreting the dream of the confined woman or that of the midwife. In some areas such as Padurenii and Hunedoarei, people still believe in Fates for which they lay the ritual table, three or seven days after a child is born. There are also cases when the side tables in the maternity hospitals become, with help of the nurses, The Fates' Table, in the third night from the birth.

The round table is akin to an altar in the form of a tiny clay object found at the archaeological site in Cascioarele in Giurgiu County, dating from the Fourth Millennium B.C. Until recently the everyday meal and the time spent around the table were sacred. Children were not allowed to talk during the meal, the bread was laid on the table and cut in a certain way. The first piece of bread was thrown under the table to satisfy the dead souls' hunger and people sitting around the table started and ended their meal by making the sign of the cross.

Around his famous "Table of Silence" Brancusi arranged twelve symbolical chairs, placed at an equal distance, one from another. Giving them the name of "chair" is a magical practice of hiding the sacred behind the profane. There is absolutely no reason to place proper chairs around an altar! When people come to an altar, they bring offerings, they pray down on their knees, standing or moving around it in a ritual circle.[145] What are labeled as "chairs" are actually sand glasses, one for each constellation of the zodiac. They divide The Table Of Silence, similar to the solar face in Gradistea Muncelului, into 12 zodiac sectors, of 60 degrees each, that are yearly visited by the solar system, including the Planet Earth.

August 29
The Midwife

The *midwife* has a strong personality, very determined in taking decisions, and respected by the whole community for her innate or acquired qualities. The midwife's empirical knowledge and the magic practices performed by her make-up a coherent whole.
At childbirth, the midwife performs all the sacred and the profane acts meant to bring the child to the world, to integrate him into the family and into the paternal descent and to guarantee a good health condition for the mother and the child. She bathes the baby immediately after birth in water which was rather colder than warm so that, later in life, "he should neither be sensitive to cold, nor easily scared," and "so that he should be lively, quick, strong and clever."

The ritual bath was done in a trough made of fir tree wood or of willow tree wood with unused water poured from a new clay pot. The objects placed in the bath water including eggs, milk, silver coins, consecrated water, sweet basil, flower and bird feathers had symbolical value:

As precious as silver,
As sweet as honey,

---

[145] Ghinoiu, 2001, p. 116-117.

As good as bread,
As red as wild rose,
As attractive as sweet basil,
As white as milk!

Before the Fates' arrival, the midwife also gives the confined woman a ritual bath in an infusion of medicinal plants. Particularly important were the instruments and the advice given by the midwife to the young mother, concerning the child's bath, hygiene, the way it should be dressed and breastfed. These instructions are extremely valuable knowledge for a traditional society lacking both a medical care system and people who could read and write.

The midwife was prepared to deal with any case of childbirth. One said of her experience: "When a woman's belly got sick and her womb came off, I knew how to fix it. Doctors operate her and take out the womb, but not me. I could fix it and she could go on having children." (Troas, Arad County)

But, in addition to the gynecological knowledge that the midwife possessed, she is also a preserver of the magic practices that were meant to maintain women's fertility, following the confinement period, after childbirth, to protect the baby against evil spirits, and to prepare the arrival of the Fates. Even after the traditional midwife was replaced with school-trained midwives, she continued to play her role as a *second midwife*. She visits the woman in her care at the maternity hospital and receives the Fates at home.

August 30
The Fates – Goddesses of Destiny

Birth is governed by numerous predetermination beliefs, mainly by those expressing the idea of destiny, on which the newly-born child depends. In folk beliefs, the Fates are mythical female representations that announce what must happen in a man's life from cradle to death. These beliefs are still present in people's conscience since they are often mentioned in everyday phrases such as: "That's my fate." "That's what the Fate sang at my birth," and other such sayings. From this, one can draw the conclusion that *fate* and its synonym *destiny* are absolute notions, sacred predetermined courses of events, from which man cannot deviate in any of the crucial moments of his life, like choosing his souse and his death.

People imagine The Fates in different ways. It can be a young virgin sister, three ghosts with women faces but always dressed in white. They bear sacred names, unknown and unuttered by the uninitiated, or names related to the role they played while predestinating: Spinner, Destiny, Death. They live in the sky or on earth. Their ritual props consist of a distaff with a flock of wool on it, a spindle and a pair of scissors. They spin the thread of a man's life – rich or poor – of his marriage and of his death, depending on their state of mind or mood. If they are furious or bitten by dogs when they arrive, they cannot be calmed down, no matter what one might lay on the table for them.

Sometimes some wool is put on the table so that the thread of life they spin may be made longer. The youngest Fate, which carries the scissors, is sometimes lame and very mean, like some other Romanian mythical representations with this handicap - Philip the Lame, Santoader the Lame. She decides what age a man will reach at his death by suddenly cutting the thread of his life, before The Spinner can twist around the spindle. The phrase often heard at someone's death "That was God's will!" is replaced in some villages from Vrancea area by the expression: "That was The Lame's will!"

August 31
The Baby's House

For people in old times, the placenta which was the shelter for the soul before birth, became, after the baby had come out of tit, a corpse that had to be subject to a funeral rite. The custom of burying the *baby's house* three days after his birth, similar to burying the dead body after death in the ground of the house, in the courtyard, in a clean place or laid floating on a running water, was praciced until the beginning of the 20th century.

"The midwife buries the child's little house in the garden, under the fence, so that no more children should be born, or under a tree which bears fruit, so that more children should be born."

"In some villages from Bucovina, the midwife sprinkles the child's house with consecrated water, puts it in a pot which she then buries in a hidden place, usually in the entrance hall, behind the door."

In Oravitei area, the placenta was given life symbolically, through a ritual sacrifice a baby boy was buried along with rooster dressed up with small clothes. If the baby was a girl, a hen was buried alongside.

SEPTEMBER

"RAPCUINE"

THE COOL MONTH

1. The Biblical New Year
2. Saint Simion of the Pole and the Rooster
3. The Code of Colors and Man's Ages
4. Days for Asking in Marriage and for Getting Married
5. The Fir and Apple Trees, Nuptial Symbols
6. Beating the Stoke
7. The Stone House
8. Birth Day of Virgin Mary
9. The Ritual of Founding the Stone House
10. The Social Motivation of Birth
11. The Lullaby
12. The Midwife and Her Husband
13. The Hazelnut Tree and the Snake
14. The Day of the Cross
15. The Snake of the House
16. The Glades Used Against Invaders
17. "Mioi" Summer
18. The Trek Cart
19. Spreading the News
20. The Turks' Bird
21. The House with a Hiding Place
22. The House with Two Entrances
23. Holidays Around the Autumn Equinox
24. The "Tecle" Celebrations
25. Unsafe Conditions for Girls and Wives
26. Memories of Ottoman Rule
27. Turks and Tatars
28. The Village Fence
29. Shepherd Roads
30. Mail Cart Road

September

is the seventh month in the Roman Almanac which starts on March 1. It is the ninth month in the Julian Almanac (Old) and in the Gregorian Almanac (New) which starts January First; and the first month in the Biblical Almanac starting September 1. Romanians call the month of September "The Cool Month" because the weather turns cold. This expression is found familiar sayings: *In the Cool Month/ Children fall on embers!* meaning that children gather around the fire. The month is also called "Nice Wine" or "Wine Time" in reference to grapes being harvested and pressed to make wine. Unlike the official New Year on the First of January, the wine growing New Year on February 2, the agrarian New Year on March 9, or the pastoral shepherd's New Year on April 23, the Christian Biblical New Year has few customs of renewal of time.

Grape picking, Dudasul Schei, Mehedinti County
(Isidor Chicet Collection)

September 1
The Biblical New Year

Until the eighteenth century the Princely Court and the Christian Church used the biblical year starting September First as the official year. The years were counted from "the creation of the world" which was said to have taken place 5,508 years before Christ's birth. In order to determine a certain Christian year one had to subtract 5,508 years from that date, if the respective event happened between January 1 and August 31, and to subtract 5,509 years, if the event happened between September 1 and December 31.[146] This calculation was made by historians when referencing documents released by the Princely Court administration prior to the eighteenth century.

God instructing Adam not to eat fruits from the 'Science' Tree' (Miniature 1844)

On September 1, the Christian Church celebrates the Pious Saint Simeon of the Pole. "He was given this name because he had been sitting on a tall pole all his life," or "Because, all his life, he had been standing on one leg on a tall pole, holding the Earth to prevent it from falling."[147]

On this day many weather observations and predictions were made.

"Saint Simeon is the master of the year. The way his day is, is what the weather will be the whole year."

"If the morning is rainy, it will be a rainy spring."

"If it is fine weather at noon, it will be a good year."

"If the whole day is rainy or sunny, the entire year will be rainy or dry."

"If Saint Simeon is gloomy, the autumn will be bad and people will hardly be able to harvest their crops."[148]

However, the most efficient meteorological predictions were deduced by observing the development stage of worms in their cocoons on oak-trees. "Those who are skillful in searching on Saint Simeon, are as

---

[146] Hasdeu, 1887, Vol. II, p. 127.

[147] Pamfile, 1914, p. 43.

[148] Niculaita-Voronca, 1903, p. 393.

good as looking into the zodiac. If the worm has already flown away on that day, it's a sign for a mostly dry year. If the worm has wings, the crops will be neither too rich, nor too poor in that year. If the worm hasn't grown wings yet, then the crops will be rich."[149] It is believed that on that day, birds, mainly sparrows, "go to fetch their measure of wealth." By this is meant that they carry in their beaks their share of crops cultivated by people to their Queen's place, where their winter food pantries are kept. Given, on the other hand that one finds few traces were in the Biblical New Year of oral traditions and customs, one can conclude that it had a minor influence on the structure of the Folk Almanac.

September 2
Saint Simeon of the Pole and the rooster

Roster On a Day-Plate, Viorel Tanasescu, Potter from Horezu, Valcea County, 2003

Saint Simeon is believed to keep the winds in a barrel and to release them whenever he thinks it's right. Once, having been angered by God who took away his only child, he kept all the winds tight in the barrel and said:

Since you have taken away my child, I am not going to release any wind in the world!

God sent word to him by other Saints, but the answer was the same:

I won't listen to him, for he didn't listen to me either when I begged him not to take my child!

Without wind on earth, "as the wind is like a bath, it cleans everything", diseases appeared and more and more people died. In order to persuade him to free the winds, God asked for help from all living creatures. When it was the rooster's turn to try to make the master of the winds change his mind, he went up to the Saint and said:

---

[149] Pamfile, 1914, p. 44.

Why don't you free the wind, dear Saint, for, look, there is so much evil the world!

I won't, because God took my child away from me! answered the Saint.

You must be joking! Look at me, how many of my children has God taken away from me? Why should I bother, as you do? As for me, I don't care a bit if a child of mine dies, I make a new one!

Saint Simeon looked at The rooster, his face lightened up, and he answered:

I think you are right. I haven't listened to anyone so far, but I shall listen to your advice.

Only then did he release the wind. For seven years, while he was mourning over his child, there was no wind in the world. That is why when someone dies, people mourn for seven years and then they forget. After the rooster helped God resolve the dilemma, God asked the rooster to come up to Him and said:

For having done such a good thing for me, I allow you to keep forty hens and go freely around in the village.

And from then on the rooster has been so proud and so dear to the hens.[150]

September 3

The Code of Colors and Man's Ages

In traditional society, age was often noted in people's clothes through certain colors, chromatic patterns or a particular cut. It was also displayed by head wear and by one's social status attending village sittings, belonging to young men's or to carol singers' groups, taking part in the ring dance, or having a reserved seat place in church. While white prevailed during early childhood, bright colors appeared gradually, especially red, getting brighter around marriage age. After marriage the colors became more sober and, towards the passage to old age, they were reduced to variations of black and white, one of the first color combinations used by man. Towards the end of life all the colors melt down to white. Through such symbolic language varied events were communicated to the community, even those considered more private or intimate such as somebody becoming pregnant. The rules for estimating age was conformed to within the same community but could differ from area to area, or even from village to village in some cases.

---

[150] The fauna legends, 1994, p. 124.

September 4
Days for asking in marriage and for getting married

Marriage was an institution strictly controlled by the church, which forbade wedding ceremonies and of course conjugal relations on Wednesday and Friday, the fasting days of the week, or during the fasting periods of the year related to Christmas, Easter, Saint Peter, Saint Mary, and also, for obvious during the more rambunctious feasting periods which excessive eating and drinking between Christmas and Epiphany, the week after Easter.

Bringing Wedding Gifts, Golos, Hunedoara County (AIEF, No. 6 881)

People's basic occupations, agriculture and animal husbandry, imposed certain regular work patterns which, in their turn, determined certain nuptial patterns, as well as most favorable nuptial moments. The traditional wedding ceremony was an event that needed time and a proper psychological preparation:

> *When it's time to get married,*
> *It's not good time to work.*
> *For, if you go to work,*
> *You only sigh from your heart!*

Plant and animal reproduction cycles together with rules imposed by the church determined nuptial seasons: one in *autumn*, lasting until Christmas Shrovetide in predominantly farming villages, and another one in *winter*, between Epiphany and Easter Shrovetide in the shepherd villages. Some secondary nuptial periods appeared in the summer, during the traditional feasts taking place at "Dragaica" on June 24 and at Santilie on July 20.

When asking someone in marriage, the most favorable days were Thursdays and Sundays. Wednesday was ill-fated for marriage as it was imagined to be a solitary widow while Saturday was dedicated to the dead. Tuesday and Fridays were also unfavorable for wedding ceremonies, which is reflected by the folk sayings: "Everything is upside down and the wedding on a Tuesday!", "Not only were they far from being young, but they also got engaged on a Friday!"[151]

September 5
The Fir-tree and the apple, nuptial symbols

The fir-tree, due to its peaked shape, its leaves shaped like needles, and its fruit-like cones, appears as an expression of masculine divinity in numerous customs belonging to the life cycle of birth, marriage, and burial. Even in contemporary speech, a young man ready to get married is described as being *manly as a fir-tree*, or *tall as a fir-tree*. A young girl, even if she is tall, will never be compared with a fir-tree! The presence of a decorated fir-tree as a masculine symbol at a wedding ceremony is practiced in southern Romania including Oltenia, Walachia, Dobrogea, southern Moldavia. In Transylvania and in Banat, however, the fir-tree was replaced with a wedding flag, while in Bucovina and in northern Moldavia it was replaced with a stick decorated with flowers.

During the wedding ceremony, the decorated fir-tree is respected and worshipped by all the participants. Special nuptial poems are dedicated to it, called *The Words of the Fir-tree* and *The Song the Fir-tree*. There is also a ritual dance called *The Fir-tree Ring Dance*. The most manly young person guards it, carries it and dances with it. He also leads the ring dances and the wedding procession. During the wedding, during moments when the groom is absent, the fir-tree keeps the bride company. The ceremony on Saturday evening taking place at the girl's house is called "*The Fir-tree Ceremony*" in Walachia, and "*The Flag Ceremony*" or "*The Tree Ceremony*" in Transylvania. The remarkable appearance of the fir-tree and its ritual dance symbolize the future husband's strong character, determination and virility.

The apple, like the fir-tree, appears in the wedding in the form of a tree, a fruit, a flower or a bough. It represents the beauty ideal of the girl engaged to be married, whose *cheeks and breasts are like apples* and whose *face is white like apple flowers*. A young man can never be compared with an apple, which is an attribute of femininity. Unfortunately, over time, the apple also acquired a pejorative sense. For instance the expression "What an apple you are!" is usually addressed to a woman who is excessively keen on making love. At some weddings, some symbols of the groom's virility combine with the symbols of the bride's femininity: the fir-tree top passes around (and through) the bride's apple or the groom's stick or cane is passed through the hole of the bride's knot-shaped bread.

---

[151] Ghinoiu, 1999, p. 136-138.

September 6
Beating the Stake

*Sowing with a Staff,
Bunesti, Valcea County
(I. Chelcea, 1965)*

An exemplary ritual, prior to creating a shelter such as a family new home, the settling of new village, is the ritual beat commonly referred to as *beating the stake* or *beating the pole*. The stake is an Axis Mundi, an image of the paternal sky mating with the maternal Earth. This magic practice, originating in the reflexes and in the to and fro movement of the sexual act, is related to building the shelter of the soul and to the first technological inventions of mankind sowing with the pole, making fire by rubbing pieces of wood, sowing with the stake or with the stick and scutching with the scutcher, or crushing seeds in a mortar with a pestle. No important construction can be raised without the foundation gesture of beating the stake or the pole.

Considering the magic practice of the ritual beat one can intuit the logic behind some old folk expressions. For example a man who speaks a lot and monotonously is compared with *a pestle*, one of the oldest technical inventions of mankind, while a woman is compared with a *scutcher*, for the same reason.

The carol singers' beat gesture and their poking with sticks in the fire, the children's beat gesture with the "sorcova" stick on the person upon whom they perform the "sorcova" ritual, or the belief that gathering nuts from a nut-tree without beating the branches of the tree will make the nut-tree fruitless the next year, are all fertility and fecundity acts which are directly or indirectly related with the ritual beat.

September 7
The Stone House

At a Romanian wedding, people always wish the newlywed couple a *stone house*. This does not refer literally to a house built of stone, but to the fact that the young couple who are getting married will set up shelter for the soul to live during its pre-existence during its intra-uterine life. This geomorphic shelter or placenta, created by the nuptial act and destroyed by breaking at birth is commonly called *shelter*, *little shelter*, the *child's house* or *little place*. It is the one which ensures protection to the embryo, to the fetus and to the baby against the aggression of infections germs and toxic substances, against violent acts, or against annoying noises or shouting during fights.

September 8
Birth day of Virgin Mary

After about a lunar month from Saint Mary's death on August 15, Christians celebrate her birth. According to the Christian tradition, Holy Mary was born in a miraculous way. Her parents, Joachim, descent of a royal family, and Anna, descent of David's family were being abused because they didn't have any children. Joachim prayed to God up in the mountains and his *barren* wife prayed in the garden to bring holy fruit to her womb. According to some folk legends, Anna became pregnant by smelling or kissing a pear-tree leaf or flower, according to others she was born of a *heartache* from a 7-year-old mother and a 77-year-old father.

Birth of the Virgin Mary by Icon Painter Savu Moga, Arpasul de Sus, 1869 (Irimie, Focsa, 1968)

The two celebrations of Holy Mary mark, in terms of almanac account, the Biblical New Year on September 1st and the assumed Creation of the World in 5508 B.C. Many characteristics typical to the Biblical New Year are taken over by two Romanian celebrations of Holy Mary. One is a great holiday held around the autumn equinox, dedicated to the death and the rebirth of a prehistoric goddess. Theologians of the Christian Church transferred the celebration of the birth of Holy Mary to September 8, who is called Our Lord's Mother, Little Saint Mary or Little Virgin Mary.

Little Saint Mary, the second in the Folk Almanac, is the astronomical delimitation between summer and winter, marked by the earth closing itself to reptiles and insects, by the departure of the migratory birds towards warmer countries, by people's changing their hats for caps, and by the organizing of fairs for trading products specific for the season.

The arrival of that day was an indication to farmers that they should start certain practical activities, such as gathering the last healing plants and fruits, *beating* the nuts off the nut-trees, harvesting grapes, sowing wheat, barley and rye, and ripping bark off certain trees that would be used for tying up vines in spring.

The two Saint Mary celebrations are strictly observed by Romanians throughout the country, especially by women who wish to have children and to have an effortless childbirth.

September 9
The Ritual of Founding the Stone House

In old times, people believed that the *stone house* was created, like any other shelter by following a ritual that included determining the favorable place for laying the foundation, usually done by a ritual hunt (the nuptial poem describes the adventure of the groom who has gone hunting), laying the foundation of the shelter by beating the stoke (the nuptial act), and giving life to the created shelter through a sacrifice.

The bringing to life of a child by man is a divine act that could be accomplished by the groom and the bride after being consecrated through the Christian *marriage ceremony* and through the pre-Christian *nuptial poem*.

After these two types of consecration, the bride and the groom become, temporarily, sacred characters that can through the nuptial act bring the baby from the beyond into our world. During the wedding everything that comes into direct contact with the bride's and the groom's sacred bodies brings luck, fertility and prosperity. The wedding guests are keen on catching and eating pieces from the knot-shaped bread or from the flat cake broken above the bride's head and thrown to the guests as sacred food. There is also the old custom of keeping the groom's shirt or the bride's blouse, sacerdotal clothes which covered the provisionally divine bodies at the wedding, to be used for wrapping the baby at birth, or for dressing with them on their death bed. One notes, too, the contemporary custom of writing the names of the bride's girl friends on the sole of her shoe to help them marry sooner.

After the ritual consecration through the religious ceremony and the nuptial poem the couple is initiated in what they have to do next through symbolic coupling, during the wedding, between masculine substitutes - the fir-tree, the flag, the cane, the stick wrapped in flowers - and the feminine substitutes - the knot-shaped bread, the apple, the bride's platter or wreath.

September 10
The Social Motivation of Birth

In the Romanian traditional village, birth represents an auspicious moment provided that the procreating couple have been ritually and religiously consecrated by the community. The couple wishes for heirs who will inherit their lives' earnings and avoid reaching old-age like *"some fruitless poplars."* When children are born, the father proves his manhood and the mother her womanhood. Moreover, the man wishes to ensure the continuity of his name and of his descent by having lots of children, grandchildren and great grandchildren. Given the social context, families with no children cannot enjoy the same consideration as those families with children. An absence of pregnancy in a family generates profound concern and a wife unable to bear children causes major problems that even lead to the family's break up.

"In the past, if the woman could not have children in seven years time, the man left her and got himself another one who would give him offspring." "Women who do not have children are amaranth weeds. They are neither honored nor appreciated by the man." (Holda village, Neamt County) "Our life changed when we had a boy and a girl. He became more considerate to me."

With children comes a peaceful and united atmosphere to a family. "The woman who has no children becomes crazy and does lots of crazy things." "There is a man in our village who drinks all the money he earns because his wife cannot give him children." "We have one man in our village who became a drunkard because his woman hasn't given him any children."[152]

September 11
The Lullaby

Child's Cradle and Bed made of Hollowed Wood, Sabaoani, Neamt County Ciubotaru, 2002)

There is no better way of expressing love for

---

[152] Ghinoiu, 1999, p. 139.

one's children than in sweet words and beautiful lullabies. They reflect a mother's love and her wishes for her child to grow-up, marry and settle down:

> *My darling, little John,*
> *My sweet swallow chick!*
> *Come, come and fall asleep.*
> *If only your mother could raise you,*
> *To let women be your wives!*

The lullaby song brings peace and quiet to a baby, especially when sung by its mother. The text expresses a variety of maternal feelings depending on whether it is addressed to boys, to girls, to twins, to fatherless children, or to illegitimate children:

> *Sleep well, mummy's little girl,*
> *Mummy's sweet pink*
> *As mummy will rock you*
> *And wash you face*
> *With spring water*
> *For you to be most beautiful!*
> or
> *Mother's two darling lads*
> *Look like flowers from afar,*
> *But, if you take a close look*
> *They are mother's greatest help!*
> or
> *Sleep well my sweet-heart,*
> *As mummy will rock you now.*
> *She will rock you with her hand,*
> *And curse you with her mouth,*
> *But she will not curse you badly,*
> *Cause it is no fault of yours,*
> *Someone else is to blamed,*
> *I am mostly to be blamed,*
> *For I did the wrong thing*
> *And now I feel so sorry!*

Unfortunately a lot of modern-day mothers do not realize that a new-born baby is stranger to everything and only recognizes his mother's voice. Those mothers, who forgo wonderful lullabies and try to calm their babies by playing the radio or television have no idea of the loss to their babies' mental well-being.[153]

September 12
The Midwife and Her Husband

The midwife and her husband represent the paternal line of the fathers' and the forefathers' spirits who ensured the baby a quite safe transfer from the intra-uterine world into the extra-uterine one. They play ceremonial and ritual roles in the most important moments in a person's life cycle (wedding, birth, funeral) and in the almanac cycle. The Romanian word for midwife, "moasa", definitely a pre-Romanian one is closely related to the same word in Albanian and probably belongs to the Ilirico-Thracian-Dacian languages.[154]

A rich body of ethnographical material confirms the fact that the midwife is to be a relative of the child's father. In some cases, the midwife and her husband are godparents when the baby is baptized. Even if traditionally schooled midwives are replaced by formally trained midwives, the former continues to play her ritual role. She goes to the maternity hospital where her relative gave birth and makes arrangements at home for receiving the Fates. In Oltenia and in Walachia, the parents take the baby to the midwife's home three years running at Christmas and at New Year, so that she can perform the ritual of "lifting the baby up to the girder" or of "touching the girder." The midwife puts the knot-shaped bread and salt on the crown of the child's head, lifts him up to the girder and wishes him:

> *May you live a long time*
> *And grow up to the girder!*

After the child's baptism the traditional midwife's tasks are taken over by the Christian tradition of *godparent*.

---

[153] Ghinoiu, 1999, p. 140.

[154] Scurtu, V., 1966, p. 15.

September 13

The Hazelnut Tree and the Snake

For a long period of time in the Romanian Pantheon, the *hazel nut tree* has been a sacred shrub, a totem of the *snake* established with profound spiritual connections. The hazelnut shrubs are a favorite summertime shelter for snakes seeking protection from thunder and lightning. This is where they gather for mating on the Day of the Cross, very close to the autumn equinox. According to some legends, the hazel-nut tree, the godfather of the snakes, protects them, gives them shelter, and helps them breed. Like any other divinity, the hazelnut tree protects its subjects, but also punishes them when they make mistakes. Some people believe that one can kill a snake or prevent being bitten by one, simply by touching it with a green hazel-nut bough.

The hazelnut tree is invoked in love charms, called *fate* charms, and also in charms performed against snake bites, against Mother of the Woods, or against the Devil, rashes or small pox. Sometimes it was invoked for winning trials in a court of law. The hazelnut stick is believed to have magic power. When propped up against a wall, it protects the house against ill-intentioned people; when held in one's hand, it leads someone to places where treasures are hidden; when ridden by a witch, it takes her in no time wherever she wants to go.

The hazelnut stick is often one of the magic props needed to perform wedding or funeral rituals. The day dedicated to gathering hazelnuts in the forest is "Probejenia" on August 6.

The hazelnut and the snake, divinities belonging to the Neolithic cultural complex, contrast with Santilie, the god of fire and of the sun, which is of Indo-European origin. When Santilie sends thunder on the earth, the hazelnut dries out and when Santilie sends lightning, the snake dies.

Snake with a Human Face on Porch Post, Maramures County
(Prut, 1972)

September 14
The Day of the Cross

The Raising of the Holy Cross on September 14 is dedicated to picking up the last healing plants: dwarf elder, rockets, belladonna, or hart's tongue. Locally the holiday is called The Vineyards' Holiday or The Day of the Snake. The Earth closes itself at The Day of the Cross, six months after opening itself for plants, insects and reptiles at Alexii Holiday on March 17th. The two holidays, one of them (Alexii) close to the vernal equinox and the other one (The Day of the Cross) close to the autumn equinox, divide the Folk Almanac into two broad seasons: summer from March 17 to September 14, and winter from September 14 to March 17.

It is believed that on The Day of the Cross the flowers complain to each other that they are starting to wither and die. On the other hand, those flowers which bloom after that day, such as the meadow saffron and the wild strawberries, are said to be unclean. They are flowers of the dead.

On that first day, the snakes, before creeping into their winter shelters, gather in the hazel-nut shrubs where they coil around each other in order to make a precious gem from the foam that covers them. From that day on people are forbidden to obey the saying "Kill the snake that comes in your way." However, there are other beliefs that encourage killing it. "On The Day of the Cross the wild beasts go into the earth, only that the snake which has bitten someone – either a man, or cattle – is not allowed by the earth to go back into it and it just wanders about in all places, turning up in a man's way to be killed." On The Day of the Cross certain apothropaic and fertilizing practices are performed in gardens and in orchards and the dead are remembered by distributing alms. (Moldavia, Bucovina) In Oltenia on The Day of the Cross, called The Vineyards' Holiday, people start to harvest grapes and to beat nuts off nut-trees.

September 15
The Snake of the House

House Snake
(Zoological Atlas, 1983)

The snake has been revered as a divinity ever since the Paleolithic age. Its more malefic significance, connected to the Biblical myth of the Creation, is a relatively late one. A belief that each house has its own protecting snake, also called *the snake of the house*, is widely documented. But a snake appearing in front of a house announces Death.

According to information recorded in Bucovina, "the snake is good for the whole household. Where there is a snake, there is good luck and prosperity and no evil and no spell can do any harm to a house! God forbid killing the snake, because someone in the family soon dies. Such snakes drink milk from the same dish as the children who would hit them on the head with their spoons to stop them. Not caring, the snakes kept on drinking from the milk pot." (Moldavia, Walachia)

In the folk beliefs the snake appeared over time in various guises. "The snake was not a snake from the beginning. It was a man who lived with God in Heaven, but God cursed him and turned him into snake when he deceived Eve." "In Heaven, with God live all creatures, but no snakes. At first, the snake could fly, it had legs and wings, it lived in Heaven and God thought it was good. But a bad spirit got into it and it taught Eve to sin with Adam. God became angry for that and drove Eve, Adam and the snake out from Heaven. God cut off the snake's legs and wings, threw it on the Earth, cursing it to creep like a rope, and, when it had a headache, it would have to appear on the road and wait for a priest to arrive and heal it with consecrated water. That is why the snake comes out on the road and people strike it in the head with a club and kill it." "The snake is the Devil's finger. He is a tricky finger and think of what he could do with it. I'd better cut it off and give myself a helping hand. And, as soon as he [God] threw it on Earth, it started to move around. It had become a snake." (Bucovina).

September 16

The "Glades" Used Against Invaders

The making of a *glade* or clearing surrounded by trees among which branches and brambles were placed, was an ingenious defense system against horse-riding invaders who came to plunder the land. From fir-tree tops people made spears pointing outwards then hid them in a fence surrounding the lawn. Such a defense lawn was set up in the village of Ieud, Maramures County, on the Cârligatura mountain top, in a place called *"In the Glades"* by the locals. In the Maramures region people call "glade" a piece of land in a forest used as a hayfield or a grazing field.

Other natural features were used by village communities in their defense battles. "Here, in Bistrita Bargaului," recounted one villager, "there were forests and swamps. When the Tatars came, passing through Tihuta, they were lured into the swamp and were defeated. From then on the place was called Tatarca and Tatarca Stones. In the past, people used to say that the treasures belonging to the ruler Petru Rares were hidden in that place."

September 17

"Mioi" Summer

The period of fifteen days between "Mioi" and Good Friday of the old style between September 29 and October 14, when a temporary warming of the weather is expected, is called *Mioi Summer*. As both on "Mioi" day and on Good Friday, there was a custom of letting the rams free in the sheep herds for reproduction. The two days were also called The Sheep's Wedding or The Rams' Rush.

September 18

The Trek Cart

Folk traditions recorded for *The Romanian Ethnographic Atlas* mention the use of a *trek cart with two shafts* by refugees from invaders, boats for transporting both cattle and food to the pond, pits in which food was hidden, and a grinding mill which was an indispensable item of the inventory carried.

"The grinding mill and a cask with cheese were put in the cart, people took their cattle and headed for the woods." (Oancea, Galati County)

"The cart had two shafts. We would put the grinding mill and the maize in it and run to the woods." (Padurea Seaca)

"In the cart we would grind the maize for the porridge." (Scornicesti, Olt County)

"When the Turks were coming, they would put the grinding mill in the cart and run to a place called Rapa Sanilii. They would stay there until the Turks went away." (Vladesti, Galati County)

Carriage of the Bird-Goddess Drawn by Swans, Banat (Serbian Region / Berciu, 1967)

"Every householder had a boat. He would put the grinding mill and the cereals in it and go to the Prut River and then on the top of the bank ridges. When they finished the grains they would go to the food pit, in the night, and get some more. They also took the cattle there. They would hide the cereals in the food pits and take refuge in the woods." (Oancea, Galați County) Terrified by the way the Turks plundered the town of Targoviste, stories are told of Paul of Alep and other Syrian clericals following the Romanian peasants' example.

"We had already sent all our things up in the mountains, some time before, with the help of that reliable abbot. He had given one, two or three bundles containing our things, to the groups of peasants living in those mountains... to keep them or to hide them in caves and in secret places up in the mountains which were known only by them."[155]

September 19
Spreading the News

The Romanian phrase *spreading the news*, literally translated as "stretching a rope all over the country," recalls a system of danger signals by lighting fires on top of high places. The smoke from those fires rose up in the air and was carried by the wind in the direction where it was blowing, leaving behind a white or grey plume in the sky. Those "ropes" of smoke were predictors of tragic events! Lamentations and cries, sounds of horns and bells, all of them announced the beginning of an anticipated ordeal. Road security was ensured and organized by every village community living along roadways, mountain passes and gorges in the Carpathian Mountains.

"Fires were set on the hillocks when the Turks and the Tatars were coming. That's how it used to be announced." (Vladesti, Galati County)

"The village guard would be on the vineyard's hill. When the Turks were coming in a dry times, the dust they raised could be seen from far away. The horn was blown and fires were lighted." (Gheraseni, Buzau County)

"From Peter's Valley they would go up to Tocatoare. That is where the oldest people in the village would beat the wooden plate when the Turks were coming." (Plopesaru, Gorj County)

"When the Turks were coming, fires were lighted on the hill and the horn was blown. People would grab their clubs and come out. If the Turks were too many, they would take refuge the woods." (Frumuselu, Vaslui County)

Even today, between Braila and Suceava, some visible hillocks of anthropogenic origin are placed according to the configuration of the land at a distance of 10 to 15 to 20 kilometers from each other. The old people maintained that, on those hillocks, there was always litter for lighting fires. The news that invaders had crossed the border was visually

---

[155] Ghinoiu, 2004, p. 33-34.

transmitted to the ruler's court in a couple of hours, which was much faster than using the traditional means of transport that would take a couple of days.

"The hillocks on Braila Road exist since the time of Stephen the Great. An observatory was set up and the garbage was set on fire when the Turks came." (Oancea, Galati County)

A row of hillocks were also built on, the east-west direction for signaling the Tatars' penetration into Moldavia.

"Braila Road, with hillocks on it, took one to Suceava. From those hillocks the coming of the Turks was announced. There was another row of hillocks coming from the Nistru River. From those the coming of the Tatars was announced by lighting fires. In Suceava one could see where the smoke was coming from and who were the enemies: the Turks from the south, or the Tatars from the east." (Vladesti, Galati County)

September 20
The Turks' Bird

Against foreign invaders, mainly Turks and Tatars, peasants saught refuge in the swamps close to the Danube and the Prut River, river meadows, marshes and flooded areas near rivers, forests, and rugged lands that were difficult to reach. Forests provided not only shelter in times of danger, but also wood for making fire and for building cottages, and food from hunting.

But because of the jackdaw, a bird that usually flies in circles around the places where people are present even in the most secret meadows in the forest, the Turks could find where the refugees were hiding. The people called it *"the Turks' bird."* The jackdaw, being a strong, cruel rapacious and invincible bird, ingrained its name in people's memory, through its own trill (ga! ga!), when it invokes rain in the hot summer days. Like angels, the jackdaw follows man constantly, flying in circles around his head. Folk sayings still used in present times such as "to be struck by the jackdaw," meaning "to get into trouble, or "watch out the jackdaw will come and get you" were used to scare naughty children.

September 21
The House with A Hiding Place

An adjustment to traditional house design was the building of an additional room with no door and no windows, called *the secret room* or *the hiding place*. Between the entrance hall and the "clean room", a tiny room had been built, with no door and no windows. The access to the hiding place was, if necessary through the attic. In times of insecurity, people would use the secret room to store a girl's trousseaux, festive clothes and food provisions. In some regions, like in Oltenia and Walachia Plains, to an entrance hall and main room was added a well hidden tiny room.

"The cottage had an entrance hall and one room," a villager recounted. "There was also a little pantry where the most valuable things were kept and where the girls could hide from the Turks. One could get into it through a very small door, painted with lime to avoid being noticed. They also put a quilt in there." (Smârdioasa, Teleorman County)

Stag and Birds on a Goblet from the Funeral Getical Thesaurus, Agighiol, IV Century B.C. (Calendar 1998, Photo by George Dumitriu)

September 22
The House with Two Entrances

The oldest traditional Romanian houses had the main entrance on the same side as the windows and the porch. The appearance of the second entrance door, situated on the back side which was not facing the road, generally on the wall oriented towards north, was a technical innovation with a well defined strategic role.

"My grandfather had a house built of beams, with two entrances. When the Turks were coming, the family escaped through the back door." (Visina, Dambovita County).

"The house would be built far away from the road, at the edge of the grazing field. Its windows were small and were covered in the evening to prevent the light inside from being seen from outside" (Frumuselu, Vaslui County)

September 23
Holidays Around the Autumn Equinox

Around the time of the autumn equinox, the Folk Almanac retains the memory of an ancient start-of-the-year celebration of the Neolithic Mother Goddess's Death and Rebirth. This was overlaid with the Virgin Mary's Death and Birth by Christian theologians. Setting first the death date on August 15, and then the birth date a lunar month later on

September 8, the Christian Church maintained the pre-Christian model. First, having reached an old age, the divinity, commonly called Great Saint Mary or Great Holy Mary, dies and then Little Saint Mary or Little Holy Mary is born. Some of the customs around the equinox specifically for the Little Saint Mary celebration were taken over from The Raising of the Holy Cross on September 14, a celebration close in time to the former one and which is better known as The Day of the Cross, or, in some places, as The Day of the Snake.

September 24
The "Tecle" Celebrations

Tecle are evil mythical representations related to fire and wolves, celebrated in shepherd communities on September 24, which took their name from the female Saint Martyr called Tecla as recorded in the Christian Orthodox Almanac. Locally, these representations are celebrated during the Ram Raisers' days of September 26 to 29. "Tecle" like "Philippies" could be calmed down through severe work interdictions on their celebration day. It was forbidden to sweep the house or to throw ashes out of the house for fear female wolves would find the glowing embers and eat them in order to be able to have cubs. In some localities, it was also forbidden to work with wool or with animal skins. (Low Carpathian Mountain areas in Walachia)

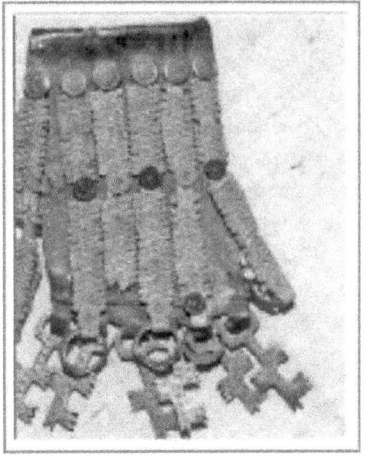

September 25
Unsafe Conditions for Girls and Wives

Rings and Small Keys Decoration Worn by Housewives, Cerbal, Hunedoara County (Isfanoni, 2004; Photo by Dan Niculescu, 1998)

One could resist the Turks and the Tatars through peaceful means or through violent battles. "When the Turks drew near, young married women and unwed girls used to smear their faces with soot and tie headscarves over their heads to look like old women, and to walk limping while carrying a bundle with a heavy stones in it." (Cavadinesti, Galati County).

"You see, up on the high mountain peaks, there were four pits where the unmarried girls would go hiding. They had clothes there and people would bring them food in the night. They would stay there until the danger was over. Every year people would repair those pits and smear them with clay. Inside they looked like huge barrels." (Cândesti, Dâmbovita County).

"When the Turks came to the Teius Valley people were taking part in a ring dance in a secluded place. The girls got frightened and threw themselves in a well. My grandmother, Stana, who died at the age of 105, used to say that, if somebody dug in that place, they would find bones and necklaces made of gold coins." (Isaresti, Olt County)

"When I was a church singer, the old priest, who died many years ago, told me that once a man came to him to confess his sins. A Turk who had come riding from remote places made him hold his horse while he went into the house and take advantage of the man's wife. The man said that he killed the Turk. After killing him, he drove away the Turk's horse and then threw the body in a precipice, covering it with stable garbage and with earth from the precipice. If someone dug in that place, they would find his bones there." (Vladesti, Galati County)

September 26
Memories of Ottoman rule

Under Ottoman Empire influence administrative units were set called "raiale." They housed Turkish officials and soldiers to ensure that the Romanian Provinces properly fulfilled their duties towards the Ottoman Porte. Those were also the places where scheming took place with Turks for the appointment of Romanian rulers. Those "raiale" were located at critical road junctions through which food and goods demanded by the Empire where transported. The same roads were used by marauding groups of Turks setting out on unexpected plundering raids. Romanian inhabitants of "raiale," such as those in the southern Dobrogea region, although benefiting from certain guarantees had to endure abuses from Ottoman soldiers and officials.

The wide dispersion of Romanian villages along the roads in Dobrogea was an outcome of plundering raids by the "Cherkezi," an Asian population tolerated by the Turks at the beginning of the Nineteenth Century.

"Some really bad people passed over here. They were killing, stealing the girls and taking advantage of the wives. They were tall, strong men and didn't eat salt. They were called Cherkezi." (Nalbant, Tulcea County)

"When the Cherkezi arrived, people would run away, hiding in the swamps, in holes where fish and crayfish usually hid. In 1877, the "Cherkezi" were driven out of Dobrogea. When they left, they took our oxen and sheep with them".

September 27
Turks and Tatars

The toponomy, the anthroponomy, and especially the expression "You run as if the Tatars were coming", or "The Tatars have set the village on fire and the old woman just sits combing her hair," reflect the deep-seated fear provoked by unexpected attacks by Turks and Tatars. The flat, broad plains of Wallachia and Dobrogea made such incursions easy and this more frequent.

Biblical characters in a Romanian "olac" (carriage) (Miniature 1844)

When the peasant uprising of 1907 repression began, authorities assumed that memories of cruelties committed by Turks would still be fresh. This allowed them to spread spurious rumors of an *imminent coming of Turks*. To make the rumor credible, authorities brought Romanian from Dobrogea dressed in Turkish clothes. An old man recalled his participation:

"I was wearing a Turkish fez on my head and I was uttering Turkish words, here and there. I didn't shoot at he insurgents. The landowners provided food and drink for us."[156]

---

[156] Babonea Anghel, 89 years old, Alimanu village, Constanta County, investigation made by the author in 1978.

September 28
The Village Fence

The village fence, also called *the village ditch*, is found in the Romanian plains of Dobrogea and in southeastern Moldavia. Until the beginning of the Twentieth Century, the ditch or the village fence served a dual role. One was economic by protecting both crops and vineyards situated outside the village from being damaged by grazing village cattle, and another for defense by hindering the penetration of malefactors, mainly Turks, who were appeared in random groups to plunder the village.

"The village was surrounded with the village fence. Each household would dig a deep ditch along the distance where his house was placed, on the field side. On the earth that was dug out and in the ditch grew plants like welted thistle, *lesser burdock* and box thorns. No man and no cattle could cross over that ditch. The only way one could enter a village was through the gate in the village fence, that was kept closed during the night." (Vladesti, Galati County)

In the village of Gropeni village (Braila County), "the defense ditch was four meters wide and about three and a half meters deep. The earth dug out from the ditch was pressed and shaped into a wall and over it fences of reed were build. In rainy weather the ditch filled with water, which dried out in periods of drought. The ditch could be crossed on *small wooden bridges* and, when the water dried out, some *small steps* made in the earth were used."[157]

September 29
Shepherd Roads

Over millennia, the constant and lengthy movement of sheep flocks between mountain and plain areas, called the Trans-Humance Movement, created *Shepherd Roads*. Folk legends explain the origin of these roads.

"Once, when they left the mountains with their sheep to go down to the plains, there was a limping sheep which remained alone. Then it left by itself it followed the same route and eventually caught-up with the others by the river bank. That is why people call that route the sheep's road."

"When the Turks came plundering the country they took away a lamb from a sheep. Followed the Turks, the sheep cried and drew its tail on the ground thus making a track, which was then called the sheep's road."

---

[157] Moraru, 1975, p. 28-29.

"A sheep goat got lost in the Balkans and found her way back home in the Carpathians all by itself. From then on people called that way the sheep's way."

"That name comes from a time when a sheep was left behind with its lambs, on the river bank and it climbed all the way up to the mountain, by itself."

"Once, a shepherd fell asleep and lost his sheep. When he woke up, he started looking for them. He followed the sheep's road and found them."

Stone cross on Sheep's Path
(AIEF Photo by Petrescu, No. 78 360)

The shepherd roads were known under various names: *The Sheep's Road, The Wool Road* (Caraula village, Dolj County), *The Butter Road* that crossed the former counties of Teleorman and Vlasca all the way to Giurgiu on the Danube River, *The Cheese Barrel Road*, evidenced at Matau, Arges County, *The Shepherd Road, The Albanians' Road*, or *The Sheep's Mountain Path*.

The shepherd roads have radial directions, starting from the shepherd villages in the Carpathians, or close to the Carpathians and reaching their terminal points situated as far as 1000 kilometers (600 miles) away. These roads follow river courses and paths. Orientation on these roads is not an easy task. To find their way shepherds raise stone crosses. These are used to orient the sheep herds and to gauge distances by counting the day's and the week's walk. The sheep herds can face serious problems when crossing wide rivers, mainly the Danube, over fords, ice drifts and raft bridges. The shepherds are skilled travelers, with inquiring minds, people who know the ways of the world and who are able, at any time to establish settlements, no matter how daring and or how remote they might be. As they used to wander long distances, covering wide territories, in older times, they would often bring news about the Turkish or Tatar armies preparing their attacks.

September 30
Mail Cart Road

In the past centuries there were two main ways of transmitting news from one place to another. One was by lighting fires on high places and another by sending people with messages and orders. The latter method became the basis of the modern mail service.

The royal couriers used to travel on horseback through villages and towns where horses were provided them. The expression *mail horse* dates back to the times when the mail horses traveled long and difficult distances and it is used for someone who is exhausted from hard work. "To make someone run around like a mail horse," means in Romanian to send someone to solve difficult problems in a short time.

When the number of couriers grew, *mail carts* came into being. These were a type of small, two-wheeled carriages used by diplomats, foreign messengers and by couriers to carry mail to neighboring countries. On occasion, foreign travelers passing through The Romanian Provinces of Moldavia and Walachia recorded ways in which transport was organized on those mail cart roads. In 1585, Francois de Piavie, Senior de Fouirquevauls, on his way from Turkey to Poland crossed Moldavia, traveling by the mail cart, which he described as a small carriage, so low and so light "that a slight wrong movement, could make one easily fall off it. There was just enough room for one person some food and a pillow." Paul de Alep, while traveling in Moldavia, in 1650, greatly appreciated the Romanian mail cart, due to which, "we were able to travel faster than the flight of a bird."[158]

---

[158] Urechia, 1911, p. 31.

OCTOBER

"BRUMAREL"

LITTLE WHITE FROSTY MONTH

1. Samedru and the Pig
2. Brasov Carriages on the Mail Road
3. The Goblin
4. The Big Road
5. The Ice Bridge
6. Fords and Bridges Across Waterways
7. Stops or "Un-yoking Places"
8. Barter
9. Vlasia Forest
10. The Inn
11. The Shepherd Civilization
12. Leading Sheep Down From the Mountains
13. The Shepherd New Year
14. Great Friday (Venera) - The Sheep's Wedding
15. Dacian and Celtic New Year
16. Anthropic Mimetism
17. Tuesday Hag
18. "Lucin"
19. Saint Peter and the Wolf
20. Painless Labor
21. The Village Word-of-Mouth
22. Samedru Fathers
23. Evil Time: Breaking the Cart
24. The Traveler and the Well
25. The Fire Rite at Samedru
26. Samedru
27. Settling Day
28. The Navel, A Stopped Up Mouth of the Body
29. Salt and Salary
30. The Salt of the Earth
31. Salt Roads

October

is the eighth month in the Roman Almanac beginning on March 1, and it is the tenth month in the Julian (old style) and Gregorian (new style) Almanacs. The common name of the month, *Little Hoar Frost*, announces the first white frost and the approach of winter. Various economic activities are typical for the period between autumn and winter. Autumn sowing of seeds is continued; crops are harvested in the fields, vineyards, orchards and vegetable gardens; grazing fields are opened for the community's cattle; sheep mate and the herds are started towards their winter places; shepherd and craft products are traded in popular fairs organized at Samedru and at Great Friday (Saint Paraschiva) and agreements made in April, at Sangiorz, are finalized. Spiritual life in October is dominated by the Shepherd holidays and customs: "Procoava", Great Friday, The End of Mioi Summer, Samedru Summer, "Lucin," The Saturday of the Dead, The Autumn Fathers, The Fire of Samedru. Saint Dumitru is the patron of the month for Macedo-Romanians and Megleno-Romanians.[159]

Samedru's Fire, Rucar, Arges County (AIEF Photo by L. David)

---

[159] MALR, 1967, Map 606.

October 1
Samedru and the Pig

The stories about *Samedru* relate to two distinct civilizations, an agrarian (harvesting) one and a pastoral (shepherd) one.

"Samedru is a shepherd who never leaves his sheep herd which he takes to graze in the middle of the forest in places where no human being has ever set foot." When he died, it was at his sheepfold.

In a legend from the Muscel region south of the Carpathian Mountains, Samedru turns into a pig which itself is an ancient mythical representation of the wheat spirit. According to the legend an old man and his old wife, who were childless, set out in the wide-world hoping to find a being that they could grow as their own child. While the old man was walking, he found a pig. At the same time coincidentally, the king of the country in which the old man and wife found themselves challenged young suitors who wished to marry his daughter to carry out some difficult tasks. None was successful except for the old man's pig. Being able to accomplish all the tasks, the pig married the king's daughter. Every night, the pig got rid of its skin and turned into a handsome young man. But one night, his wife threw his skin into the fire. Quite upset, the young man told her that he was Samedru and that he would go away. But only by searching and finding him, would she be able to give birth to their child. It was said that it took her nine years to find him and then lived together happily ever after.

October 2
Coachmen

The livelihood of Romanian *coachmen* drew the attention of a French traveler passing through Walachia and Moldavia at the beginning of the Twentieth Century. He wrote that though having traveled in carriages for over 40,000 leagues, he had never met coachmen like the Moldo-Walachian ones anywhere in the world. He thought that even the most indifferent and the dullest person could not help enjoying the spectacle put on by the Moldo-Walachian coachmen with their skill, livelihood, quickness and high spirits. However, he noted, they were also notorious for using bad language. People used to say about coachmen that "they were people whose flesh had been cut off their legs, so that they could run as fast as a horse, without feeling tired." Since they spent most of their time on the road and were very little time at home, the word *coachman* was commonly used about someone who neglected his family and his household.

In 1840 the ruler of Walachia decided to introduce *Brasov carriages* to transport travelers on the main mail roads. Each carriage was covered with a tarpaulin and could transport six people. Ion Ghica, a Romanian writer, economist and politician, described a journey he made from Bucharest to Iasi before 1848.

"After paying visits to the officials, which meant running around for about 10 days, one Friday afternoon at 3 o'clock, I finally heard some clatter of hoofs and saw eight horses with two coachmen and a riding courier come into the yard. In no time, they had harnessed the horses, two by two, to a kind of light carriage, that could easily be drawn just by one horse; in a twinkling of the eye, we were at the end of the Outer Fair Bridge, which is now the [Mosilor] Barrier; the coachmen were shouting and snapping their whips in the streets of Bucharest, so loudly that they rose the whole city, men and women rushing to the doors and windows of their houses, to see who was passing by ..."[160]

October 3

The Goblin

The witch or person who sells his or her soul to the devil receives from him a little devil named *Goblin* as a reward. The Goblin can be gotten by other means too. If an egg of a black hen is wrapped in hemp and carried in the armpit a Goblin chick will hatch; or someone unaware may take the Goblin by stealing an object from someone who had the devil.

The Goblin, or Nichipercea, Sarsaila, The Little One, is a small, strong, knowledgeable, lively, tricky and a discoverer of new things devil, It has a chick's face which can turn into a fly, cat, dog, rabbit, he-goat, horse. It can satisfy any wish, binds lovers or breaks their love, brings disease, ailments, death, predicts the future.

In exchange for fulfilling wishes, the recipient must take care of Goblin' s food, drink and cigarettes. If this is not obeyed troubles can occur even the death of the one who bought the Goblin. When its master is on the death bed, the Goblin torments him or her and when he or she dies takes him or her directly to hell. That is why those who had the Goblin and had advantages tried, when old, to get rid of it by selling it or confessing to the priest and having services in the church.

---

[160] Ghica, 1959, p. 108-109.

October 4
The Big Road

The ways of communication that were more highly trafficked were called, until our time, *big roads*. Outlaws used to rob people at the *big road*. When the big roads had to cross over waterways, carriages used floating bridges, for which a fare had to be paid. But most often carriages were driven directly through water, wading through it, or people waited until winter came, when they could traverse over ice bridges.

Wood carriage on the 'Big Road'
(Ethnographic Atlas of Romania, Vol 2, 2005)

More precise details about crossing over water courses and about charging for crossing over bridges are given in a document issued during Stephen the Great reign, on 3 July 1460: "In Cernauti, for one carriage, be it German or Armenian styled, they have to pay four coins, but only when crossing on floating bridges; when the water is frozen, or when carriages made through it, they shall pay nothing." Due to favorable conditions for trading, most of the Romanian boroughs and towns developed near running water fords where the riverbed was wider and the speed of the water was lower, thus making it easier for the carriages to cross.[161]

October 5
The Ice Bridge

At Romania's geographic latitude rivers sometimes freeze over in winter, a climate feature that was taken advantage of for local transport. Yet, crossing rivers on ice bridges involved serious risks as people and their sledges did fall into the icy water. Drowning was considered one of

---

[161] Ghinoiu, 2004, p. 45.

the most terrifying ways of dying. For those who disappeared in the icy waters and frozen to death a proper funeral ceremony was difficult to perform.

On the lengthy Danube River, ice packs often started appearing downstream in November and would eventually form firmly interlocked ice bridges. On such a bridge Michael the Brave's army of 60,000 warriors crossed over into the Balkans on its way to Turkey in 1594. In contrast, foreign armies from the Mediterranean area moving north of the Danube always organized them only during the summer in order to avoid the cold winters requiring extensive preparations and special battle techniques. Some of the great rulers who embarked on northward expeditions included Darius I, the Persian king in his war against the Scythians, Alexander the Great, the Roman Emperor Trajan, later Byzantine emperors and Sultans of the Ottoman Empire on frequent occasions.

October 6
Fords and bridges across waterways

Ferry boat on the Somes River (Ethnographic Atlas of Romania, Vol 2, 2005)

The Romanians' sense of cautiousness when crossing a waterway is rendered by the expression: "It is safer to walk along a river a whole day than drown in the morning." This traces back to old methods of travel when the best way of crossing a river was at a *ford* where the river is less deep. This occurs at wider points in the river's course and one can walk, ride or drive a carriage drawn by cattle across it. Irrespective of their orientation on land, the trade roads would always bundle together at those points along rivers in which were located the most important and passable fords.

The simple and efficient method of cutting a long tree and propping it across a river, between its two banks, thus obtaining an improvised bridge to walk on, is used even today in most villages in the mountain, hill and plateau areas. Between crossing the river in a boat and crossing it on a real bridge, there was an intermediary stage, namely using the mobile bridge, that was a kind of footbridge laid on a couple of boats, which was moved from one bank to the other. The floating bridge is an ancient technique that survives until our days. It is used by villagers for their local transport needs and could be easily removed in case of danger.

Whether it is people going to work in the field, carts filled with produce and hay, or cattle being taken to the grazing fields, all cross from one bank to the other on these "vessels" whose steersmen served too as "bridge" tax collectors. It is quite likely that in places where rivers flowed through gorges or deep valleys with steep slopes, bridges were made from rawhide. According to some legends from the ethnographical Muscel Area, when the legendary ruler Negru Voda was forced to withdraw with his troops from the Tatars, to Cetatuia, in Dambovita County, he had a bridge built across the water with animal skins.

October 7
Stops or "Un-yoking Places"

People traveling in ox-drawn carts, horse-carriages on old roads would stop from time to time at *"un-yoking places"*, so-named because there the oxen were freed from their yokes. Those rest stops were placed at the edge of settlements in areas protected from strong winds and with an accessible source of water. When evening came, every rider, coachman or ordinary traveler on foot stopped there, ate a meal, and rested together with their animals and thus be best prepared to continue their trip the next day.

Resting Place for Animals & Travelers
(AIEF Photo by Vladutiu)

Alongside their carts, travelers prepared their corn meal and other foods. This opportunity was used to inform one another about weather conditions and distances between villages. Those stops were small nuclei of social life where the transporters' interests intersected with locals' interests. Such crossroads, river fords and mountain passes in the Carpathians thus served as routes by which culture and civilization were spread. Over the centuries people stopped for longer periods and where commercial life took root prosperous trading villages or towns ensued.

October 8
Barter

Apples for Corn Barter in Olt County (AIEF Photo by L. Vladutiu)

The exchange of goods called *barter* is a verbal agreement between two parties who exchange things between themselves. As a human activity, barter preceded modern commerce in which money is the common medium of exchange. In medieval times, due to lack of cash even Romanian rulers resorted to barter. Old documents, for example, record the Moldavian ruler Stefan Tomsa as ordering three carts filled with tin from Bistrita in exchange for cattle, or the case of Alexandru Lapusneanu who promised wine to Romanians living in the Bistrita region in exchange for oil and other produce.

At the beginning of the Twentieth Century, most people living in Carpathian and Sub-Carpathian mountain areas bartered their handicrafts made of wood, animal produce, fruit and distilled plum brandy for wheat, maize, barley, rye, and oats from the plains and low plateau regions.

October 9
Vlasia Forest

Travelers often grouped together in defense against robbers as well as to help one another find their way on country roads or to cross large rivers. Hence the Romanian expression: "To get oneself a travel companion." Additional precautions had to be taken against robbers especially when tradesmen were traveling the 50 kilometer (30 mile) Bucharest-Ploiesti road which crossed through *Vlasia Forest*. A history of unfortunate experiences on that road is the origin of the colloquial expression: "To rob someone as in Vlasia Forest."

Basic preparations were carried out by those taking long voyages. Before setting off on a long voyage for the purpose of selling their goods in exchange for money or produce, handicraftsmen would gather food provisions for people and their animals as well as pots for cooking food, mainly a cast iron kettle for making cornmeal, and some tools for repairing their carts. Departure from home took place according to a certain ritual, which included a psychological preparation in anticipation of probable hardships. *Drum Bun* meaning "Travel the road well!" is a wish addressed today to travelers even in present times. If a handicraftsman managed to sell his goods quickly, he would help his travel companions with their own trading activities, or he would wait for them in a neighboring village so that they could make the return trip as a group.

October 10
The Inn

Inns or lodges were most often located at crossroads along the roads traveled by the most important tradesmen, officials and foreign diplomats. The ancient "Hanul lui Manuc" in Bucharest is one of the last large gated-inns of this type in Romania to survive as a hostelry. Rooms, located around a large courtyard, served as secure accommodations for travelers, vehicles and goods during the night. The inns not only offered guest rooms but also stables and, in many cases, workshops for repairing carts and carriages. Large protective gates made it easier to guard against robbers and in winter time to be protected against severe snow storms or wolf attacks. Throughout the year, the inns were always animated with travelers. People met and made friends and often plotted political intrigues.

Writers connected inns with mysterious happenings, as in I. L. Caragiale's short story "Manjoala's Inn", or with profound meanings, as in Mihail Sadoveanu's "Ancuta Inn." In the latter's case, the inn was the metaphor of a much wider world. Ancuta's Inn was like a fortress accommodating both storytellers and listeners who were offered wine from the Low Country in new red clay pots: "You see, that inn was not just an inn, it was a fortress. It had thick walls and gates bound with iron padlocks that I had never seen before in my life. People, animals and carriages could find a safe shelter there and no one had to worry a bit about robbers", or "Such fortress walls, such iron bars, such wine cellars and such wine could not be found anywhere else, nor such sweet and careful atmosphere, not to mention the dark eyes; I would just sit and watch them until the time came for me to leave for the land with no snow storms."[162]

October 11
The Shepherd Civilization

Figurines made of green ewe cheese, Neruja, Vrancea County (Cherciu, 2003)

A special lifestyle was inspired by shepherds. For the most efficient use of grazing fields or hayfields many times located far from the precincts of the village, the shepherds built special shelters for people and for animals, dug wells, and created pathways for their sheep. These were also used to transport salt. The abundance of natural resources created favorable conditions for the development of home industry in wool processing, in making wool products as well as animal skins and furs. The transfer of herds to and from high mountain pastures played a special role in the shepherd culture. Practiced into present times, this type of shepherding called 'transhumance' reached its climax in the middle of the Nineteenth Century. Huge sheep flocks covered many hundreds of kilometers spanning.

In their search of grazing fields, Romanian shepherds roamed vast areas from the Sub-Carpathian areas and those from the regions south of the Danube River and would spend the summer in the high Carpathians pastures stretching up to Moldavia and Silezia or southward to the Dinaric Mountains of the Balkans, the Pindus, and the Rodope, or eastward to the Caucasian Mountains. Winters were spent in the plains close to the shores of the seas: The Mediterranean, The Caspic, The Adriatic, the Ionic, the Aegean and in the Caspian Steppe regions stretching up to Crimea and to the Northern Caucasus. In this manner shepherds created lengthy communication routes, set up villages and towns, and contributed to maintaining the spiritual and cultural unity of Romanians and of South-Eastern Europe peoples.

---

[162] Sadoveanu, 1973, p. 4.

October 12
Leading Sheep Down From the Mountains

The period for starting to lead sheep herds down from the mountains, starting around Great Saint Mary in mid-August 15, lasts into October. During ensuing weeks, once in the villages, the herd is scattered, meaning that individual owners picks up his marked sheep, the cheese produced is allocated and shepherds receive their pay. Celebrations between owners and shepherds follow the settlement of mutual affairs. Unfortunately, often on these occasions misunderstandings arise from which certain sayings originated.

At sheepfold set up,
Dogs will fight;
While at sheepfold break up,
Masters will fight!
or
In spring, dogs will fight,
In autumn, masters will quarrel!

Transhumance in Nucsoara,
Arges County
(AIEF Photo by I. Ghinoiu, 1975)

Shepherds have to face hard conditions some natural such as rainfalls, snow, snowstorms, hundreds and thousands of kilometers on foot, others from man-induced banditry. All of this makes for a heavy burden even for the shepherds reputed capacity for mental and physical endurance. In addition, the long absence of the shepherd husband from home means that all the household responsibilities are left in the wife's charge:

When you go away with your sheep,
I must take care of all the needs.
In winter you are at the riverbank,
In summer you are up in the mountains,
You and I are never together!

October 13

The Shepherd New Year

The Romanian Shepherds' Almanac is divided into two equal seasons: *the shepherd summer,* between Sangiorz on April 23, and Samedru on October 26, and *the shepherd winter,* between October and April. Midsummer is marked by Santilie on July 20, honoring a Christian Saint who is selected to take over the tasks of a prehistoric god of the Fire and of the Sun. Mid-winter is marked by the Wolves' Sanpetru the night of January 15 to 16, when this feared divinity gives the wolves their expected year's worth of sheep, cattle, and humans.

The starting points of the Shepherd Seasons (Sangiorz and Samedru) and their midpoints (Santilie and the Wolves' Sanpetru) are key moments in planning the shepherd's full activity. Counting the days in a two-season almanac year, summer and winter could start both at Sangiorz, after the sheep give birth to their lambs, the lambs have been weaned and the herds have been taken up to the mountains, and at Samedru after the sheep are taken down from the mountains and mated. The beginning of any of these two seasons is marked by elaborate ritualized events which included sacrifices of a lamb at Sangiorz and of a ram at Samedru.

The shepherds' flocks, sterile during the shepherd summer, are fertilized at the start of winter, while the farmers' crops are sterile in winter and fertile in summer. This is why, unlike the agrarian New Year celebrated at Dochia's symbolical death and rebirth from March 1 to 9 when the grass starts to show its blades and the forest comes to leaf, the shepherd's New Year begins around Samedru between 14 to 27 October in the period when sheep mate and trees shed their leaves.

October 14

Great Friday (Venera) - The Sheep's Wedding

The folk feast taking place at the *Great Friday* (14 October) is dedicated to Saint Friday, the mythical representation associated with the Goddess Venera (in Romanian "vineri" means Friday) in the Roman Pantheon that was initially the protector of vegetation and fertility. At Romania's geographic latitude, the reproduction cycle of sheep and goats can start in spring or in autumn. But for economic reasons, shepherds keep females separate from males during the summer until Great Friday and sometimes even until Archangels on November 8.

The days during which the rams are let free in the sheep flocks for mating are called *The Sheep's Wedding* or *The Ram Rush*. By this timing, the lambs and the kids born in spring can benefit from the warm season and greater abundance of food and thus more fit to survive the winter season. After a 21-week period of gestation, from Great Friday until March, the lambs and the kids are born when there are clear signs that the weather is getting warm. Weaning, that is separating the lambs and the kids from the sheep and the goats to make them feed on their own takes place at Sangiorz.

Venus on seashell, from the Casa della Venere in conchiglia, Pompeii. Before AD 79

On day during which the ancient Goddess Venera was celebrated, the Orthodox Church overlayed the celebration of the Christian Saint Parascheva. Similar in stature to the Virgin Mary, being called Great Saint Mary in the Folk almanac, the Goddess Venera acquires her own greatness and is called Great Venera or Great Friday.

There are ethnological arguments confirming the fact that the great pilgrimage to the Three Hierarchs Church in Iasi on October 14, whose patron is Saint Parascheva, when hundreds of thousands of people honor a late Christian replica of the cult dedicated to the prehistoric Mother Goddess, represented under various names in the Folk Almanac as Virgin Mary, Dochia, Old Fairy, Mother of the Forest, Great Friday. She is invoked for healing diseases, helping girls to get married and women to give birth to children. Great Friday has taken over some of the features of the usurped Goddess Venera and, in time became a major almanac reference point demarking important shepherd activities of which sheep mating is critical.

Between the actual day of the week "Friday" and the event "Great Friday," there is no special connection. Great Friday is a holiday with a fixed date and can fall on any given day of the week.

October 15
Dacian and Celtic New Year

Dacian sanctuary at
Sarmizgetusa
(AIEF Photo by E. Tarcomnicu,
L. David 2002)

Like the Romanians who preserved a lot of customs typical of the shepherd New Year, the nations of Celtic designation had a shepherd almanac consisting of two seasons: Summer from Armindeni on May 1 to All Saints' Day November 1, and Winter from November 1 and May 1. The fact that only a few days differentiate the Dacian territory (present-day Romania) from the Celtic ones is explained by the distinction in geographic latitude and in local climate conditions in which modern-day descendants of the Dacians and of the Celts live. On the Isle of Man, a place which best preserved and defended the ancient traditions against later invaders, on November 1 (old style) local groups sing a song called Hogmany that started with the words "Tonight is the New Year's Night, Hogunaa!"[163]

October 16
Anthropic Mimetism

At the point of juncture between Europe, Asia and Africa, three fertile *cornucopias* existed in ancient times: the lower river basins and deltas of the Danube, of the Tigris and Euphrates and of the Nile. In each case the indigenous populations in their struggle for survival had several options: to capitulate in front of frequent invaders and thereby adopt the coward's attitude of "those who bend their heads, no sword shall cut their heads," or to defend themselves with their lives, or to find diplomatic solutions leading to agreements, compromises, tributes, or reconciliations; or to watch for the enemies' intentions and to prepare for a final confrontation in which defeat of the aggressor was assured; or to avoid unnecessary loss by withdrawing into inaccessible refuges and outwait the enemy.

Ruling out extreme solutions, namely surrendering without any opposition or fighting when there was no chance of victory, the Carpato-Danubian population chose other forms of resistance through reconcilia-

---

[163] Frazer, 1980, vol. V, p. 25-27.

tion, sometimes a temporary one, following the saying "become the devil's brother until you have crossed the bridge." In short, it meant compromise, temporary payment of tribute, self-isolation (simulating death), and the voluntary acceptance of modest living conditions.

Well documented is the vital role played by *pit house villages* which were used as strategic shelters until the nineteenth century. Dwellings, as well as churches, mills, stables, pubs and inns, were built underground. Protection was provided also by forests, mountains, as well as the Danube River with its broad delta and swamps. Resorted to for millennia, these survival solutions instilled widely shared reflexive behaviors and attitudes. This is exemplified by the Jews' history and by the Romanians' history. In times of deep crisis, they sought exile in places situated close to or further away from their land of origin in Palestine. Romanians did the same. Often, Jewish people chose to fight and punish the enemy according to the principle "eye for an eye" while Romanians chose to fight and then to reconcile, compromise or pay tribute to the enemy. Labeled 'anthropic mimetism' by academics, it influenced both peoples' behavior and mentality in different ways but in each case the attitude adopted ensured survival.[164]

October 17

Tuesday Hag

Tuesday Hag is a female mythical representation of Tuesday. In some areas she was called Tuesday Evening. In the folk imagination she looks like an old woman who has devilish powers, or like a ghost woman or "strigoi" who lives in remote forests or in the sky. She roams in villages during Tuesday to Wednesday nights which is why she is also called Saint Wednesday in search of women who work during her evening. If the house doors are not open, she uses all kinds of tricks to get inside and resorts to various ways of torturing women who are disobedient and disregard her power. Although identified under the name of Tuesday Hag or Tuesday Evening, mainly in Transylvania and in Banat, she also appears sporadically along some old shepherd roads frequented by Transylvanian shepherds in Walachia (Muscel, Arges, Dambovita, Ialomita, Braila), in Dobrogea (Constanta) and in Moldavia (Neamt, Tecuci, Covurlui, Botosani).[165] Her character and behavior merges with another Romanian mythical character, Thursday Hag or "Joimarita."

In the Folk almanac there are other Tuesdays holidays. The *Pots* Tuesday or "Spolocania", the second day after Shrovetide, when people

---

[164] Ghinoiu, 2002, p. 120-121.

[165] Evseev, 1997, p. 227-228.

wash their pots with lye to prepare them for use during the fasting period, or replace them with pots used exclusively during the fast period. The *Hearth* Tuesday, when people make prehistoric clay pans for baking bread on a hearth; The *Beak's* Tuesday, when the Calus Beak dies symbolically.

October 18
"Lucin"

Lucin was a holiday celebrated during the time when wolves gathered in packs for reproduction and it was dedicated to a shepherd divinity. Both the name and the celebrating date were taken from the Orthodox Almanac of October 18, Saint Apostle Luke. In order to prevent the dangers provoked by wolves, certain magic practices used to be performed such as tying up the teeth of combs used for carding the wool, or forbidding any type of activity connected with processing wool, animal hair and skins (Banat).

October 19
Saint Peter and the Wolf

Unlike the bear that usually steals one or two sheep from the shepherd when it gets a chance, the wolf kills everything it can find by tearing it apart. That ferocious and senseless killing was often described in folk legends. Such occurrences are reported to this day.[166]

"Having lots of sheep, Saint Peter built himself a sheepfold and, near it, an enclosure with a fence woven only of violets and other beautiful flowers. He used that enclosure to keep his sheep, while he was away, paying visits to God to ask for advice. Once, it happened that Saint Peter was again visiting God and he stayed there for a longer time than usual. In the meantime his sheep got hungry, ate up the fence and went to the grazing field by themselves where the wolf came, put down ninety-nine of them and killed them. When it was about to kill one more, Saint Peter arrived and, seeing how many sheep had been killed by the wolf, he got angry and cursed: 'As soon as you have killed one more sheep, you shall die! And for having killed my best sheep, you shall always be chased by dogs.' From then on, the wolf dies as soon as it has killed a hundred

---

[166] In 2008 in Simon (Bran), wolves killed 15 sheep and lambs one night in a shepherd's hilltop barn [recorded by Dan Dimancescu]

sheep. But it can seldom get to kill so many, because it is usually chased away by the dogs."[167]

October 20
Painless Labor

A mother's consciousness of pain at birthing increased as civilization evolved. What is considered *painless labor* is usually attributed to the animal world though confirmed with primitive populations. In modern cultures, pain intensity depends to a large extent on types of education, life experience, and particularities of the social environment.

Customs related to childbirth as recorded by ethnographers indicate the possession of detailed knowledge concerning the physiological processes that occur when giving birth to a child. Often the psychological preparation of future mothers starts in childhood when little girls were encouraged to play specific games with dolls and look after their younger siblings. More commonly, they performed household activities normally done by mothers. In this manner maternal feelings were gradually induced. As for fear of giving birth and all the prejudices related to it, they were unknown in the traditional village. Folk beliefs had an incredible psychological effect as they instilled confidence that everything would go well. For example, the surprise caused a mother by a midwife suddenly slamming a door shut at a carefully chosen moment, could induce the birthing of her child.

In the Padureni area, an interesting technique for controlling labor pains, called *"cuvatul"*, was recorded. While the woman was giving birth, the man would moan, scream and cry, thus simulating the labor pains in a room next door. In the villages from Tara Almajului, people used to say that when women were in labor, they were allowed to beat their husbands. In the Somes Valley area, men performed sympathetic ritual acts while their wives were in labor. Practices with analgesic effects were applied:

"When a woman feels labor pains in the back and in her belly, then another woman should take an axe and pass it around the loaded woman's waist and say":

> *"If it is a little boy,*
> *"Let him come out to get the little axe!*

"The custom is repeated in case a girl would be born. She takes a distaff and passes it over the woman's waist and says:

---

[167] Fauna Legends, 1994, p. 56-57.

"If it is a little girl,
"Let her come out to get the little distaff!"

Fear and anxiety as much as cultural beliefs and motivations can influence labor pains. Folk practices used during birthing, managed to inhibit some subjective factors and enhance others which could induce *painless labor*, a condition sought by many nowadays.

October 21

Word-of-Mouth

Rural civilizations possessed a very efficient system of information sharing and of communication: *word of mouth*. However in contemporary times, as other methods of communication appeared, this expression acquired a pejorative meaning. Communicating all sorts of news at the house gate or water well, in pubs, at church, or fairs, ensured cohesion among social groups that made up the folk culture. The *word of mouth* was highly effective since it combined the total transparency of the news as expressed in the saying "her husband does not know what the whole village knows" or with the capacity of keeping the most important secrets by saying "his mouth has neither eaten any garlic nor does it smell of any garlic".

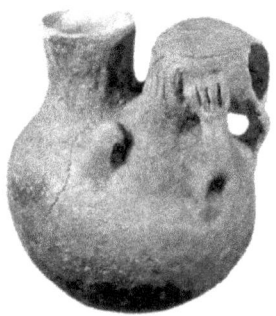

The "Shouting-Man", Vinca-Turdas Culture, Vth Millennium BC, Parta, Timis County (Miclea, Florescu, 1980)

In the Romanian language there are numerous colloquial expressions and sayings which reflect subtleties particular to *word of mouth* communication, e.g. "to spoil one's mouth" (to speak in vain), "to speak with half of a mouth" (to speak unconvincingly), "to keep one's mouth on someone" (to insist on convincing someone of something), "to put a padlock on someone's mouth" (to be careful of what you say), "to lack mouth" (to lack the courage of saying what you know), "to satisfy people's mouth", "to have a free mouth", "to have a good mouth", "to have a bad mouth", "to be a chatter mouth."[168]

---

[168] Ghinoiu, 2001, p. 85.

October 22

Samedru Fathers

The practices connected to the cult of the dead, held on the Saturday before Samedru Day, are called Autumn fathers, Great Fathers or Samedru Fathers. On this day offerings are distributed as alms (boiled wheat, knot-shaped bread, milk, butter and cheese) and the spirits of the dead are invoked to bring health, prosperity and growth to the house:

> *Old fathers and forefathers,*
> *May always be happy,*
> *And bring plenty to my house,*
> *Lots of food on the table,*
> *Lots of help in the field of flowers!*

October 23

Evil time: Breaking the Cart

In the Folk Almanac, the end of every period of time, such as day, week, month, season, or year, has a less favorable character reflecting that time has 'grown old' and therefore must die first in order to be born again. It is more difficult to notice this feature in the case of shorter units of time, like the day or the week, but it is easier with longer ones such as seasons or the whole year. However, the rituals for the end and for the beginning of the week must follow the general rules: Saturday has an ill-fated character ("the three evil moments"), Sunday celebrates the victory of the good forces over the evil ones which have accumulated during the previous week, and Monday marks the beginning of the week under the most favorable signs for human activity. Gradually, the time of the week matures. Thursday is the most powerful day but by the middle of the week time starts to degrade, which is an indispensable condition for its renewal.[169]

October 24
The Traveler and the Well

Each guest-house or well-established inn, and even the simplest stops had access to a safe water source. However in flat plains, springs were rare and underground water was sometimes deep down. The situation was different in the mountains, hills and in plateaus areas where water was plentiful, the only problem being that it had to be found at a place as close to a spring as possible. Romanians used various ways of reaching the underground water and of using spring water, by building small wells, chutes, large wells with seeping levers, hooks, chains, or wheels. A lot of folk legends and beliefs are connected to 'wells'. These legends contain the names of the people who built them or those in the memory of whom the wells were cleaned and were used again.

In times when pollution was yet to affect water quality, people would drink water directly from rivers. People believed that "as long as the water has passed over nine rocks, it is good to drink." Today, one still sees many roadside wells with a lengthy lever or 'sweep' which is a prehistoric vestige, a reminder of the primitive method of lifting loads, pails of water in our case, using minimum effort. Many writers, ethnographers, architects and painters have found inspiration in the well with a sweep, as a place where people sit and meditate, meet or rest for a short while.

Roadside 'sweep' well Teleorman Valley (Walachia) by D. Dimancescu 2008

---

[169] Ghinoiu, 2001, p. 43.

October 25
The Fire Rite at Samedru

The night of October 25-26, in villages from the northern parts of Arges and Dambovita counties and in a portion of Valcea County, a ceremony is held as spectacular as the New Year's celebration. All villagers go up to a high place, such as a mountain, a hill or a hillock, where an enormous bonfire is set alight. In the old forms of the ritual, the trunk of a tree cut from nearby woods is placed to be set on fire in the middle of the pile of wood and needle leaves, the tree trunk is representative of the phytomorphic (plant) god who died and was reborn every year.

Around the fire fueled with dried wood, straw and hemp residues, all the participants chant together the consecrated formula: "Come to Samedru Fire!" At the death of the shepherd year, women distribute pretzels, fruit and drinks. While the tree trunk, the phytomorphic body, burns out, people enjoy themselves by eating, drinking, telling jokes and dancing. Even old women participate in the cheering and dancing. The most exciting moment of the ceremony is when the burnt tree falls to the ground thus marking the symbolical rebirth of the dead god. The direction on which the divine body falls marked by the embers indicates which of the girls or of the young men will marry in the New Year. When the ritual is over, people take embers home to use as fertilizer for their gardens and orchards.

The original significance of the ritual is no longer known today but the custom is still practiced in many villages from the northern parts of Arges, Dambovita and Valcea Counties.[170]

---

[170] Ghinoiu, 1997, p. 77.

October 26

Samedru

Samedru, a god in the Romanian Pantheon symbolically sacrificed in the spectacular nightly ceremonial, took his name and his date of celebration from Saint Dumitru, the Great Martyr from Thessalonica who is present in the Orthodox Almanac. Together Sangiorz and Samedru divide the Shepherd Year into two symmetrical seasons: Summer from April 23 to October 26 with Santilie as its midpoint on July 20, and Winter from October 26 to April 23 with Winter Sanpetru as its midpoint on January16. Sangiorz and Samedru are in opposition to each other, since the former locks winter in and covers the trees in the forest with leaves while the latter locks summer in and makes the leaves of the forest fall. In folk legends and beliefs, Samedru is an ordinary cattleman, or a Saint who roams the Earth sometimes accompanied by Sangiorz. As a mythical character, he turns into a pig during the night, the pig being an ancient agrarian divinity. Samedru also appears in some Transylvanian traditions where he is compared to Prince Charming of the fairy tales.

October 27

Settling Day

The New Saint Dumitru, a divinity invoked by lots of women to help cure diseases, took his name and the celebration date from the Holy New Saint Dumitru from Basarabi on October 27 who is present in the Orthodox Almanac. According to some beliefs from Muscel, he is alleged to be Samedru's brother.

The day before, Samedru, was considered an important settling day when people finish paying off all their debts, rents, loans, season jobs and all further business that had been agreed upon six months earlier at Sangiorz on April 23. It was a day for making new deals, occasions marked with drinks and entertainment. The shepherd origin of this custom is evidenced by the six months duration of deals that were equal in time to summer which started at Sangiorz and ended at Samedru. It is also evidenced by the saying: "At Sangiorz dogs would fight, At Samedru masters would quarrel!" This referred to spring, when the sheep flocks are formed and dogs fight because they are not familiar with each other, while in autumn masters fight because the deals that had been made at Sangiorz were not respected.[171]

---

[171] Ghinoiu, 1997, p. 225.

October 28
The Navel, A stopped up Mouth of the Body

The navel is one of the mouths of the human body which the midwife stops up at birth, by tying it up with a hemp thread. The navel is like a sacred gate separating the intra-uterine life or pre-existence from the extra-uterine life or existence. Unlike the ascending mouth where the parents' and the forefathers' souls come out at death and the descending mouth where the children's, the grandchildren's and the great grandchildren's souls come out at birth, the navel remains a closed gate well bolted up at birth in order to prevent any attempt of the soul to return to the intra-uterine paradise. The umbilical cord was usually tied by the midwife at a three-finger distance from the new-born baby's body with a white hemp thread and then cut at a palm's measure.

In some cases, three to nine knots were made on the remaining umbilical cord attached to the baby. When the dried out navel was removed, the mother kept it to be given to the child when he was three or four years old. The child would then undo the knots and find out all the secrets of the birds. The knots could also be undone by a young man before enrolling in the army, or before getting married. Some midwives kept record of the children she had helped to be born by making a knot for each child on a thread. That thread with knots was placed in the coffin when the midwife died. During the wake some women tried to stealthily add knots on the thread, one for each abortion they had had.

October 29
Salt and Salary

Salt-Lick for Goats and Sheep (AIEF No. 37 493)

Salt was one of the most common and valued 'currencies' used by mankind. From *barter*, the first form of exchange by which one could obtain any goods if one had salt comes the word *soldier* and the name of the pay he receives (*"solda"* in Romanian) - both words originating in the Indo-European *sare* and in the Latin *sol, salis*. History records several ways of obtaining it. Nicolae Perianu, governor of Severin, asked King

Sigismund to pay certain militaries by giving them money or salt; in other cases foreign travelers related that in the time of Alexandru Ipsilanti salt was exchanged for fish. In some cases it was cut into same sized and weight lozenges and used as currency.[172]

Romania possesses the largest deposits of salt and rock salt and of salt-springs in Europe. Archaeologists found that around every salt mountain or salt spring existed one or more prehistoric settlements. Along both sides of the Carpathian Mountain spine one can count two-hundred salt mountains. To these are added the salt springs called "*slatine.*" Together the network of salt mining roads, the techniques used for extracting salt from salt-mines and salines, the Romanian toponomy and anthroponomy related to salt, and the role played by salt in both ritual and magic practices as well as in the Romanian folklore make up a great spiritual treasure.[173]

October 30

The Salt of the Earth

An element indispensable for life, salt was considered in ancient times as a gift from the gods. People used to sprinkle salt over the offerings they brought to their gods. Its ritual function is still preserved today in association with bread and as a symbol of respect and appreciation shown to a guest. In many areas across the globe, the lack of salt caused migratory movements. In some cases, wars were fought over a salt mine without which reproduction of mammals, including humans, life be impossible. Peasants, knowing the effect of salt on cattle breeding, have always been careful about placing salt blocks in stables and in the sheep pens. The chronicles mention types of salt extraction practiced by peasants in the so-called "*salt-cliffs.*" Those peasants were entitled to use the salt for their own needs.

There is enough salt on the globe, though its geographic distribution is unequal. Europe possesses the richest deposits. This explains, perhaps, the cause for successive migratory waves from Asia towards Europe since prehistoric until modern times?

---

[172] I. Simionescu, 1938, p. 392.

[173] Ghinoiu, 2004, p. 20.

October 31
Salt Roads

Transporting salt to the sheep pens
(Ethnographic Atlas of Romania, Vol 2, 2005)

    To support salt mining, a network of roads was developed bearing various names found on maps old and new: Salt Road, Saltmen Road, Salt-Mine Road. On these roads, salt supplies were carried to villages and towns all over the country. Great amounts of salt were transported in carts, on the major trade roads, to Turkey, Poland and to the Habsburg Empire. Salt was bartered for shepherd products and, later on, towards the turn of the 20th century, it was exchanged for money. Salt was also transported on rafts on the rivers Olt, Mures, Cris and most likely on the Trotus and Siret.

    In Walachia and in Oltenia, the Salt Roads followed a north-south direction. In Moldavia, from Targu Ocna some salt roads headed east, towards the winter places of sheep in the Ponto-Caspian steppes; others headed west, towards Transylvania, through the Oituz Pass and others headed north towards the Ukraine following the Siret River valley. On maps, the salt roads appear in the form of broken lines, as their entire length could not be marked. The only certain places are their starting points: the Salt Mine areas, along the Carpathian Mountain foot-hills. The shepherd economy could not have developed without that system of salt roads which was used to drive sheep to and from the mountains. Even today, the transport of salt blocks to mountain sheep folds remains a shepherd's greatest concern.

NOVEMBER

"BRUMAR"

THE WHITE FROSTY MONTH

1. Cosmadin
2. Evening, Midnight and Dawn
3. A Legend About How People Multiplied
4. The Wolf as a Soul's Guide
5. The Fetal Cry and the "Strigoi" (ghosts)
6. The Wolf's Holidays
7. Archangel Forefathers
8. The Archangels
9. The Rams' Flat Cake
10. The Hedgehog, God's Advisor
11. Robbers' Day
12. Saint Peter's and Saint Andrew's dogs
13. Philippies, A Divine Pack of Wolves
14. Christmas Shrovetide
15. "Gadinet" (Another Word for Wolves)
16. The Wind as a Young Man Ready to Marry
17. The Wax Cane
18. Evil Time
19. Covasa, A Ritual Drink
20. Andrew's Little Flat Cake
21. Ovidenia
22. The Limping "Gadineti" Wolf
23. Spirits of the Wood
24. Werewolves
25. The Giant's Daughter
26. The Man and the Tree
27. Divination Acts
28. Andrew's Lament
29. The Strigoi Night
30. Saint Andrew, the Dacian New Year

November

is the ninth month in the ancient almanac with the year beginning on March First. Its colloquial names announce the White Frosty Month, The Great White Frosty Month, Hoar Frosty Month and or Wine Maker because of wine fermentation in barrels. Preparations for winter intensify and the village becomes the center of activity. The month contains numerous pre-Christian holidays, many of them dedicated to the wolf which was a totem of the Geto-Dacians (Autumn Philippies, The Wolf's Day, The Limping Phillip, The Night of the "Strigoi"). During this month are the Christian holidays of Cosmadin, Archangel Fathers, Archangels Shrovetide, Ovidenia and Saint Andrew.

Above: Carpathian Mountain Wolf
(Zoological Atlas, 1983)

November 1
Cosmadin

*Cosma and Damian,
Two Saint Doctors
(Silvia Ciubotariu, 2005)*

A holiday celebrated on a November 1, Cosmadin is a blending of two Christian Saints' names: Cosma and Damian. In their time they were doctors who treated people without charging money. That is why they were called "Saint Doctors curing for Free" and why Cosmadin day is seen as a favorable for practicing folk medicine. The two saints were invoked in charms against typhoid fever and against falling sickness (epilepsy). The holiday was practiced in Moldavia, Bucovina, Transylvania and in Banat.

November 2
Evening, Midnight and Dawn

*Shepherd Mandau, 114-years old
(AIEF Photo By R. Vulcanescu 1963, No. 6 471)*

Three giant terrifying brothers, *Evening, Midnight and Dawn,* can do people a lot of harm. One behind the other, they walk from east to west as the night does. If a daring young man is quick enough, he can catch up with Midnight and use him for whatever he needs. Whenever nights seem to be longer than others, it means that a young man stopped Midnight to do a job for him.

"A man on his death bed told his sons that his last wish was to have a fire made on his grave, out of 99 carts with wood and 99 carts with straw. After their father's death, his sons were not able to find a fire anywhere. However, they saw some burning flames on a mountain peak. Crancu, the youngest son, headed there at once and, on his way, he tied up Evening, Midnight and Dawn. When he reached the fire, seven giants who were guarding it promised to give him glowing embers if he would bring them the daughters of the Green King. Helped by Evening, Midnight and Dawn, Crancu killed the giants, got into the chambers of the King's daughters and took the youngest one's ring. Then, he set the three giants free so that they would continue to measure the time for people, took a glowing ember and returned to light his fire."

November 3
A Legend About How People Multiplied

In old times, when communication was much simpler, people spent their free time telling stories. The topics and the inspiration sources were unlimited.

One story recounts how people multiplied on Earth. "When God expelled Adam and Eve from Heaven, he gave them a patch of land to till and to get what they needed for their living. The Devil came up to them and said: 'How will you manage with only that little patch of land? You will need a lot more to be able to feed your children! I could give you land, if you gave me your dearest thing in the world!' Adam and Eve thought for a while, and then said: 'We shall give you what you ask for!' The Devil told them that they could till as much land as they wanted and, in exchange, he wanted their two children. Feeling helpless, Adam and Eve gave him the children and the Devil took them to Hell, his kingdom. Hearing of this, God got very angry. To recover the children back, He sent Saint Basil to serve the Devil for three years - in those times, a year was equal to three days. Saint Basil went to the Devil and served him for one year and then for one more year. The Devil never asked him why he was doing it. When the Saint had finished his third year service, the Devil finally asked him and found out his purpose. When he realized that he had been deceived, the spiteful Devil beat Saint Basil black and blue, but he gave him back the children. Saint Basil brought them back to Earth and from them the world was eventually filled with people".

November 4
The Wolf as the Soul's Guide

The Wolf's Fang plant used in folk medicine (Nitu, 2003)

A divinity of the Dacians and of their Romanian descendants, the wolf both punishes man and protects him. It is said to be the only animal that can see devils and tear them to pieces. If a child gets a disease, the wolf can frighten it away. On Luncani Platform, a place situated very close to the Dacian forts in Orastie Mountains, the newborn baby was fed for the first time through with a *wolf mouth, a* device made from the jaw and the skin of a wolf. In several ethnographical areas the names of seriously ill children were changed to Wolf or Bear to scare away diseases and death. The high recurrence of these two names among Romanians speaks to the wide extension of this magic practice.

In the *Romanian Book of the Dead,* mainly in the "Zori" songs, the wolf guides souls on the roads separating *Our World* from *The Beyond.* In some villages from southwestern Romania, the dead man was advised in the funeral songs sung before burial to make friends with the otter, as it knew the way on water, and with the wolf, as it knew the way on land:

The wolf will come,
In your way
To scare you.
Be not afraid,
Make it your brother,
Cause it knows well
The paths in the woods
And it'll help you out,
On a clear road,
To meet a prince
Who will take you to Heaven,
Where the true life is;
On the hill
Where there's joy,
That's where you should rest;
In the field

With peonies,
That's where you long to be.
(Oltenia, Eastern Banat)

November 5
The Fetal Cry and the 'Strigoi'

A criterion used by Romanians to identify whether a "strigoi" (ghost) is present in the maternal womb was the baby's cry before being born, a phenomenon known in medicine as *vagitus uterinus* or *the fetal cry*.[174] A widespread popular belief about a baby who cries before being born is that it turns into a "strigoi." The fetal cry had been long noticed by ordinary people in the 24-week of intra-uterine life before doctors and psychologists acknowledged its existence or importance. This curious phenomenon was proven to be real, although it has been unjustly considered a superstition.

The hero of a well-known Romanian fairy tale, "Never-ending Youth and Everlasting Life," starts crying before being born and does not stop until his father, the King, promised him never-ending youth and everlasting life. The same theme appears in other fairy tales as well: *Red King, The Strigoi Woman, Death Voice, Saint Archangel and the Carpenter*.

Romanian people divide evil spirits by gender into male ones, *the moroi or strigoi*, which are more active in the cold season between Samedru (October 26) and Sangiorz (April 23), and female ones, *the Iele*, that appear only in the warm season between Sangiorz and Samedru. The absence of the strigoi in the summer is due to Santilie who strikes them with his whip of fire (lightning) as he does to devils. By their origin, the strigoi are of two kinds. There are *dead strigoi (moroi)* and *live strigoi (moroi)*. The belief in strigoi or in moroi is related to the immortality of the soul. If the wicked people's souls can survive after death as strigoi and moroi, there are even more reasons for the good ones' souls to live on.

November 6
The Wolf's Holidays

By virtue of Romania geographic location, wolves generally gather in packs around October followed by a period in which they roam and familiarize themselves with one another. Moving about, they attack in groups, "make friends," and form male-female pairs. After about a month, at Autumn Philippies (November 14-21), mating begins and lasts until the

---

[174] Schiopu, Verza, 1997, p. 63.

Winter Philippies (January 29-31), with some variations depending on the geographical latitude and altitude. After a 62-63 day gestation period, the female gives birth in late spring. During the summer wolves lead a family life (the male, the female and their cubs). In autumn, when the pack is formed, the new generation of wolves take part in attacking and capturing prey. Some important folk customs and celebration follow the natural behavior of the wolf.

The holidays at the end of November (Autumn Philippies, Ovidenia and Saint Andrew) and at the beginning of December (Saint Nicolae, Bubat's Days and Varvara) are dedicated to the wolf. The customs, rituals and the magic practices carried out during these holidays make up the rituals of the Dacian New Year. They include nightly feasts (Strigoi Night, Watching the Garlic) remiscent of ancient orgies. Central in these events is the belief that during the nights of Saint Andrew and Ovidenie graves open up and dead people arise, that animals speak, and that charms and witchcrafts are effective especially those for finding marriage partners. The midpoint in the celebration period of the Dacian New Year is St. Andrew's Day (and night).[175]

November 7
Archangel Forefathers

Food offerings distributed for the dead as alms on the Eve of Archangels' Day or on that day, November 8, are called *Archangel Forefathers*. Candles are burned for the living and for those who died in horrific circumstances (frozen, drowned, struck by lightning, or killed by wild beasts). The custom has been evidenced in Moldavia and in Bucovina.

November 8
The Archangels

The Saint Archangels in the Palesti Church, Vrancea County (Cherciu, 2003)

The Holy Archangels Mihail and Gavril are commonly called the *Archangels* to be celebrated on this day. In folk traditions the Archangels, who wield swords, are leaders of the angels and they are charged with

---

[175] Ghinoiu, 2003, p. 361-368.

transporting souls of the dead. In some areas where they were considered patrons of the sheep flocks, they were celebrated over two days November 8 and 9. Archangel Mihail, more present in the Romanian folklore than Archangel Gavril, sometimes carries the Keys to Heaven. He watches a sick person by standing by the head if the person is dying and by the feet if the person is to get well and live longer.

The short autumn period with clear sky and warm weather which appears around The Archangels' Day (8 November) is called *The Archangels' Summer* in Transylvania.

November 9
The Ram's Flat Cake

On Archangels' Day, when in some ethnic areas the rams were mixed with sheep in the flock for reproduction, a special bread called the *Ram's flat cake* made from maize or wheat flower was baked. In order to find out if sheep would be well or not after 21 week gestation period, the Ram's Flat-cake was thrown in the middle of the flock and if it fell with the face up, it was a good sign, if not, it was a bad sign.

November 10
The Hedgehog, God's Advisor

In some folk legends God is not the only creator of the world. To fulfill its creation He asked for help from various living creatures, especially from the *hedgehog* whom God had endowed with intelligence.

"When God built the world of earth, there was a little left and He did not know what to do with it. So He sent the bee to the hedgehog to ask him for advice as He knew it was smart. The hedgehog told the bee: 'Why does he ask me? He is God. He should know better. Shall I teach Him what to do?' The bee pretended to leave but hid itself in the door's hinge. Soon the hedgehog started to speak to himself: 'I can't understand what kind of a man God is! When He created me He couldn't make me any uglier, I look like a ball of thread, and now he comes to me to tell him what to do! Can't he make some hills and some mountains!' Hearing the hedgehog's words, the bee immediately ran and told God and He did as the hedgehog said."[176]

---

[176] The Legends of the Cosmos, 1994, p. 169.

In animal fairy tales, the hedgehog is so intelligent that it can cheat even the most cunning animal such as the fox. He is able to punish the wolf and can run faster than the stag.[177]

November 11

Robbers' Day

The day in the Folk almanac dedicated to Mina, the character who can prove a villains' guilt and who takes the name and date of celebration from Saint Martyr Mina (November 11) in the Orthodox Almanac, is called *Robbers' Day* in Moldavia. One of the magic practices performed for finding out the truth about robbers, killers and malefactors, during the period from November 11 (Mina) to December 25 (Christmas), was by intentionally lighting candles at the wrong end. By doing so, people believed they could change the enemy's thoughts, or could direct the young boys' attention toward girls who liked them. On that day, prayers were requested from the priest for getting married, for finding out certain secrets and for curses to come true.

November 12

Saint Peter's and Saint Andrew's Dogs

Carpathian shepherd dog (Photo by Isidor Chicet)

A very long time ago, as the story goes, Saint Peter was a fisherman. Occasionally along with Saint Andrew, he was also a herdsman. Hearing of the Christ's wonders, they gave up fishing, left their sheep to be watched by their dogs and joined the disciples following Jesus. Some time later, other shepherds drove away their dogs into the wild and took their sheep. Angry at being chased away, the saints' dogs attacked the sheep, eating and killing as many of them as possible. These dogs became wild dogs and finally turned into ferocious wolves.

---

[177] Barlea, 1986, p. 11-12.

When Saint Peter died and arrived in Heaven, he remembered his dogs and sent them manna from time to time to appease their hunger. Saint Andrew called them every year on the night of November 30, when his day is celebrated, and blessed them so they might breed. On the same night, it is said, they also received permission to go find their prey.[178]

November 13
Philippies, A Divine Pack of Wolves

The Autumn *Philippies*, themselves terrifying personifications of wolves, are a divine pack, whose chieftain, *The Great Philip* or *The Limping Philip*, is celebrated at *Ovidenie* (November 21) or at *Saint Andrew* (November 30). When the gestation period for the wolves ends, at *Winter Circovi* (January 16-18), the herdsmen celebrate another patron of the wolves on *Winter Sânpetru* (January 16). People believe that, in the night of Philippies she-wolves search feverishly for glowing embers. Those who do not manage to eat fire, a symbol of virility, remain barren for the whole year. On Philippies Day, in order to prevent the wolves from breeding excessively, women do not take ashes out from the house and do not lend fire to their neighbors.

November 14
Christmas Shrovetide

Christmas Shrovetide, a nightly celebration (November 13-14) marks the beginning of a six-week period of Fasting November 15 to December 24, is an occasion for family parties. In some areas, Christmas Shrovetide is preceded by Shrovetide Eve (November 13) and followed by rites of purification on "Spolocanie Day" (November 15). In these mid-November days, Autumn Philippies is celebrated through ritual for protection against evil spirits by making loud noises and shooting, or smearing the doors, the gates and the windows with garlic; or by taming birds, mainly sparrows, by feeding them with the leftovers from the nightly feast so that they would not damage the crops, or turning all the pots in the house upside down to prevent evil spirits from hiding in them, or by prophesy rituals allowing the foretelling of marriage partners and the abundance of crops.

---

[178] Fauna Legends, 1994, p. 46-47.

November 15
"Gadinet" (another word for wolf)

During the holidays dedicated to wolves (Winter and Autumn Philippies, the Great Philip, Saint Andrew, Winter Saint Peter), people avoided uttering the word "wolf" and if they had to refer to it, they used the word *Gadinet*. They believed that the mere utterance of its name caused the wolf to hear it and to *come visit* the stables and the sheepfolds. In other parts of the country, the nickname Gadinet, used during the holidays dedicated to the wolf, means a one-year old pig.

November 16
The Wind as a Young Man Ready to Marry

In some folk legends. the wind is personified into a playful and handsome young man who lives with his mother in the sky. He is unmarried and is looking for a wife. When he runs around in the world and we say that the wind is blowing, he is actually searching for a wife. When he gets tired he stays in his home resting or doing household chores. When he feels like going out and searching for a wife, he starts puffing again.[179]

November 17
The Wax Cane

Funeral candle in the length of the deceased to light the way to heaven, Vartoapele, Teleorman County (Ghinoiu, 2004, Photo by Em. Parvu)

The candle or *wax cane* coiled up in a spiral the length of the deceased person, which is lighted at certain moments of a funeral ceremony, symbolizes the long way separating *our world* from *the beyond*. It bears other names, depending on the geographical area: skylark, flat cake, or spiral candle because of its circular shape. In the "Zori" (Dawn) funeral songs, the dawning divinities are begged to allow the deceased some time to

---

[179] The Legends of the Cosmos, 1994, p. 197.

make his spiral candle:

> *Zori, Zori,*
> *Dear sisters,*
> *Don't you hurry,*
> *To come over us,*
> *Before the Fair Wanderer*
> *Has prepared*
> *His little wax flat cake.*
> *May it light his way...*[180]

The spiral candle is made after a person dies by a 'clean' woman, usually a forgiven woman, out of a straight yarn the length of the deceased. It is lighted at certain moments during and after the funeral thus allowed to burn little by little for forty days. During the same period incense is burned at the grave until the soul reaches Heaven. In some areas, a spiral candle that has not fully burnt out at the funeral is placed on the dead man's chest in the coffin, or given away as alms, or turned into a wax cross and kept as a luck totem in the house.

In funeral songs, the deceased is repeatedly guided ("Go straight on/ And then to the right", and so on) in a certain way, which if transposed graphically would make up a spiral, which is the mythical road represented by the cane or the spiral candle. The spiral is one of the most representative motifs in Neolithic art from Cucuteni and in the folk arts present, too, in many other ancient cultures. When it appears on sewing, on decorated eggs, on pottery, it is called the dead man's way, the lost way, or the endless way.

November 18
Evil Time

The malefic spirit which harms, mutilates and kills those who come in its way is commonly called *Evil Time* or Weak Time. One can recognize its presence by the shrill sound it produces when it flies. It can appear at any time of the day or any time in the year. But, unlike Sundays, Mondays, Wednesdays, Thursdays and Fridays, when there can be only one ill-fated occurrence, Tuesdays and Saturdays can have three Evil Time occurrences.

To protect themselves from the harm which could be done by Evil Time, people cross themselves, knock on wood and call out: God help us! If someone was seized by Evil Time it can be driven out of the

---

[180] Brailoiu, Constantin, 1981, p. 110.

person's body with the help of a charm. But it also had the advantage that if it left in the body it will go to much better places:

Evil Time that cripples,
Evil Time that strikes,
Evil Time that scares,
Evening Evil Time,
Midnight Evil Time,
Day-time Evil Time,
Go up on the mountain,
Go inside the mountain,
For that's where your gardens are,
Where tables are laid,
With chairs around them,
And glasses filled for you,
All made ready for you.

Then it is reminded of the risks it faces, if it ever comes back:

Keep staying there,
Don't even think
About my John.
As if you don't go away,
If you don't stay away,
I'll grab ninety-nine spears
And drive them into you,
And scare you off
And drive you away...[181]

November 19
Covasa, a Ritual Drink

An ancient felting mill for crushing seeds
(AIEF, No. 6326, A. Chevallier, 1916)

At Ovidenie or at Saint Andrew around the Tutova Hills area, a fermented drink called *covasa* is made. The drink had a sweet-sour taste, similar to that of millet-beer. Ethnographic records describe two methods of preparing covasa, one using

---

[181] Evseev, 1997, p. 99.

corn and wheat flour and the second using only maize flour. In the first case, a type of porridge is made from equal quantities of maize and wheat flour mixed with hot water. After two hours the mixture is put into a cask, lukewarm water poured over it, and then stirred until a viscous liquid results. This is passed through a sieve of the same type used for maize flour and then let to ferment in a fairly warm place. A day later, it is boiled in a cast-iron kettle, over moderate fire, until becoming thicker. Covasa is kept in crocks and bowls and is also given away to neighbors in order "to help cows give plenty of rich fat milk."[182]

In other villages, covasa is called millet-beer and was made only of maize flower. Hot water is poured over the maize flower and from that mixture four flat cakes are made, two of which are baked. When the baked cakes cool off, they are kneaded together with the other two in a cask and hot water is poured over the mixture. Next, it is stirred, a few slices of lemon are added and the mixture is let to ferment until the next day when ready to be consumed. In the Covurlui region, from Central Moldavia, they said that "it was every man's duty to drink covasa that day so as to be protected from strigoi."[183]

November 20
Andrew's Little Flat Cake

On Saint Andrew's Day, the most likely Dacian New Year's Day, the preferred magic practices related to predicting the future spouse. When it was right time for a young girl to marry, she would prepare a little thin flat cake from wheat and flour and a lot of salt, called *Andrew's little flat cake*. In a state of physical and spiritual cleanness she would bake it then eat it before going to bed so as to dream of her future husband

In other cases, young girls returning home from the nightly celebration called "Watching the Garlic" on November 29-30, would sow a clove of garlic in a ball of dough. Judging from the way the garlic shoots grew, certain matrimonial predictions would be deduced.[184]

The end of November was also favorable time for meteorological and astronomical observations. Some old people watched the sky in the night of Ovidenie on November 21 or of Saint Andrew on November 30 and predicted what the year had in store. Would the year be rich or poor, rainy or dry; would there be peace or war?

---

[182] Pamfile, 1914, p. 145.

[183] Pamfile, 1914, p.146.

[184] Pamfile, 1914, p.140-141.

The custom of planting wheat grains in a clay pot with earth in it, for predicting how rich the crops will be in the coming year, is still practiced.

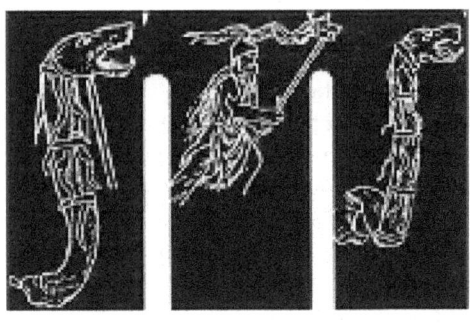

November 21
Ovidenia

A Dacian banner with dragon & wolf heads

The holiday dedicated to Holy Mary's Coming into Church, called *Ovidenia, Obrejenia* or *Vovidenia*, corresponds in the Folk Almanac to the celebration of a frightening divinity of the wolves, the Limping Philip or the Great Philip. In the northern Bucovina region, people believed that Jesus Christ was born on that day. The Ovidenia celebration together with Autumn Philippies, the Strigoi Night, Saint Andrew and Saint Nicolae, all covering a period between November 13 and December 6, make up a scenario for the ritual renewal of time which is probably the Dacian New Year. During the Ovidenia night, when according to the belief "the sky opened and animals could speak," people would watch over a bowl with healing water lighted by a coiled up candle. On that occasion, spells, charms and marriage predictions would be made, as well as weather forecasts and observations. Funeral meals were prepared and alms offered on that day for the children who died before being baptized and for those who drowned or who died without a lighted candle. Since the strigoi were thought to roam about freely, people smeared garlic on the window frames, the door cases, the stoves and the ovens, which were connected to the outside through the chimney. For protection of cattle against wild animals, any kind of activity that involved processing wool or animal skins was forbidden. From Ovidenia until Sangiorz, women were not allowed to wash their laundry in the river.

November 22
The Limping 'Gadinet'

Since the wolves prowled more dangerous during their days of celebration, people tried to tame them by calling them "gadinet" as a term of endearment. The strongest and the most ferocious of them was the *Limping "Gadinet"* celebrated at Ovidenie and at Saint Andrew. In those particular days, the stiff neck of the wolf was believed to become mobile, and so "the wolf could see its tail." In some shepherd communities, severe work interdictions were imposed, mainly those related to processing wool and animal skins. In parallel ritual acts for protection were performed against evil spirits. This involved smearing the cattle's horns, the gates and the doors with garlic, or tying up the teeth of the combs used for carding wool.

November 23
Spirits of the Woods

The *spirits of the woods* are mythical representations that are believed to dwell in trees and in the Hag of The Woods plant (*Lathraea Squamaria* L.). They can take the shape of an animal (mare, buffalo cow or cow), or of a fearful human (Hag of the Woods, Girl of the Woods, Forest Father, Man of the Woods, Forest Plague). One can come across these ghosts during full moon nights in forests, shrubs, fields and crossroads where they come to punish by scaring, mutilating, striking dumb women who spin on Tuesday, men who whistle or sing in the forest waking up the Hag of the Woods' children, lumberjacks who do not obey the rules governing care of forests and also those who pick fruit in the forest on forbidden days. The spirits of the woods, mastered by the Hag of the Woods, make up a real pantheon of the wood culture that dominated the Carpato-Danubian-Pontic land mass over a long span of time.

November 24
Werewolves

Werewolves are monsters who eat and darken the Moon and the Sun. They appear in the third or the seventh child born of an unmarried girl, or in the strigoi born with a tail. They dwell in the sky, among the clouds or above the clouds. When they bite the Moon and the Sun during eclipses, people scare them away by beating on old iron sheet objects. They also try to drive them away by genuflecting and by praying to God. In wintertime werewolves can turn into humans and descend over the fields and do harm to those who cross their way. Most often they appeared as wolves and were called *pricolici* or *varcolaci*.

November 25
The Giant's Daughter

Devil mask created by Paul Buta (Buta, 2001)

The belief in giants (ogres) is frequently recorded in the Romanian folklore. Legends say that giants carried earth in their lap to raise knolls found in the Carpathian region. Some anthropic landscape forms have been confirmed as funeral tumuli dating back to the Bronze and Iron Ages. The same giants allegedly build the ancient Dacian settlements ("davae") and fortresses, which were discovered on the Romanian territory. The giants' huge size was recounted in stories comparing them to normal human beings.

"Once, a *giant's daughter* was walking in the field and she found a plough with six oxen and two men who were plowing. The girl played with them, took them in her lap, brought them home to her mother and said to her: 'Look, mother, I have found some small worms that were scraping the earth.' 'These are humans, my dear daughter. Take them back where you found them, as they shall be masters of the world when the time comes.'"

November 26
The Man and the Tree

In certain ritual and ceremonial contexts, man and tree are often intertwined. The tree can substitute and shelter the man symbolically, and it can also become his brother, sister of wife.

There are great spiritual differences between leaf-bearing forests and coniferous forests. Deciduous trees whose leaves grow and fall every year express the idea of immortality through death and perpetual rebirth. The deciduous tree is the symbol of measured human time, while the fir-tree symbolizes the everlasting time. The apple tree dominates customs related to birth and marriage, whereas the fir-tree is predominant in funeral customs. The sacred places of the Romanian voivodes such as Stephen the Great, Mircea the Old and Avram Iancu (The Prince of the Western Carpathians) were marked by planting of venerable oak trees and not by fir-trees.

"What is a tree with its legs upwards?" is a Megleno-Romanian riddle to which the answer is *man*. The riddle refers to the tree branches oriented upwards and can be connected with the colloquial word "*crac*" meaning leg. The same word can also be related to the etymology God Christmas and to the Christmas *log* (tree log), which is usually burned in the stove in the night of December 24. The custom of cremating the divinity in its phytomorphic state on Christmas night was practiced until the Nineteenth Century when it was replaced with the ritual of trimming the fir-tree which became a European custom.

About the Christmas tree, the author of folk stories Petru Ispirescu said long-ago in a lecture: "When I was a child, I once saw a decorated tree in a house and I stopped to stare at it. I reckoned that must have been the tree for Christmas. I had never seen a fir-tree decorated like that, except at funerals, as where I came from no one had ever seen or mentioned about a Treee for Christmas..."[185]

November 27
Divination Acts

The spirits of the dead, hovering around in the night of Saint Andrew, created favorable conditions for certain *divination acts*. Those performed in specific locations such as the well, the pigpen, the household fence and gate, or the table filled with garlic, had only one purpose. This was to predict whom a young girl's future husband would be and what qualities he might posses. Would he be young or old, handsome or ugly, rich or poor. Magic acts were carried out in secret, either individually by each girl, or by several persons. An interesting custom was the one recorded in the former county of Covurlui called "making the flat cake of Saint Andrew. "The unmarried girls who get together at the house of one of them to make the flat cake of Saint Andrew, bring water in their mouth. For the knot-shaped bread of Saint Andrew, they bring untouched

---

[185] Ispirescu, 1998, p. 25. [Petru Ispirescu 1830-887]

water. For the flat cake equal amounts of water, salt and flour measured with a nutshell were mixed. Each girl bakes her own flat cake on the stove and then eats it. In that night she expects to dream of a young man who will come to bring her water and quench the thirst she feels from the salty flat cake."[186]

November 28
Andrew's Lament

Old-man mask used during the wake of a funeral, Toplesti, Vrancea County (AIEF)

For ancient man, the death and the rebirth of their worshipped divinity was ritually substituted by a sacred sacrifice such as a tree, an animal, a bird, a human being or a symbolically personified object. The Christian celebration of Saint Andrew eventually overlaped the celebration of the Dacian New Year called *Andrew's Lame* that is witnessed among Romanians living in Transnistria.

Girls would make a doll of rags, which was called *Andrew (Andrei)* to symbolize the old year, lay it on a bench (bed) as though a dead person and would then lament over it. One Dacian New Year tradition, which might have migrated from autumn to the contemporary celebration of the New Year which is celebrated at the winter solstice, is the sacrifice of the pig.

November 29
The Strigoi Night

The presence of the two aged saints, Father Andrew and Father Nicolae, and the beginning of winter when packs of wolves move about, reflect the aging of the calendar year. Order steadily deteriorates to the point during the Strigoi Night of November 29 when a symbolic state of

---

[186] Pamfile, 1914, p. 140-141.

chaos is reached similar to that which existed before the creation. It is a terrifying night, as the spirits of the dead come out of their graves, and together with the live strigoi start fighting one another along village borders and at crossroads. The bloody dueling, with sharp blades and scythes stolen from the peasants' households, last until dawn. But when the roosters sing, the space is purified and the spirits of the dead return to their graves. The living strigoi's souls regain their bodies and go back to their beds.

In some cases, the strigoi act violently against those who fail to taken any protective measures by smearing their bodies, doors and windows with garlic. Such dangers escalate on November 30 dedicated to the wolf at Saint Andrew. Then, it is said, the neck of the wolf becomes flexible and thus easier to catch its pray.[187] As a result, people take supplementary measures for protecting their cattle and to perform various magic practices meant to defend them against wolves. At no time of the year are people more likely to turn into "pricolici," humans with a dog or wolf appearance as on the Eve and Day of Saint Andrew.

November 30
Saint Andrew, the Dacian New Year

The customs and the holidays held at the end of November and the beginning of December correspond in timing to the Thracian Dionysiac country feasts and to the Roman Saturnalia feasts. During this period, theologians of the Christian faith decided to celebrate Apostle Andrew who propagated Jesus Christ's faith in the Danubian Basin and Black Sea areas during the first decades of the first millennium A.D. The new Christian holiday settled into believers' consciousness along with characteristics of the usurped god, as confirmed by ancient ritual acts and magic practices carried out in the night of November 29 and 30.

The three-week period starting with Autumn Philippies (November 14) and ending with Saint Nicolae (December 6) dedicated to the wolf overlaps with *the Dacian New Year*. On the date of the Dacian New Year two more Fathers have appeared: Father Andrew (November 30) and Father Nicolae (December 6). With time, these traditions became the contemporary Christmas and New Year, while others of prehistoric origins, such as the days dedicated to the wolves and to the strigoi, remained unchanged. Father Christmas Eve and Father Christmas, two aged representations, are celebrated: on December 24 and 25. By virtue of their old age after 365 or 366 days, death of one year is followed by the rebirth of the almanac new year.

---

[187] Pamfile, 1914, p. 135-137.

According to Mircea Eliade, the Dacians called themselves "wolves", or "people who are like wolves." It was the wolf that the Dacians chose to be their totem, and not any other animal such as the strongest of them, the bear. He based his theory on several arguments: the information left by Strabon referring to the fact that the Dacians were called *dáoi*. This was drawn from observations recorded by Hesychius that *dáos* was the Phrygian word for "wolf" and that the Indo-European root *dháu* - meaning to squeeze or to strangle - was derived from *Dáousdava*, the town or fortress of wolves). This was as well as the name of a town situated in Moesia Inferior, south of the Danube).

DECEMBER

"UNDREA"

1. The Night, A Time of Great Transitions
2. Foretelling the Year
3. Camberwell Beauty, the Devil's Daughter
4. Varvara
5. Holy Mary and Saint Nicolae
6. Father Nicolae
7. The Old Style Winter and Summer
8. Gogea
9. Ana Zacetenia
10. The Vulture
11. God and the Hedgehog
12. Sweet Basil of Love
13. The Pantheon from Târgu Jiu
14. Swollen Tonsils
15. Calloused Skin
16. The Hiccup
17. The Christmas Log
18. The Clucking Hen
19. Siva
20. Ignat
21. The Pig Dissatisfied with God's Decisions
22. The Opening of the Graves
23. The Opening of the Sky and the Burning of the Treasures
24. Christmas Eve Father
25. Father Christmas
26. Craciuneasa (Father Christmas' Wife)
27. Christmas Knot-Shaped Bread
28. Christmas Burial
29. Buhai
30. The Meteorological Almanacs
31. The New Year's Party

December

is the tenth month in the Roman Almanac which begins March First, and the twelfth month in both the Julian and Gregorian almanacs that starts January 1st. For country people, day-to-day work life becomes more relaxed as spiritual events related to Christmas and New Year intensify.

Group of carol singers at the "Dimitri Gusti" National Peasant Museum (1996)

The common name Neios indicates the abundance of snow in this month, while the other names: Andrea, Indrea and Undrea remind one of Saint Andrew celebrated the last day of November. Throughout December several starting points for winter have been documented over time: December 1 (official almanac), December 6 – Saint Nicholas (folk almanac), and Winter Solstice (astronomic almanac).

There are folk holidays and customs specific to the end of the year as well as for the beginning of the New Year, the latter having been celebrated at Christmas before being moved to January 1. The most important holidays of the month are Bubatul, Sava, Father Nicolae, Ana Zacetenia, Modest, Ignat, Father Christmas Eve, Father Christmas and Christmas Burial.

December 1
The Night, A Time of Great Transitions

The nightly holidays and customs are linked to an ancient lunar and agrarian cult, dating far back in the times when time was measured in nights and not in days. The night is the ritual time considered most favorable for significant events in man's life and in the life of his divinities to take place. In the peaceful darkness of the intra-uterine life, man spends his heavenly pre-existence time. The family events include predicting children's fate the third night after birth (The Fates' Table), the nuptial act and the beginning of a new vital cycle in the wedding night, and the death watch with games and masks in the night before the funeral

It is notable, therefore, that the most important holidays in both the Folk Almanac and the Church Almanac are nightly ones such as New Year's Eve (the Birth of the Year), Christmas (The Birth of Jesus Christ), Easter (Christ's Resurrection), Saint Andrew (Strigoi Night), The Fire of Samedru, and others. Those holidays belonging to the family cycle mirror examples of divinities who die and are reborn in the night.

December 2
Foretelling the Year

The magic practices of foretelling the year, for example predicting the harvest of fruit-trees, are performed on Saint Andrew, Varvara, Sannicoara and Epiphany holidays which mark the end of The Old Year and the start of The New Year. Boughs cut from various fruit trees are placed in a pot with water at room's temperature in the night of these holidays. Judging from the way the leaves and the flowers grow, it could be gauged whether the year would be rich or poor in fruit. In some regions, children use these boughs in blossom as a "sorcova" in one of New Year rituals (Moldavia, Walachia, Oltenia, Southern Transylvania). Similarly, foretelling the field harvests is made by planting wheat grains in a clay pot.

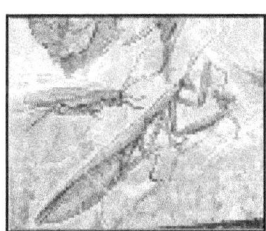

December 3
Praying Mantis, the devil's daughter

The Camberwell Beauty
(Zoological Atlas, 1983)

The *Praying Mantis* (in Romanian "nun"), the carnivorous insect with front legs like hooks for catching the pray, appears in some folk legends personified as the Devil's Daughter.

"They say that the Devil, God help us, had a wicked daughter, so wicked that there was no one worse than her in the world. Well, the time came when the Devil, devilish as he might have been, seeing that there was no way he could tame his daughter, decided to take her to a monastery to become a nun. He hoped that in this way, his crazy daughter would change for the better and be more pious. But the girl didn't change a bit.

"God became very upset seeing that a Devil's Daughter was living in a monastery and that the wicked Devil's offspring kept doing things her own way. In anger He turned her into an insect. The other insects called her 'nun; and from then on, that insect has been called 'nun' until today."[188]

December 4

Varvara

As an anthropomorphic representation, *Varvara* appears in several forms in the folk tradition as a fairy, as an old woman, as a master over children's diseases. Some of her features belong to the Mother Goddess. In some villages from the southwestern part of the country, the holiday, also called Smallpox Days, lasted three days and was observed by mothers as they wished to protect their children from smallpox.

Varvara took her name and her celebration date from The Great Saint Martyr Varvara, December 4 in the Orthodox Almanac. On her celebration day, to prevent smallpox from growing and getting hard as kernels, children were not allowed to eat beans, lentil, peas, maize or pumpkin seeds, neither boiled or baked. (Bucovina, Moldavia, Basarabia)

Varvara is also celebrated by miners as a patron of the mines. She is said to show miners where to dig for gold.

December 5

Holy Mary and Saint Nicolae

The main method for ranking mythical representations in the Romanian pantheon is based on their power and functions. Some of them release rain, others stop it; some of them help the young girls to marry

---

[188] Legends of the Fauna, 1994, p. 280.

and mothers to give birth to their children; others cause people to become ill and even to die; some of them guard and carry the Sun in the sky while others devour it during eclipses. Thus, in some legends, *Saint Nicolae*, patron of the sailor, saves people from drowning while *Holy Mary* drowns them.

"The drowned ones belong to Holy Mary, they are her people in the beyond. She is happy when someone drowns. She makes those who are in danger of drowning sink deeper into the water. When you pass by a water course, never pray to Holy Mary to help you, because it's not a good thing to do. You should pray to Saint Nicolae. A man was once swimming across a wide river and he was praying Holy Mary to help him all the time. But the more he was praying the deeper he was sinking, as She was drawing him down. Then, all of a sudden he cried:

"Saint Nicolae! Don't leave me, help me!" and he rose above water at once."

"Saint Nicolae is master of the water, otherwise why would sailors celebrate his day by organizing great feasts?!"

"Saint Nicolae stopped the water during the deluge, or else Noah's Ark would have sunk."

"Saint Nicolae looks after those who cross the water." (Moldavia, Bucovina)

December 6
Father Nicolae

The divinity belonging to the generation of aged saints, who took over the name and the celebration date of Saint Nicolae on December 6 from the Church Almanac is called Sannicoara (Transylvania) and Father Nicoale (Muntenia) in the Folk Almanac.

Saint Nicolae,
Noble Icon Palesti Church
Vrancea County (Cherciu, 2003)

Saint Nicoale was a real character, a bishop from Myrna who defended the faith in Jesus Christ and died, it is surmised, in the year 342 A.D. According to Romanian traditions, his duties were unusual for a saint. He appeared on a white horse in reference to the first snow which falls in December; he watched the Sun that tries to creep around him and travel northward so that the world will be devoid of light and heat; he was the Devil's spy; he was the master of the water and the patron of the sailors whom he saves from drowning; he protected soldiers who fought in war and invoke him during the battles; he helped widows, orphans and poor girls wanting to get married; he brought gifts to children in the night of December 5 to 6, but he also punished children who were lazy and naughty.

On this holiday victory of good forces over evil ones, of light over darkness is celebrated. "At Saint Nicolae the night turns towards day as much as the chick turns in its shell", says a proverb from Muscel.[189] In comparison with other Christian Saints, Father Nicolae is well favored by God. On Christmas night, when the sky opens at midnight, the Saint can be seen sitting at a magnificent table next to God.

December 6 marks the end of the cycle of customs dedicated to the wolf and to the Dacian New Year such as the Autumn Philippies, the Limping Philip, Ovidenia, The Strigoi Night, Saint Andrew or Father Andrew, and others.

December 7

The Old Style Winter and Summer

Ancient ways of dating the changing of seasons, before the almanac was modernized, are described in an old legend.

"They say that a long time ago, when people were more virtuous, the sun rose earlier; until noon they had plenty of time to work. In the summer it travels higher and in the winter it travels lower. On Ana Zacetenia day, December 9 the solstice day in the old style, it jumps towards summer as much as the rooster jumps on the threshold, and the day starts to grow until Epiphany, when it becomes one hour longer. At Stretenie Day on February 2, the winter meets the summer; when the sun climbs higher and higher and the night becomes smaller and smaller, then winter starts its journey. The longest day is at Saint Onofrei (June 12), and after that day the sun starts to withdraw going towards winter, which means that from Saint Pantelimon on July 27 onwards summer starts its journey and autumn begins. Then the water gets cold, the stag goes out of the river, the sky configuration changes, summer changes for winter, the two seasons meet and say: 'Well, dear summer, you may leave now, for I, winter, will take your place!'"

---

[189] Codin, Mihalache, 1909, p. 91.

December 8

Gogea

Gogea is the magic practice of forcing fate, notably of predicting who the future spouse will be. It is carried out during the nights of the main holidays of the year (Christmas, New Year, Epiphany, Shrovetide, Easter) in Banat and in Transylvania. The ceremony is attended not only by unmarried young men and women, but also by people of various ages and social status. The usual ritual objects involves two wooden twigs with green bark, substitutes of the predicting divinity, one for the men and one for the women, one or two containers with water (wooden pails or plates), and a bed sheet or a large trough made of willow tree or of poplar tree. In Bihor region, when night falls, the participants gather at the diviner's house where the host being is called Gogea, Vergelator or New Year's Announcer. After a small party, the ceremony begins with each of the young men and women throwing their rings into the wooden pail with water. Gogea, covering himself with a sheet or hiding under the trough in order not to be seen by the audience, stirs the water with the two twigs while invoking the divinity to bring rich crops in the new year.

Meanwhile, the young participants sing a ritual song asking Gogea to take out the rings, symbols of marriage. Taking one from each pail containing women's rings and men's rings, the participants are asked identify their rings in pairs. In this manner could be predicted who would marry whom. The procedure was repeated until Gogea had finished taking out all the rings and pairing up all the participants.

In Bucovina, young men would choose the host for the ceremony, buy drinks and pay for the musicians. The during the New Year's evening, the sound of horns and trumpets calls people to gather for the ceremony of Vergel. The New Year Host also called Vergelator places a wooden pail with water on a table in which each participant throws a particular object, a ring, an earring, a button. The Host then hits the pail rim with the twigs producing a sound similar to the beating of the church board while reciting a carol wishing prosperity in the New Year. Then, after a chaste 10-13 year old boy takes out an object from the pail and the owner identifies it, Vergelator predicts the kind of luck which would be brought to that person by Saint Vasile, the first Saint to be celebrated in the new year. The procedure is repeated until all the objects have been taken out from the water and until all the luck-bringing Saints from the Folk Almanac had been invoked. The ceremony ends with a feast at which the participants enjoy themselves by singing and dancing.

The custom survives to this today, but in a different form. During New Year's Night people play cards, dice, backgammon, roulette and may eat a special pie in which predictive messages have been placed.

December 9

Ana Zacetenia

The ninth of December, the winter solstice day in the old style almanac and the day in which the sun begins its ascension towards summer, is an important landmark in measuring the almanac time. Eventually Christian theologians transferred the celebration of Holy Mary's Conceiving by Saint Ana over the astronomical phenomenon of the winter solstice on December 9.

December 10

The Vulture

Vulture on the Walachian Stem
(Pravila, 2004)

The vulture, present on monuments commemorating heroes, on the Romania Coat of Arms, and on funeral poles in cemeteries, is a substitute for the souls of the dead fathers and forefathers. In the prehistoric sanctuary from Çatal Hüyük (VII millennium B.C.), where the vulture appears as a rapacious bird attacking beheaded bodies, it represents the Goddess of Death. Carnivorous animals and birds tearing the flesh off abandoned dead bodies is mentioned as a funeral ritual by Christian theologians in connection with Judgment Day. People who practice that type of ritual believed that the dead would not be able to reach the happy realm of the souls if they were in flesh and blood.

Romanian curses meant to result in someone's death also contain elements hinting at various funeral rituals, mainly the burial one ("may earth eat you up!", "may earth swallow you up!") and the cremation one ("may fire burn your body!"). But in some folk death curses, predator birds are invoked such as the raven or the vulture to tear off the flesh of those who separate lovers:

> *May the ravens drag the flesh*
> *Of those who separate lovers,*
> *Into the beech-tree forest,*

And drag their bones under the trees

May the ravens tear off
The flesh of those who separated us,
And carry it far in the valleys,
And drag their bones through the trees;
May God scatter their flesh over the beech-trees,
And drag their bones through the trees,
As they separated two lovers."[190]

In some funeral songs from the *Romanian Book of the Dead* the vulture is included in the funeral ritual, as the bird which caries the dead people's souls into the world beyond.

December 11
God and the Hedgehog

Two of the reflexes by which the hedgehog defends itself, rolling its body into a ball and emanating a foul odor, are explained in a funny way by a legend recorded in Boureni, Dolj County: "

God summoned the hedgehog to Him and said:
I thought I should have you design the Earth.
How could I, a small animal, design such a large earth,
with all the valleys, the hills, the mountains and the rivers?
Don't worry! I shall help you!
Oh, well, that's better!

Now, the hedgehog, being so happy for receiving such an important task, prepared a basket with eggs to take it to God as a gift. When he reached God's palace and saw God, so very old and with white hair and white beard, sitting on His royal throne, the hedgehog was so impressed and so nervous that he tripped over the threshold and fell on the basket full of eggs. At that moment, God exclaimed: "Yuck! You couldn't find a better place to let that stinking air out!" The hedgehog felt very ashamed, lowered his head, looking at his feet." And from then on the hedgehog would roll itself into a ball as soon as he saw a man and had the bad habit of releasing a bad smell.[191]

---

[190] Ispas, 1989, p. 27.

[191] The Legends of the Fauna, 1994, p. 112-113.

December 12

Sweet Basil of Love

Sweet basil, a strongly scented herb of the *Labiatae* family originating from India and China, is planted by girls and women on Sangiorz Day (Saint George). Due to its diuretic, antispasmodic and anti fever qualities, sweet basil is used in folk medicine and in Christian Cult practices as well as in families following almanac customs.

The tradition recounts that the sweet basil first grew on the tomb of a young girl, when it was watered with her lover's tears, whose name was Basil. In order to gain healing qualities and predicting power, the *sweet basil of love* had to be planted in the morning of Saint George Day, then weeded, watered, gathered and kept according to certain rules. The plant is said to hold miraculous powers. It helps young girls to find out how their future husband will be (young or old, handsome or ugly), and enhance their attractiveness to young men. This is reflected in the folk saying: "They are attracted to each other, as love is attracted by the sweet basil."

Although not bearing a beautiful flower, sweet basil is among the dearest plants to Romanians. Every girl who wears it in her waist-band, on her bosom, in her hair, or puts it under her pillow during the night preceding the major holidays - Christmas, New Year, Epiphany, Easter, Sangiorz - would dream of her future husband or having luck in love and marriage. This plant is commonly used in rituals connected with births, marriages and funerals. It also appears in fairy tales and in a dance song that bears its name.[192]

December 13

The Pantheon from Targu Jiu

The vast open air sculpture complex in Targu Jiu created by Brancusi is similar to the temples of prehistory. The disposition of its components from east to west marks man's journey from birth to death. The critical moments of the human existence (birth, marriage and death) are indicated by miniature symbolized 'temples': The Table of Silence, The Kiss Gate and The Infinite Column.

Like the Fates' Table around which the fates foresee the newborn baby's future, The Table of Silence is the oracle where the fate of an entire nation was predicted. From the table of destiny, placed by Brancusi on the Jiu River bank, near "The running water/ Never flowing back" of the soul, unfolds, from east to west on a distance of 1,653 m, man's life

---

[192] Evseev, 1997, p. 212-247.

consisting of some decades, with the three physical and psychical thresholds: birth (The Table of Silence), marriage (Kiss Gate) and funeral (The Infinite Column). The end of this particular road, marked by The Infinite Column, becomes, through the cyclic vertical disposition of the rhombohedrous of this funeral pole, the beginning of the soul's ascending road, from man's terrestrial time in our world towards the everlasting time in the beyond.[193]

December 14
Swollen tonsils

Swollen tonsils is the name commonly used for tonsillitis caused by bacteria, viruses or fungi. In some charms performed against tonsillitis, nine young sons of Ciandalina or Mandalina are mentioned. After removing the swelling from the throat by means of various healing techniques such as herb tea, throat wash with plum brandy mixed with oil, a compress with crushed onions mixed with oil, or a compress with fried onion or with warm maize porridge sprinkled with salt, friction, massage, the nine brothers are then sent to "death" through the psychotherapy of the charm. Tonsillitis being mainly a children's disease the therapeutic techniques are accompanied by short stories which captivate them and sooth their suffering. In a charm against *"Lizard"* (a local name of tonsillitis), the disease is driven away from the body as a result of the dialogue between the lizard and the spellbinder:

> *Flat lizard, have you been to the lake?*
> *Yes I have.*
> *Have you caught any fish?*
> *Yes I have.*
> *Have you boiled it?*
> *Yes I have.*
> *Have you salted it?*
> *Yes I have.*
> *Have you eaten it?*
> *Yes I have.*
> *Have you left any for Nick?*
> *Sorry, I forgot to*
> *And the swelling disappeared.*

---

[193] Ghinoiu, 2001, p. 143.

December 15

Calloused Skin

The personification of the suffering caused by the hardening of the skin on the palms, or on the feet as a result of repeated rubbing, is commonly called *hard flesh* or *corn*. Its treatment with a compress of onion macerated in plum brandy is accompanied by a charm:

> *Hard flesh,*
> *Hard flesh,*
> *Roaming about in the world,*
> *It rubbed itself here and there*
> *And it stopped just here,*
> *But Nick came up to us*
> *And cried to us in suffering.*
> *We began our spell*
> *Right away,*
> *With our words*
> *We cursed it,*
> *And drove it far away,*
> *Over nine seas*
> *And nine countries...*

December 16

The Lion

Lions lived in the Balkan area until the middle of the first millennium. Social memory of its existence remains is retained in Romanian toponymy such as the Dolj County village of Leu, meaning lion in English, in charms and spells, and in certain pre-Christian corrals. In the charm for fright, the lion is a spirit that induces disease, but in the charm for the evil hour the induced sufferings are sent back to the lion:

> *Let you vanish yourselves*
> *And go*
> *To the Lion Emperor*
> *Because there he is waiting for you*
> *With laid tables*
> *With burning torches ...*

In one of the most beautiful Romanian corrals, that of Lion, the mythical character confronts the hero:

Raise you Lion
Mad dog
Let's fight
With swords to cut ourselves!
Let's fight because it's fairer
As God let it be!...
(Tohanu village, Brasov County)

December 17
The Christmas Log

The *Christmas Log*, long a substitute of the dead god, is represented by an oak-tree trunk cut in the forest and brought home to be burnt on the night of December 24-25. The cut tree (actually the log) symbolizes the yearly death of the native god Christmas, who, before the Christian era, was reborn through the incineration ritual practiced by the Geto-Dacians. The log has funeral significance in Romania. Hence the expression "To find someone lying like a log" refers to a man who died without a lighted candle at his deathbed, while "to tie someone up like a log" refers to someone who is immobilized and cannot move, as if he were a dead man.

When a family's genealogical tree is drawn up, the log is the name of the forefather from which the lines of descendents emerge. In the Mehedinti area a custom was recorded by which a log of cherry (*quercus cerris*) was burnt on Christmas Eve and on Christmas Day and the embers were kept to be used for healing certain diseases. Decorating the Christmas tree was a practice that overlapped the native custom of incinerating the dead phytomorphic body, namely the Christmas log. Starting with the second half of the Nineteenth Century, the western European tradition of trimming the Christmas tree spread across the country from north to south and from towns to villages. The custom of burning the Christmas log, which has disappeared today, was practiced by Romanians, Macedo-Romanians, Latvians and with Serbo-Croatians. In France, the "Bûche de Noël" (Christmas Log) pastry remains a widely-held tradition.

December 18
The Clucking Hen

A log burning was called by some Megleno-Romanians *Clucking Hen*. At Christmas-time. a man holding the Clucking Hen (log) in his arms, along with his children, called the Hen's Chicks, with boughs in their hands and his wife, carrying a tray filled with special fasting food and all sorts of fruit, pears or raisins, go to a pole placed in the middle of their farmhouse courtyard where the horse used for threshing wheat was tied. There they lay a flat cake with a silver coin in it on a tray and then thank the Hen:

"Dear God, dear God, come and eat the rich dinner we have prepared in good health and in good luck; we thank you for all these gifts that you have given us!"

Next, the head of the family calls his children, imitating the hen calling its chicks. They answer as chicks and re-enter the house where the Clucking Hen (Log) is set afire and burn during all the days left until Epiphany. The ashes are kept and later thrown at the foot of fruit-trees. During this period of time, members of the family each eat a clove of garlic to ensure good health throughout the year. They divide the flat cake into several pieces: one for the Hen, one for the cattle, and one for each member of the household. The one finding the silver coin would have luck in the New Year. The next morning when returning from church, family members step over a piece of iron so that they should be in good health in the new year and entered their home carrying a piece of wood (a twig, a chip, a sliver). They put the wood on the fire and pray: *May God bring good luck!* Following a meal and a nap, they eat a plentiful dinner and go out to visit relatives and friends greeting them with the formula: *"Bird, bird! May God bring you luck!"* (The custom was recorded with Megleno-Romanians).

December 19
Siva

The pig, due to its prolific birthing - 10-18 piglets at a time - and to its short gestation period of three months, three weeks and three days was compared to the wheat ear. In ancient times it was associated with the divinities of vegetation: Demeter, Persephone, Attis, Adonis, Ossyris, Dionysus. Those who worshipped God Attis and those who worshipped God Adonis refused to eat pork, because it personified the respective god himself. In ancient Egypt, although the pig was considered a disgusting animal, people would sacrifice it and eat it within a ritual dedicated to God Ossyris on a certain designated day of the year. Several millennia after the pig was confirmed as a divinity, the Romanians still maintain many aspects of its cult. They sacrifice a pig in a ritual manner on Pigs' Ignat December 20, prepare food from its meat (sausages, pig's trotters, black pudding), and imitate its voice with an instrument called *surla* (fife). The custom is practiced in Europe only by Romanians and Macedo-Romanians and in Asia by Indians.

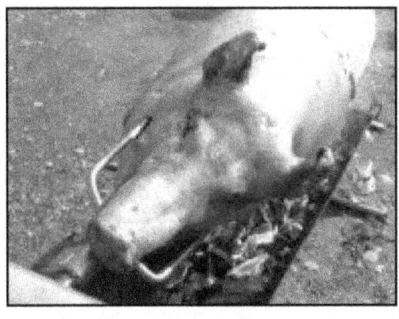

The pig appears in nursery rhymes and in children's games (Playing the Pig, or the Sow) and most significantly, the pig is present in a special carol, called Siva, recalling the great Indian God Shiva. The Siva custom was practiced until the middle of the Twentieth Century at the New Year. The Siva Carol is symbolized by the head of the pig which sacrificed at Ignat. In Romania, the custom has a rich vocabulary: Siva, Siva's Baby, or Vasilica, Sila. The Siva ceremonial consists of several elements:
- the pig's head decorated with rings, earrings, bracelets and flowers is displayed at a window or in a house chosen for the ceremony;
- the carol which narrates Siva's life in the heavenly beech-tree and oak-tree forests is sung;
- the pig dies a violent death and its inanimate body is burned (singed);
- singers descend to the valley to drink water;
- Siva is judged by a jury which often includes The Old Christmas and Holy Mary;
- the carol singers wish "Happy New Year!" to their hosts from whom they received gifts.

Over the last century, the Siva Carol was taken over by Roma (gypsies) who turned it into a commercial event.[194]

December 20

Ignat

Originally related to the cult of fire and sun, *Ignat* took its name and celebration date from Saint Ignatie Teofan in the Orthodox Almanac, also The Pigs' Ignat. The sacrifice of a pig as well as the incineration ritual

---

[194] Ghinoiu, 2001, p. 175.

(singing of the pig) on Ignat Day (*Ignis*=fire) are prehistoric practices that still survive. Ethnologic arguments support the theory that the ritual sacrifice of the pig was carried out in spring during wheat period. Like other customs typical for the New Year Holiday that used to be celebrated in spring ("sorcova," the sowing custom, "plugusorul"), the ritual sacrifice of the pig was transferred from the vernal equinox to the winter solstice.

All the beliefs, customs and magic practices related to predicting a violent death such as using fat to perform spells and charms as well as to prepare certain medicines, making ritual food out of selected vital organs of the animal, uttering particular magic formulas, are relics of the sacrifice by substitution of the god who dies and is reborn yearly at the winter solstice. The custom is found, in various stages of regression, throughout Romania.

December 21
The Pig Dissatisfied with God's Decisions

As a prehistoric divinity of wheat, as a sacrificed offering at Christmas and as a symbol of the Year that dies and is reborn after 365 days, the pig is depicted in some Romanian traditions as unhappy with God's decisions or being usurped by God.

"When God finished creating all the living creatures of the world, He summoned them to let each of them know what their fate would be. He told the horse that it would help man, it would be ridden by him, it would be clad in mail and taken to the battle field. He told the dog that it would guard man's house, it would be fed, beaten and stroked by man. And so He went on telling each creature about their duties in the world. All the animals obeyed God's decisions, for who could dare to stand against God Almighty? Only the poor pig kept grunting in discontent, sounding like a broken drum. When its turn came and when it heard what its fate would be, it started to grunt even worse. When God saw how shameless the pig was, He punished it to grunt all its life, and to look for what it lacked, namely shame, in the ground. That is why the pig is always grunting, whether it is hungry or not, and is always looking for shame in the ground..."[195]

---

[195] Legends of the Fauna, 1994, p. 78-79.

December 22

The Opening of the Graves

One set of beliefs holds that spirits of the dead return on the eve of major holidays throughout the year - Christmas, the Forty Four Martyrs, Sangiorz, Sanziene, Samedru - to meet and to enjoy themselves with living ones. The innocent souls of the dead are welcomed with good food laid out on tables in people's houses (The Eve's Meal in Bucovina and Moldavia), or in their courtyard (The Fires at Joimari in Walachia and in Oltenia). Canes are made for them which are struck in the graves (western Oltenia and eastern Banat) to be used by them while they travel on earth. Their shelter is purified by burning incense beside their graves and distributing alms on their behalf. On such occasions they are asked to help solve problems such as a girl's marriage, ensuring bountiful crops and productive sheep flocks, men's health, or punishment of enemies. However on certain dates and at midnight on New Year's Night, Sangiorz, Pentecost, or Saint Andrew, the spirits of the dead are forced by various means such as the Calus Dance, cries and loud noises produced by whips, bells, to return to their underground dwellings.[196]

December 23

The Opening of the Sky and the Burning of the Treasures

A widespread belief once prevailed that during the nights of the great holidays and mainly on New Year's night, the sky and graves opened themselves, that animals could speak and that treasures started to burn. If people looked up in the sky, in those particular nights, they might for a moment see God sitting at the regal table together with His closest saints. If so, any wish would come true. Once, it was said, there was a man waiting at his window and watching for the sky to open. When that happened he asked God to make him smarter. But when he wanted to close the window, he could not because his head was too big for the window frame. The poor man had to wait until the next year when the sky opened again in order to ask God to change him back and make him as smart as he had been a year before.[197]

When the treasures start burning, people say that the buried money starts dancing or washing itself. People could find treasures by orienting themselves according to those flames which were *bluish* and had

---

[196] Ghinoiu, 1997, p. 63.

[197] The Legends of the Cosmos, 1994 p. 61-62.

no heat. The most favorable time for "burning" and "washing" money was each night before one of the major holidays of the Year - Christmas, New Year, Saint George, Easter, Sanziene. Treasures could be *clean* if not influenced by any spell or curse or *unclean* if cursed. Few treasures could be discovered or dug out if under spells dedicated to the devil.

December 24
Christmas Eve Father

Christmas Eve Father is a mythical representation in the Romanian Pantheon. He is Father Christmas' brother and is very old, having come close to death after 365 days. One day younger than his brother, Christmas, he is celebrated on December 24. The legend says that Holy Mary was in labor pains and asked Christmas Eve Father to give Her shelter. But he told Her that he was too poor and had no place for Her. He asked Her to go to his brother and neighbor, Father Christmas, who was richer than he. He sent Her from number 24 house to number 25 house (the numbers of the houses being similar to the particular days in December). In other legends Christmas Eve Father is a shepherd or a watchman for Christmas's sheep flocks. That is an interesting example of the way most abstract philosophical notions of time and space have been humanized and introduced in the cultural fiber of a nation.

December 25
Father Christmas

Christmas is a phytomorphic solar god, typical for the territories inhabited by the Geto-Dacians that was identified with the Roman god Saturn and with the Iranian god Mithra. For over a millennium Christians celebrated the New Year on Christmas Day, December 25, very close to the winter solstice, in Rome until the Thirteenth Century, in France until the year 1564, in Russia until the time of Peter the Great, and in the Romanian Provinces until the end of the Nineteenth Century.

The Romanians still keep those times fresh in their memory, since, in some villages from Banat and from Transylvania, the New Year's Day on January 1 is called Little Christmas. The term *old father* infers that the worshipped god must die to be reborn at New Year. The Roman Saturnalia, then the birth of Mithra, the solar god or Iranian origin, and, after the Christian faith appeared, the birth of Jesus Christ, overlapped the native Christmas holiday. All the customs held at Christmas, New Year and Epiphany make up together the scenario of the death and the rebirth

of the divinity. Numerous rituals celebrate this transition and beliefs illustrating the degrading of time and the chaos existing before the Creation:
- excessive eating, drinking, feasting, an avalanche of bad language;
- the ritual "Perinita" dance, the dances with masks;
- the death of the Old Year, marked by turning off the lights at midnight on Christmas and New Year;
- the birth of the New Year, marked by turning on the lights;
- people's cheering, hugging and congratulating each other, signifies that the world has been saved from destruction;
- the evil spirits being chased away by cries, bangs and loud noises produced by whips, horns and "buhai" (an instrument imitating the roaring of a bull);
- nightly illumination;
- purifying people by sprinkling water on them and by young men bathing in cold river water;
- purifying the air by disorienting or chasing horses;
- agrarian and shepherd customs like Plugusorul, Semanatul, Sorcova, and Vasilca.

The fact that the Christian customs overlapped the ancient pre-Christian ones, the Greek-Roman and oriental customs overlapped the native ones (Geto-Dacian) generated a spiritual phenomenon unique in Europe.

December 26
Craciuneasa (Father Christmas' Wife)

In the legends, Christmas's wife and the midwife of the Holy Child, Jesus Christ, is called *Craciuneasa*. She is a well-intended mythical representation, who gives Holy Mary shelter and helps Her to give birth to the Holy Baby, without Christmas knowing about it. When her husband finds out, he punishes her severely by cutting off her arms from the elbow. But Virgin Mary puts the arms back and even makes them shine like the Sun.

December 27
Christmas Knot-Shaped Bread

The preparing and the sharing of *knot-shaped breads* is one of the most long-lasting and well known Romanian customs. The Christmas knot-shaped bread is sacred food, made from leavened dough, by *clean* women (meaning women with no menstruation), eaten at ritual meals and feasts. It was given to carol singers and given away as alms for the spirits of the dead. The Christmas knot-shaped bread has different forms: circle, horseshoe and star, meaning the *Sun, the Moon* and the stars in the sky; as a doll and the figure eight, representing the anthropomorphic body of the Indo-European and Christian deity; as a filled circle, with no hole in the middle, imagining the geomorphic Neolithic deity; as different sacred animals and birds (the bull, or the hoopoe).

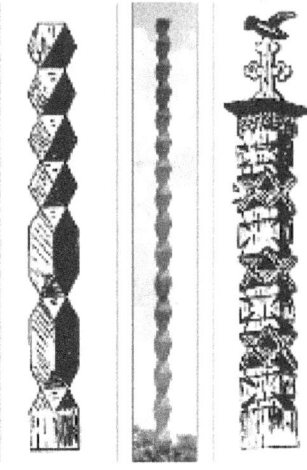

Brancusi Column of the Infinite (center Comarnescu, 1972) between two funeral pillars (Pavelescu, 2004)

The making, offering of wishes, and receiving of the Christmas knot-shaped bread as well as sharing and eating it are ceremonial moments of deep spiritual experience. In Moldavia and Bessarabia, the Christmas knot-shaped breads, named *little Christmas*, were preserved till Forty Martyrs, the New Agrarian Year in the old almanac, when they were set on the horns of oxen or on plough handles. The Christmas knot-shaped breads were given to animals for eating or were buried in furrows.

December 28

Christmas Burial

As carried out by young men from the Somes valley on December 28, the simulated burial of the Old Year and the rebirth of the New Year was called *Christmas Burial*. Young men meet at *the house of the game*, where they chose one who will play the role of Dead Christmas. He is laid on a wooden ladder (the funeral stretcher) and covered so as not to be recognized. While accompanying *the dead man* to the river on his last journey, the procession *sings a funeral song*. The priest and church singers perform the funeral service and musicians play music specific to unmarried dead people. The ritual text, sung on the melody of the funeral song, reveals the significance of the custom:

> *Dear Christmas,*
> *Dear Old Man,*
> *Today we bury you.*
> *Come, come everyone,*

To carry Christmas to the valley,
To put him in the ice hole
And lay a log over it.
Oh, Christmas
Oh, Old Man
Farewell, go from us,
Go on Saturday water,
And do not come back,
As a new Christmas will come,
A better one than you.

When the procession reaches an ice hole on the river, the dead man is absolved of his sins and then thrown from the ladder onto the ice. In that moment the Dead Christmas is reborn and promptly stands up to be seen by those gathered around. The New Christmas, accompanied by the young men, singing and playing joyful songs, returns to the village where they have the funeral meal which is in fact a lively feast.[198]

December 29
Buhai

Buhai Instrument,
Campulung Moldovonesc, Suceava County
(AIEF, Photo by G. Habenicht, 1970)

Before the introduction of the Christian religion, *buhai*, the Romanian folk name for bull synonymous with "Plugusor" (Moldavia), used to be one of the zoomorphic substitutes of the Thracian god Dionysus and of the Iranian god Mithra, sacrificed on December 25. The same name, buhai, is also used for the ritual musical instrument used by the group who perform the buhai or plugusor at New Year. It is decorated on the outside and is carried by one member of the group, or, if it is too large, it is carried in a sledge or a cart drawn by oxen or by horses. With the buhai instrument, the sound of a roaring bull (ancient agrarian divinity) is imitated during the performance.

The buhai is made from a wooden container made from a small barrel or cask from which the top and bottom have been removed. One of the openings is covered with a tightly stretched animal skin - sheep

---

[198] Medan, 1978, p. 91-99.

skin, goat skin or veal skin) - in which a narrow hole is made. Through that hole a tuft of horse hair is passed. By pulling the tuft of hair with wet hands, a deep gravely sound is created. This emulates the roaring of an infuriated bull. The instrument recalls the bloody scene in which a bull was once sacrificed, as a substitute of god Dionysus and of god Mithra, over which the Christians later transposed the celebration of the Birth of Jesus Christ. The "buhai" was in evidence among Romanians and Macedo-Romanians from southeastern Europe and adopted by neighboring cultures.

December 30
The Meteorological Almanacs

At Christmas and at New Year, old villagers predict, through ingenious means, if the months of the year will be rainy or dry. These meteorological predictions are called almanacs made of onion leaves, of nutshells, or even of glowing embers. The most well-known almanac is the one made of onion leaves. The method consists of several steps:
- large onion is divided into two equal parts;
- twelve onion leaves (cups) are chosen;
- the inside skin is removed from the cups;
- each cup is given the name of a month of the year;
- equal quantities of salt is put in the cups;
- the cups each representing a month are lined up, starting with January and ending with December, and are placed in the pantry or between the windows of a room;
- the next morning one can see, from the amount of water in the cups, which will be months of rain and which ones will of drought.

For a short-term forecasts of a week, day and even hour of a day, another type of almanac is used. Living creatures are looked to as oracles. This is based on the well-documented fact that animals and insects - pigs, mice, bees, roosters, ants and others - change their behavior according to changes in atmospheric pressure or humidity levels.

December 31
The New Year's Party

Winter feasts bear procession, Danmanesti, Bacau County (Ciubotaru, 2002)

The New Year's Party is the nightly holiday dedicated to the oldest god of mankind, the Year, personification of the Sun. He is called Old Year before he dies at midnight and New Year as soon as it is reborn. The Year, father of the great gods of mankind - Zeus, Saturn, Christmas, Shiva, Mithra - is born, grows, becomes mature, ages and dies. After 365 days he is reborn. Following their position in the calendar, Saints are older or younger ones. Saint Vasile (January 1) is, according to the folk legends, a young man who sits on a barrel, who loves women and enjoys himself; Dragobete (February 24), Dochia's son, represents the god of love in the Carpathian regions; Sangiorz (April 23) and Santoader are young men, riding on horseback; Santilie (July 20) and Samedru (October 26) are mature men. They are followed by elder saints: Father Andrew (30 November), Father Nicolae (December 6) and Father Christmas (December 25). The growing old age of those divinities finally announces the death of the Year, identified in the folk culture with Christmas.

For over one millennium and a half, until the Nineteenth Century, Romanians celebrated the New Year on Christmas Day. New Year celebration, after being separated from the Christian holiday of Jesus' Birth and after being transferred to January 1 when the Roman celebrated the January Calends, was called Little Christmas, Christmas Burial, Year Burial, and finally New Year's Party. The holidays belonging to the New Year cycle are divided by the New Year's night into two symmetrical parts. The customs, the ritual acts and the magic practices reflect, in the first part of the cycle, fear, disorder and chaos caused by the fact that The Old Year becomes old and dies, while, in the second part, after New Year's midnight, it reflects optimism, joy, order and balance.

The first part, between the ritual sacrifice of the pig at Ignat and New Year's Midnight, overlaps the days preceding the winter solstice, when the night grows longer and when it gets colder and darker. These natural phenomena made people fear that the world would be destroyed and that the time would come when the Sun disappeared from the sky forever. Then comes the spectacular phenomenon of the winter solstice when the Sun starts to go up in the sky, and when the days gradually become longer. The second part of the cycle, governed by optimism, generated by the rebirth of the Year, is the period between New Year's Midnight and Epiphany.

Through such holidays and customs, Romanians make it easier to cope with the implacable course of time. This is accomplished by humanizing natural phenomena that happen independent of their will: the ritual sacrifice of the pig, preparing the ritual food of wheat (knot-shaped bread, flat cakes), of pork (sausages, pig's trotters); the belief that the graves open and that the spirits of the dead return among the living ones; the numerous parties and feasts with excessive food, drinks, with enjoyment, trivial gestures, abusive language, "Perinita" dance, all of them being surviving relics of the ancient orgies; the young men groups who express, in their carol singing and in their ritual acts, the yearly dramatic birth and rebirth of the divinity; and, finally, turning off the lights at midnight to symbolize the total darkness and chaos caused by the death of the divinity. After a few moments, the lights are turned on again, which means that the god Year is reborn, and, together with it, the time and the surrounding world. People believed that, in that favorable moment, the sky opened, the treasures started to burn and the animals could speak. The evil spirits are driven away with all kinds of loud sounds (cries, bells, whips), the rich harvest is invoked by various customs (Plugusorul, Seminatul, Sorcova) and by ritual acts; people try their luck, they also predict the future spouse and make meteorological almanacs (of onion leaves, of nutshells, etc.); people reconcile and become more tolerant; they also start work symbolically.

Due to the fact that the New Year's celebration is an ancient one and to the fact that Christ's birth celebration has been transferred from January 6 to December 25, overlapping the holiday of god Christmas, the order of these ritual scenarios is not entirely respected.

BIBLIOGRAPHY

An extensive academic literature exists in Romania. Cumulated over many decades, serious and substantial ethnographic and sociological studies were undertaken in late nineteenth century as well as the inter-War period between the 1920s and 1940s. These were expanded and built-on during the Communist regime though in many cases with a forced aim of establishing a 'pure' Romanian ethnic and folk origin. Academic interest and research in ethnography and sociology has been sustained in recent decades.

Adascalitei, Vasile, *Istoria unui obicei. Plugusorul*, Iasi, Editura Junimea, 1987.
Badescu, Ilie, *Teoria Latentelor,* Bucharest, Editura IDOGEP – EUXIN, 1997.
Berciu, Dumitru *La izvoarele istoriei. O introducere în arheologia preistorica*, Bucharest, Editura Stiintifica, 1967.
Bernea, Ernest, *Contributii la problema calendarului în satul Cornova,* în „Arhiva pentru Stiinta si reforma sociala", Anul XX, nr. 14, 1932.
Biltiu, Pamfil, *Armindenuli in Zona Lapus*, în REF, nr. 3, 1993.
Bîrlea, Ovidiu, *Mica enciclopedie a povestilor romanesti,* Bucharest, Editura Stiintifica si Enciclopedica, 1976.
Bîrlea, Ovidiu, *Eseu despre dansul popular romanesc,* Bucharest, Editura Cartea Romaneasca, 1982.
Bogdan, Ion, **Olos**, M., **Timis**, N., *Calendarul Maramuresului*, Baia Mare, 1980.
Boroneant, Vasile, *Arheologia pesterilor si minelor din Romania*, Bucharest, Institutul de Memorie Culturala, 2000.
Brâncus, Grigore, *Vocabularul autohton al limbii romane*, Bucharest, Editura Stiintifica si Enciclopedica, 1983.
Bratiloveanu-Popilian, Marcela, *Obiceiuri de primavara din Oltenia. Calendarul ortodox si practica populara*, Bucharest, Editura „Constantin Matasa", 2001.

Brailoiu, Constantin, *Opere*, vol. V, Bucharest, Editura Muzicala, 1981.
Buhociu, Octavian, *Folclorul de iara, ziorile si poezia pastoreasca*, Bucharest, Editura Minerva, 1979.
Burghele, Camelia, *In numele magiei terapeutice*, Zalau, Editura Limes, 2000.
Butura, Valer *Enciclopedie de etnobotanica românească*, Bucharest, Editura Stiitifica si Enciclopedica, 1979.
Butura, Valer, *Cultura spirituala românească*, Bucharest, Editura Minerva, 1992.
Buta, Paul, *Alaiuri de masti*, Galati, Centrul Cultural „Dunarea de Jos", 2001.
Candrea, Ion Aurel, *Iarba fiarelor. Studii de folclor,* Bucharest, Cultura Nationala, 1928.
Caraman, Petru, *Pamânt si apa. Contributie etnologica la studiul simbolicei eminesciene,* Iasi, Editura Junimea, 1984.
Cârciumaru, Marin, *Marturii ale artei rupestre preistorice în Romania*, Bucharest, Editura Sport-Turism, 1987.
Caatori straini despre Tarile Romane, vol. VI (partea I Paul de Alep, partea a II-a Evlia Celebi), Bucureati, Editura Stiintifica si Enciclopedica, 1976.
Chelcea, Ion, *Obiceiuri de peste un în doua sate din Almaj,* in „Sociologie romaneasca," nr. 34, 1939.
Ciubotaru, Ion H., *Folclorul obiceiurilor familiale din Moldova. Marea trecere*, Iasi, in „Caietele Arhivei de Folclor", vol. VII, 1986.
Ciubotaru, Ion H., *Catolicii din Moldova. Universul culturii populare*, Iasi, Editura Presa Buna, 2002.
Ciubotaru, Silvia, *Nunta în Moldova*, Iasi, Editura Universitatii „Al. I. Cuza," 2000.
Cojocaru, Nicolae, *Traditii la cultul crestin*, Suceava, Editura Lidana, 2004.
Comanici, Germina, *Ramura verde în spiritualitatea românească*, Bucharest, Editura Etnologica, 2004.
Conea, Ion, *Clopotiva. Un sat din Hateg*, vol. II, Bucharest, Institutul de Stiinte Sociale al Romaniei, 1940.
Constantinescu, Nicolae, *Lectura textului folcloric*, Bucharest, Editura Minerva, 1986.
Cotta, V., **Bodea**, M., *Vânatul României*, Bucharest, Editura Agrosilvica, 1969.
Cretu, Vasile Tudor, *Ethosul folcloric – sistem deschis,* Timisoara, Editura Facla, 1980.

Cristescu-Golopentia, Stefania, *Gospodaria în credintele si riturile magice ale femeilor din Dragus (Fagaras)*, Bucharest, Editura Paideia, 2002.

Cuceu, Ion, *Probleme actuale in structura culturii traditionale*, Cluj-Napoca, Presa Universitara Clujeana, 2000.

Cuceu, Ion, **Cuceu**, Maria, *Vechi obiceiuri agrare romanesti*, Bucharest, Editura Minerva, 1988.

Dancus, Mihai, *Contributii la cunoasterea unui obicei de Anul nou in Maramures*, in „Anuarul Muzeului Etnografic al Transilvaniei pe anii 1971–1973," Cluj, 1973.

de Alep, Paul, în *Calatori straini despre Țările Române*, vol. VI, Bucharest, Editura Stiintifica si Enciclopedica, 1986.

Densusianu, Ovid, *Graiul din Tara Hategului*, Bucharest, 1915.

Densusianu, Nicolae, *Raspunsuri la un chestionar istoric din Muntenia, Moldova si Dobrogea*, mss. 5359, Biblioteca Academiei Romane, 1893–1897.

Dictionar de istorie veche a Romaniei (Paleolitic – sec. X), Bucharest, Editura Stiintifica si Enciclopedica, 1976.

Drogeanu, Paul, *Practica fericirii*, Bucharest, Editura Eminescu, 1985.

Dumitrescu, Vladimir, *L'art preistorique en Roumanie*, Bucharest, 1937.

Durand, Gilbert, *Structurile antropologice ale imaginarului*, Bucharest, Editura Univers, 1977.

Eliade, Mircea, *Aspecte ale mitului*, Bucharest, Editura Univers, 1978.

Eliade, Mircea *De la Zamolxis la Genghis Han*, Bucharest, Editura Stiintifica si Enciclopedica, 1980.

Eretescu, Constantin, *Folclorul literar al romanilor. O privire contemporana*, Bucharest, Editura Compania, 2004.

Evseev, Ivan, *Dictionar de magie, demonologie si mitologie romaneasca*, Timisoara, Editura Amarcord, 1997.

Fochi, Adrian *Datini si eresuri populare de la sfarsitul secolului al XIX-lea: raspunsurile la chestionarele lui Nicolae Densusianu*, Bucharest, Editura Minerva, 1976.

Francu, Teofil, George Candrea, *Romanii din Muntii Apuseni*, Bucharest, 1888.

Galusca Crismaru, Tatiana, *Rituale pastorale*, in FEF, nr. 1, 1979.

Ghinoiu, Ion, *Varstele timpului*, Bucharest, Editura Meridiane, 1988.

Ghinoiu, Ion, *Obiceiuri populare de peste an. Dictionar*, Bucharest, Editura Fundatiei Culturale Romane, 1997.

Ghinoiu, Ion, *Lumea de aici, lumea de dincolo*, Bucharest, Editura Fundatiei Culturale Romane, 1999.

Ghinoiu, Ion, *Zile si Mituri. Calendarul taranului roman*, Bucharest, Editura Pro, 2000.
Ghinoiu, Ion, *Panteonul romanesc. Dictionar*, Bucharest, Editura Enciclopedica, 2001
Ghinoiu, Ion, *Calusul. Istorie si documente*, Slatina, Editura Fundatiei „Universitatea pentru Toti," 2003.
Gimbutas, Marija, *Civilizatie si cultura. Vestigii preistorice în sud-estul european*, traducere de Sorin Paliga, prefata si note de Radu Florescu, Bucharest, Editura Meridiane, 1989.
Gimbutas, Marija, *Civilizatia Marii Zeite si sosirea cavalerilor razboinici*, Bucharest, Editura Lucretius, 1997.
Golopentia, Sanda, *Learn to sing, my mother said*, Baia Mare, Editura Ethnologica, 2004.
Gourhan Leroi, Andre, *Gestul si cuvantul*, vol. III, Bucharest, Editura Meridiane, 1983
Graur, Tiberiu, *Sistemica culturii populare*, in „Anuarul Muzeului Etnografic al Transilvaniei pe anii 1974–1977," Cluj–Napoca, 1977.
Hasdeu, Bogdan P., *Etymologicum Magnum Romaniae. Dictionarul limbii istorice a romanilor*, tom. II, Bucharest, Socec, 1887.
Hedesan, Otilia, *Pentru o mitologie difuza*, Timisoara, Editura Marineasa, 2000.
Herseni, Traian, *Forme stravechi de cultura poporana romaneasca*, Cluj-Napoca, Editura Dacia, 1977.
Ionica, Ion I., *Drâguş – un sat din Tara Oltului. Manifestari spirituale. Reprezentarea cerului*, Bucharest, Institutul de Stiinte Sociale, 1944.
Ionita, Maria, *Cartea Valvelor*, Cluj-Napoca, Editura Dacia, 1982.
Irimie, Cornel, **Focsa**, Marcela *Icoane pe sticla*, Bucharest, Editura Meridiane,1968.
Ispas, Sabina, *Lirica de dragoste. Index motivic si tipologic*, IV, (S–Z), Bucharest, Editura Academiei, 1989.
Isfanoni, Doina, *Interferente între magic si estetic*, Bucharest, Editura Enciclopedica, 2002.
Isfanoni, Rusalin, *Padurenii Hunedoarei*, Bucharest, Editura Mirabilis, 2004.
Jula, Nicolae, **Manastireanu**, Vasile, *Traditii si obiceiuri romanesti. Anul Nou în Moldova si Bucovina*, Bucharest, Editura pentru Literatura, 1968.
Kahane, Mariana, **Georgescu-Stanculeanu**, Lucilia, *Cântecul Zorilor si Bradului. Tipologie muzicala*, Bucharest, Editura Muzicala, 1988.
Kernbach, Victor, *Dictionar de mitologie generala*, Bucharest, Editura Albatros, 1983.

Kligman, Gail, *Nunta mortului. Ritual, poetica si cultura populara in Transilvania*, Iasi, Editura Polirom, 1998.
Larionescu, Sanda, *Cultul martilor la sarbatorile de peste an în câteva sate din jud. Caras-Severin. Text, functie si limbaj*, Timisoara, in „Tibiscus," Etnografie, 1976–1978.
Legendele cosmosului; Legendele faunei; Legendele florei: Editie critica si studiu introductiv de Tony Brill, Bucharest, Editura „Grai si suflet – Cultura nationala," 1994
Micul Atlas Lingvistic Roman, Serie Noua, vol. II, Bucharest, Editura Academiei, 1987.
Manolache, Dumitru, *Andrei, Sanpetrul lupilor*, Bucharest, Editura Anastasia, 2000.
Marian, Simion Florea, *Ornitologia*, vol. I, Siret, 1883.
Marian, Simion Florea, *Inmormantarea la romani*, Bucharest, Editura Lito-Tipografia „Carol Göbl," 1892.
Marian, Simion Florea, *Sarbatorile la romani. Studiu etnografic,* vol. I-III *(Carnilegile)*, Bucharest, Institutul de Arte Grafice 1898.
Marza, Traian, *Lioara – un gen muzical inedit al obiceiurilor de primavara din Bihor*, în „Lucrari de muzicologie," vol. V, Cluj, 1969.
Medan, Virgil, *Obiceiul Ingroparii Craciunului la Nires*, Dej, in „Samus," an. II, 1978.
Mehedinti, Simion, *Civilizatie si Cultura. Conceptii, definitii, rezonante*. Ingrijirea editiei, studiu introductiv si note de Gheorghita Geana, Bucharest, Editura Trei, 1999.
Miclea, Ion, **Florescu**, Radu, *Stramosii românilor. Vestigii milenare de cultura si arta: Daco-romanii; Preistoria Daciei; Geto-dacii; Decebal si Traian*, Bucharest Editura Meridiane, 1980.
Moise, Ilie, *Contributii privind cunoasterea obiceiului Prinsul verilor si varutelor*, in „Studii si comunicari", Sibiu, Asociatia Folcloristilor si Etnografilor, 1981.
Moraru, Georgeta, *Cercetari etnografice in Gropeni*, in volumul *Studii de etnografie si folclor în zona Brailei*, Braila, 1975, p. 28-29.
Mutu, Gheorghe, *Din mitalogia tracilor,* Bucharest, Editura Cartea Romaneasca, 1982
Muzeul Satului. Tezaurul Romaniei, Bucharest, Editura Kina, 2004.
Naides, jud. Caras-Severin, informatie de teren inregistrata în anul 1981.
Niculita-Voronca, Elena, *Datinile si credintele poporului român adunate si asezate în ordine mitologica*, Cernauti, Tipografia Isidor Wiegier, 1903.

Nitu, Georgeta *Plante din flora spontana cu utilizari în gospodaria taraneasca din Oltenia*, Craiova, Editura Helios, 1999.

Oisteanu, Andrei, *Motive Si semnificatii simbolice în cultura tradițională romaneasca*, Bucharest, Editura Minerva, 1989.

Olinescu, Marcel, *Mitologie romaneasca*, Bucharest, Editura Casa Scoalelor, 1944.

Olteanu, Antoaneta, *Metamorfozele sacrului. Dictionar de mitologie populara*, Bucharest, Editura Paideia, 1998.

Oprisan, Horia Barbu, *Monografia folclorica a Teleormanului*, Casa Creatiei populare, Alexandria, 1971.

Pamfile, Tudor *Sarbatorile de vara la romani. Studiu etnografic,* Academia Romana, Colectia „Din viata poporului roman," Bucharest, Socec, 1910.

Pamfile, Tudor *Sarbatorile de toamna si postul Craciunului*, Academia Romana, Colectia „Din viata poporului roman," Bucharest, Socec, 1914.

Pamfile, Tudor *Cerul si podoabele lui dupa credintele poporului roman,* Academia Romana, Colectia „Din viata poporului roman,"Bucharest, Socec, 1915.

Pamfile, Tudor, *Mitologie romaneasca. Dusmani si prieteni ai omului,* Academia Romana, Colectia „Din viata poporului roman," Bucharest, 1916.

Pamfile, Tudor, *Boli si leacuri la oameni, vite si pasari*, Bucharest, Editura Saeculum I.O., 1999.

Panea, Nicolae. *Gramatica funerarului*, Craiova, Editura Scrisul Românesc, 2003.

Papahagi, Pericle N. *Meglenoromânii. Studiu etnografico-filologic*, fara alte date pe coperta.

Papahagi, Tache, *Mic dictionar folcloric,* Bucharest, Editura Minerva, 1978

Parau, Steluta. *Lumina si culoare in amenajarea estetica a spatiului romanesc traditional de locuit la romani*, Galati, Editura Fundatiei universitare „Dunarea de Jos," 2001.

Parvan, Vasile, *Contributii epigrafice la istoria crestinismului dacoroman,* Bucharest, Socec, 1911.

Parvu, Constantin *Universul plantelor. Mica enciclopedie*, Bucharest, Editura Enciclopedica, 2000.

Pavelescu, Gheorghe, *Cercetari asupra magiei la romanii din Muntii Apuseni,* Bucharest, Institutul Social Roman, 1945.

Patrut, Picu, *Miniaturi si poezie. Comori ale artei populare romanesti*, Bucharest, Intreprinderea poligrafica «Arta Grafica,» 1985.

Petrescu, Paul, **Secosan**, Elena, **Stoica**, Georgeta, **Ciobanu**, Pavel, *Arta populară din Mehedinti*, Comitetul de Cultura si Educatie Socialista. Centrul de Indrumare a Creatiei Populare si a Miscarii Artistice de Masa Mehedinti, Drobeta-Turnu-Severin, 1983.
Petrovici, Emil, *Folclor din Valea Almajului*, in „Anuarul arhivei de folclor," an. III, 1935.
Pippidi, Dumitru M., (coordinator), *Dictionar de istorie veche a Romaniei*, Editura Stiintifica si Enciclopedica, 1976.
Pop, Mihai, *Mitul marii treceri*, in *Folclor literar*, vol. II, Timisoara, 1968.
Popa-Lisseanu, *Mitologia greco-romana in lectura ilustrata*, editia a VII-a, Bucharest, Tipografia Ion C. Vacarescu, 1928.
Popescu, Alexandru, *Traditii de munca romanesti*, Bucharest, Editura Stiintifica si Enciclopedica, 1986.
Radulescu, Nicolae, *Sulul – un obicei inedit din ciclul calendaristic*, in REF, nr. 1, 1969.
Radulescu-Codin, C., **Mihalache**, D., *Sarbatorile poporului cu obiceiurile, credintele si unele traditii legate de ele. Culegere de prin partile Muscelului*, Academia Romana, Colectia „Din viata poporului roman," Bucharest, Socec, 1909.
Sanie, Silviu, *Culte orientale în Dacia romana. Cultele siriene si palmiriene*, Bucharest, Editura Stiintifica si Enciclopedica, 1981.
Scorpan, Constantin, *Cavalerul trac*, Constanta, Muzeul regional de arheologie Dobrogea, 1967.
Simenschy, Teofil, *Cultura si filosofie indiana în texte si studii*, I, Bucharest, Editura Stiintifica si Enciclopedica, 1978.
St. Lazar, Ioan, *Calatorie de recunoastere*, Rm. Valcea, Editura Patrimoniu, 2003.
Stahl, H. Henri, *Eseuri critice*, Bucharest, Editura Minerva, 1983.
Stoica, Georgeta, **Horsia**, Olga, *Mestesuguri artistice traditionale*, Bucharest, Editura Enciclopedica, 2001.
Stoica, Georgeta, **Petrescu**, Paul , **Bocse**, Maria, *Dictionar de arta populara*, Bucharest, Editura Stiintifica si Enciclopedica, 1985.
Saineanu, Lazar, *Basmele romane*, Bucharest, Editura Univers, 1978.
Schiopu, Ursula, **Verza**, Emil, *Psihologia varstelor. Ciclurile vietii*, Bucharest, Editura Didactica si Pedagogica, 1997.
Seuleanu, Ion, *Poezia populara de nunta*, Bucharest, Editura Minerva, 1985.
Stefanuca, Petre V., *Cercetari folclorice în valea Nistrului de Jos*, in „Anuarul Arhivei de Folclor," an. IV, 1937.

Teodorescu, Dem. G., *Incercari critice asupra unor credinte, datini si moravuri ale poporului roman,* Bucharest, 1874.

Tufescu, Victor, *Oameni din Carpati,* Bucharest, Editura Sport-Turism, 1982.

Vaduva, Ofelia, *Pasi spre sacru. Din etnologia alimentatiei romanesti,* Bucharest, Editura Enciclopedica, 1996.

Vuia, Romulus, *Originea jocului de Calusari,* in „Studii de Etnografie si Folclor," vol. I. Editie îngrijita de Mihai Pop si Ioan Serb, Bucharest, Editura Minerva, 1975.

Vulcanescu, Mircea, *Dimensiunea românaesca a existentei. Schita fenomenologica,* in „Caiete critice," nr. 12, supliment la „Viata romaneasca," 1983.

Vulcanescu, Romulus, *Mitologie romaneasca,* Bucharest, Editura Academiei, 1985.

www.ingramcontent.com/pod-product-compliance
Lightning Source LLC
Chambersburg PA
CBHW022103150426
43195CB00008B/242